# WORD BY WORD

Second Edition

ENGLISH/JAPANESE

ワード・バイ・ワード イラスト英和辞典

Steven J. Molinsky • Bill Bliss 著

Uta Bryce 訳

イラスト
Richard E. Hill

Dedicated to Janet Johnston in honor of her wonderful contribution to the development of our textbooks over three decades.

*Steven J. Molinsky*
*Bill Bliss*

Word by Word Picture Dictionary, English/Japanese, second edition



Pearson Education, 10 Bank Street, White Plains, NY 10606

Editorial director: Pam Fishman
Vice president, director of design and production: Rhea Banker
Director of electronic production: Aliza Greenblatt
Director of manufacturing: Patrice Fraccio
Senior manufacturing manager: Edith Pullman
Marketing managers: Kyoko Oinama, Oliva Fernandez
Editorial assistant: Katherine Keyes
Senior digital layout specialist: Wendy Wolf
Text design: Wendy Wolf
Cover design: Tracey Munz Cataldo
Realia creation: Warren Fischbach, Paula Williams
Illustrations: Richard E. Hill
Contributing artists: Steven Young, Charles Cawley, Willard Gage, Marlon Violette
Reviewers: Kenichi Kamiya, Osaka Institute of Technology, Kaori Wada, Ritsumeikan Asia Pacific University
Project management by TransPac Education Services, Victoria, BC, Canada with assistance from Yu Jian Yo, Studio G, & Robert Zacharias

**ISBN 0-13-193542-9**
Longman on the Web
Longman.com offers online resources for teachers and students. Access our Companion Websites, our online catalog, and our local offices around the world.

Visit us at longman.com.

Printed in the United States of America
2 3 4 5 6 7 8 9 10 – QWD – 11 10 09 08 07

# 目次

# 『ワード・バイ・ワード イラスト辞典』第二版にようこそ！

本書は、学習者がダイナミックでコミュニカティブな経験として単語を学習をしながら、日常生活、地域社会、学校、そして仕事の場面で使われる英語を無理なく習得することを目的として構成されています。

THE LIVING ROOM 21

リビング／居間

各課のページは使いやすく、生き生きとした楽しいイラストが満載で、どのレベルの学習者も容易に利用することができます。

| | | | | | | | | |
|---|---|---|---|---|---|---|---|---|
| 本棚／書棚 | 1 | bookcase | 壁 | 10 | wall | ソファ | 20 | sofa/couch |
| 写真 | 2 | picture/photograph | 天井 | 11 | ceiling | （観葉）植物 | 21 | plant |
| 絵 | 3 | painting | カーテン | 12 | drapes | センターテーブル | 22 | coffee table |
| マントル（炉棚） | 4 | mantel | 窓 | 13 | window | じゅうたん | 23 | rug |
| 暖炉 | 5 | fireplace | 2人掛けソファ | 14 | loveseat | ランプ | 24 | lamp |
| 暖炉ガード | 6 | fireplace screen | 壁面ユニット家具 | 15 | wall unit | ランプのかさ | 25 | lampshade |
| DVDプレーヤー | 7 | DVD player | スピーカー | 16 | speaker | サイドテーブル | 26 | end table |
| テレビ | 8 | television/TV | ステレオ | 17 | stereo system | 床 | 27 | floor |
| ビデオデッキ | 9 | VCR/video cassette recorder | マガジンラック | 18 | magazine holder | フロアランプ | 28 | floor lamp |
| | | | クッション | 19 | (throw) pillow | ひじ掛けいす | 29 | armchair |

138のトピックから4,000語以上を収録しており、詳細な研究をもとに組み立てられた各課で、学習者の文法および単語力を同時に高めていきます。

A. Where are you?
B. I'm in the living room.
A. What are you doing?
B. I'm dusting* the **bookcase**.

* dusting/cleaning

各ページの会話例文は、それぞれの語句が実際のコミュニケーションの中で使われる例を示しています。学習者はこれらの例文をもとに新しい会話文を作成しながら、ダイナミックかつインタラクティブな単語練習をしていきます。

A. You have a very nice living room!
B. Thank you.
A. Your ________ is/are beautiful!
B. Thank you for saying so.

A. Uh-oh! I just spilled coffee on your ________!
B. That's okay. Don't worry about it.

Tell about your living room.
(In my living room there's ..............)

追加例文は、学習者が習得した単語をより広範囲の文脈で使用したり、ほめる、謝る、情報を得るなどの重要な基礎的コミュニケーション力を高められるよう構成されています。

各課に設けられたライティングやディスカッション問題は、学習者が自分自身、自分の文化や国についての経験、考え、意見、情報を他人と分かち合いながら、学習した語句やテーマを実生活に結びつけていかれるよう工夫されています。

# ティーチング計画

ティーチャーズ・ガイドは、『ワード・バイ・ワード』各課の教授法を段階的に説明をしています。以下に、各レッスンの語句を導入し練習する際に有用な方法をいくつか紹介していますので、ご参考ください。

**1 語句のプレビューイング：** レッスンに入る前に、学習する課の語句に関して生徒が知っていることをブレインストームによって引き出し、ボードに書き出してみます。また、『ワード・バイ・ワード』のOHPシートやイラストを見せ、なじみのある語句を確認させます。

**2 語句の導入：**『ワード・バイ・ワード』のOHPシートやイラストを使い、各語句のイラストを指さし、その語句を言い、クラス全体または一人ずつに繰り返させます。（オーディオ・プログラムの単語リストを聞かせてもよいでしょう）生徒が導入された語句を理解し、正しく発音しているかを確認します。

**3 語句の練習：** クラス全体で、ペアで、あるいは少人数のグループで学習した語句を練習します。語句を言うか書き出すかして、生徒に該当するイラストを指さすか、その番号を言ってもらいます。逆に、イラストを指さすか番号を言って、生徒にその語句を言ってもらってもよいでしょう。

**4 会話例文の練習：** 会話例文のなかには、その課の単語リストに出てくる最初の語句を使ったものと、語句を挿入してダイアログを作るものがあります。

a. プレビュー：生徒に例文の隣のイラストを見せ、誰が話しているのか、どんな場面での会話だと思うかをディスカッションさせます。

b. 例文を示すか、オーディオCDを一度または数回かけて、生徒が会話の状況と語句の意味を理解しているか確認します。

c. 生徒にクラス全体または一人ずつ会話の各文を繰り返させます。

d. 生徒はペアを組んで会話例文を練習します。

e. 生徒のペア1組を選び、単語リストから別の語句を使って会話させます。

f. 生徒はペアで、単語リストから別の語句を使っていくつかの会話文を作り練習します。

g. ペアを何組か選び、自分たちの作った会話文を発表させます。

**5 会話の追加練習：** 多くの課では、学習する語句を使ってさらに会話練習ができるよう、空所を補う形式のダイアログが2つ用意されています。生徒は使いたい語句を自由に使い、会話練習します。生徒が追加練習を始める前に、オーディオ・プログラムの会話文を例として聞かせてもよいでしょう。

**6 スペリング練習：** クラス全体で、ペアで、あるいは少人数のグループで学習した語句のスペリングを練習します。最初にまず先生が語句を言い、生徒にそのスペリングを声に出して言ってもらうか書いてもらいます。

**7 ディスカッション、作文、日誌、学習記録のテーマ：** 生徒にクラス全体で、ペアで、あるいは少人数のグループで問題（ページ下部）に答えてもらいます。または、問題を宿題とし、その答えをクラスで発表してもらい、クラス全体で、ペアで、あるいは少人数のグループで話し合ってもよいでしょう。こうした作文は生徒の英語学習の進歩度を示すよい例となります。

**8 ティーチャーズ・ガイドは、**学習者の単語学習を強化し、発展させる豊かなリソースを提供しています。

**『ワード・バイ・ワード イラスト辞典』第二版にようこそ！** 本書はあらゆるレベルの英語学習者を対象に、日常生活における英単語4,000語以上を生き生きとした楽しいイラストと各語句を用いて使える会話文のレッスンを併用しながら紹介しています。本書は、学習者が日常生活、地域社会、学校、仕事、さらには海外旅行の場面で使われる英語を無理なく習得することを目的として構成されています。また、この二カ国語版では、日本語が併記してあり、イラストと日本語の両方で語句の意味を確認することができます。

**『ワード・バイ・ワード』**では収録単語を17のテーマに分類し、学習者に最も身近な環境から世界へと広がるトピックを通じて、詳細な研究をもとに組み立てられたそれぞれの課で、学習者の文法および単語力を同時に高めていきます。始めの課では家族や日常生活について学び、続いて地域社会、学校、仕事、ショッピング、レクリエーションなどについて学びます。『ワード・バイ・ワード』は学習者の単語力発達にとどまらず、語彙習得、リスニングおよびスピーキング能力、ライティング／ディスカッションのテーマを統合する、総合的なコミュニケーション力を高めるプログラムとしても有用です。

『ワード・バイ・ワード』の各課はそれぞれ独立しているため、最初から順番に学ぶことも好きな順序で学ぶことも可能です。ご使用になる方の便宜を図り、『ワード・バイ・ワード』では２通りの索引を掲載しています。1つは巻頭の目次でページ順に、もう1つは巻末のテーマ別索引でアルファベット順になっています。さらに、付録には単語索引も掲載されているので、これらを組み合わせることにより、学習者や先生は、すべての収録単語とトピックを容易に見つけられるようになっています。

『ワード・バイ・ワード イラスト辞典』は、様々なレベルに対応できる印刷／メディアサポート教材を提供する、「ワード・バイ・ワード単語増強コース」の中心教材です。

各レベルのワークブックは、学習者のニーズに合わせて様々なオプションを用意しています。初級／中級用のボキャブラリー・ワークブック (Vocabulary Workbook) は、学習者の興味をかき立てる単語、文法、リスニング練習が特徴です。リタラシー・ワークブック (Literacy Workbook) は、特にアルファベットになじみのない学習者や英語の語彙、リーディング、ライティングに対して初級以前の導入が必要な学習者のために全体的なスキル (言語技能) 練習を提供しています。

CD-ROM付きのティーチャーズ・ガイドおよびレッスン・プランナー (*Teacher's Guide and Lesson Planner with CD-ROM*) には、レッスンプランの提案、コミュニティ・タスク、インターネットのウェブリンク、複製可能なマスターコピーなどが含まれており、先生がレッスンの準備に多くの時間をかけなくてもよいよう配慮されています。重要な単語増強アクティビティのための段階別ティーチング計画が付いたアクティビティ・ハンドブック (Activity Handbook) は、ティーチャーズ・ガイドに含まれています。

オーディオ・プログラム (Audio Program) には、インタラクティブな練習に使うすべての語句と会話、そして付録の教材として、楽しい音楽を使って単語練習するためのワードソング (WordSongs) の数々が含まれています。

さらに、副教材として、カラーOHP シート (Color Transparencies) 、ゲームカード (Vocabulary Game Cards) 、テスト・プログラム (Testing Program) もあります。

### ティーチング計画

『ワード・バイ・ワード』では、語句を文脈の中で紹介しています。各ページの会話例文は、それぞれの語句が実際にコミュニケーションの中で使われる例を示しています。これらの会話例文は、学習者がダイナミックかつインタラクティブな練習をするための基礎となります。さらに、各課に設けられたライティングやディスカッション問題は、学習者が自分自身、自分の文化や国についての経験、考え、意見、情報を他人と分かち合いながら、学習した語句やテーマを実生活に結びつけていかれるよう工夫されています。このようにして学習を進めていくことにより、学習者はまさに単語ごとに (word by word) 互いについて知ることができるのです。

『ワード・バイ・ワード』の使用にあたっては、先生ご自身の教え方や学習者のニーズや能力に合ったアプローチや方法を確立することが重要ですが、以下に、各レッスンの語句を導入し練習する際に有用な方法をいくつか紹介していますので、ご参考ください。

1. **語句のプレビューイング：** レッスンに入る前に、学習する課の語句に関して生徒が知っていることをブレインストームによって引き出し、ボードに書き出してみます。また、『ワード・バイ・ワード』のOHPシートやイラストを見せ、なじみのある語句を確認させます。

2. **語句の導入：**『ワード・バイ・ワード』のOHPシートやイラストを使い、各語句のイラストを指さし、その語句を言い、クラス全体または一人ずつに繰り返させます。（オーディオ・プログラムの単語リストを聞かせてもよいでしょう）生徒が導入された語句を理解し、正しく発音しているかを確認します。

3. **語句の練習：** クラス全体で、ペアで、あるいは少人数のグループで学習した語句を練習します。語句を言うか書き出すかして、生徒に該当するイラストを指さすか、その番号を言ってもらいます。逆に、イラストを指さすか番号を言って、生徒にその語句を言ってもらってもよいでしょう。

4. **会話例文の練習：** 会話例文のなかには、その課の単語リストに出てくる最初の語句を使ったものと、語句を挿入してダイアログを作るもの（多くの場合、[ ]内に示された番号の語句を用いて会話練習することができます。[ ]がない場合には、その課の語句すべてが挿入可能です。）があります。

   会話例文の練習には、以下のステップが有効です。

   a. プレビュー：生徒に例文の隣のイラストを見せ、誰が話しているのか、どんな場面での会話だと思うかをディスカッションさせます。

   b. 例文を示すか、オーディオCDを一度または数回かけて、生徒が会話の状況と語句の意味を理解しているか確認します。

   c. 生徒にクラス全体または一人ずつ会話の各文を繰り返させます。

   d. 生徒はペアを組んで会話例文を練習します。

   e. 生徒のペア1組を選び、単語リストから別の語句を使って会話させます。

   f. 生徒はペアで、単語リストから別の語句を使っていくつかの会話文を作り練習します。

   g. ペアを何組か選び、自分たちの作った会話文を発表させます。

5. **会話の追加練習：** 多くの課では、学習する語句を使ってさらに会話練習ができるよう、空所を補う形式のダイアログが2つ用意されています（ページ下部の黄色い部分）。生徒は使いたい語句を自由に使い、会話練習します。生徒が追加練習を始める前に、オーディオ・プログラムの会話文を例として聞かせてもよいでしょう。

6. **スペリング練習：** クラス全体で、ペアで、あるいは少人数のグループで学習した語句のスペリングを練習します。最初にまず先生が語句を言い、生徒にそのスペリングを声に出して言ってもらうか書いてもらいます。

7. **ディスカッション、作文、日誌、学習記録のテーマ：**『ワード・バイ・ワード』の各課には、ディスカッションや作文のための問題が用意されています（ページ下部の青い部分）。生徒にクラス全体で、ペアで、あるいは少人数のグループで問題に答えてもらいます。または、問題を宿題とし、その答えをクラスで発表してもらい、クラス全体で、ペアで、あるいは少人数のグループで話し合ってもよいでしょう。

   生徒に書いたものを日誌として記録してもらうこともできます。時間に余裕があれば、生徒全員の日誌に目を通し、生徒の書いたものにコメントするだけでなく、先生自身の意見や経験を書き加えてもよいでしょう。また、生徒の学習成果を記録している先生には、こうした作文は生徒の英語学習の進歩度を示すよい例となります。

**8. コミュニケーション・アクティビティ：** CD-ROM付きのティーチャーズ・ガイドおよびレッスン・プランナーは、いろいろなゲーム、タスク、ブレーンストーミング、ディスカッション、全身を使ったアクティビティ、絵描き、ジェスチャー、ロールプレイなど多様なアクティビティを紹介しており、生徒の学習スタイルや特技を生かして学習できるようになっています。それぞれの課でこの中から1つか2つくらいのアクティビティを選び、クリエイティブで楽しい授業を通して生徒の意欲を高めながら単語学習を強化してください。

**『ワード・バイ・ワード』**は、コミュニカティブで実生活に役立つ、生き生きとした英単語学習の実現を目的としています。私たちがつくったこのコースの本質をお伝えする上で、私たちが信じる教育理念、すなわち単語学習とは本来インタラクティブなものであり、生活に密着し、学習者の能力や学習スタイルに柔軟に対応し、そして何よりも楽しくあるべきであるということをご理解いただければ幸いです。

**スティーブン・J・モリンスキー**

**ビル・ブリス**

***Welcome to the second edition of the WORD BY WORD Picture Dictionary!*** This text presents more than 4,000 vocabulary words through vibrant illustrations and simple accessible lesson pages that are designed for clarity and ease-of-use with learners at all levels. Our goal is to help students practice English used in everyday life, in the community, in school, at work, and in international travel.

**WORD BY WORD** organizes the vocabulary into 17 thematic units, providing a careful research-based sequence of lessons that integrates students' development of grammar and vocabulary skills through topics that begin with the immediate world of the student and progress to the world at large. Early lessons on the family, the home, and daily activities lead to lessons on the community, school, workplace, shopping, recreation, and other topics. In addition to developing students' vocabulary, the text also serves as a comprehensive communication skills program that integrates vocabulary learning, listening and speaking skills, and themes for writing and discussion.

Since each lesson in *Word by Word* is self-contained, it can be used either sequentially or in any desired order. For users' convenience, the lessons are listed in two ways: sequentially in the Table of Contents, and alphabetically in the Thematic Index. These resources, combined with the Glossary in the appendix, allow students and teachers to quickly and easily locate all words and topics in the Picture Dictionary.

The *Word by Word* Picture Dictionary is the centerpiece of the complete *Word by Word* Vocabulary Development Program, which offers a wide selection of print and media support materials for instruction at all levels.

Workbooks at different levels offer flexible options to meet students' needs. Vocabulary Workbooks at Beginning and Intermediate levels feature motivating vocabulary, grammar, and listening practice. A Literacy Workbook provides all-skills practice especially appropriate for learners who are not familiar with the alphabet or who need a pre-Beginning-level introduction to English vocabulary, reading, and writing.

The Teacher's Guide and Lesson Planner with CD-ROM includes lesson-planning suggestions, community tasks, Internet weblinks, and reproducible masters to save teachers hours of lesson preparation time. An Activity Handbook with step-by-step teaching strategies for key vocabulary development activities is included in the Teacher's Guide.

The Audio Program includes all words and conversations for interactive practice and —as bonus material—an expanded selection of WordSongs for entertaining musical practice with the vocabulary.

Additional ancillary materials include Color Transparencies, Vocabulary Game Cards, a Testing Program. Bilingual Editions are also available.

## Teaching Strategies

*Word by Word* presents vocabulary words in context. Model conversations depict situations in which people use the words in meaningful communication. These models become the basis for students to engage in dynamic, interactive practice. In addition, writing and discussion questions in each lesson encourage students to relate the vocabulary and themes to their own lives as they share experiences, thoughts, opinions, and information about themselves, their cultures, and their countries. In this way, students get to know each other "word by word."

In using *Word by Word*, we encourage you to develop approaches and strategies that are compatible with your own teaching style and the needs and abilities of your students. You may find it helpful to incorporate some of the following techniques for presenting and practicing the vocabulary in each lesson.

1. **Preview the Vocabulary:** Activate students' prior knowledge of the vocabulary by brainstorming with students the words in the lesson they already know and writing them on the board, or by having students look at the transparency or the illustration in *Word by Word* and identify the words they are familiar with.

2. **Present the Vocabulary:** Using the transparency or the illustration in the Picture Dictionary, point to the picture of each word, say the word, and have the class repeat it chorally and individually. (You can also play the word list on the Audio Program.) Check students' understanding and pronunciation of the vocabulary.

3. **Vocabulary Practice:** Have students practice the vocabulary as a class, in pairs, or in small groups. Say or write a word, and have students point to the item or tell the number. Or, point to an item or give the number, and have students say the word.

4. **Model Conversation Practice:** Some lessons have model conversations that use the first word in the vocabulary list. Other models are in the form of skeletal dialogs, in which vocabulary words can be inserted. (In many skeletal dialogs, bracketed numbers indicate which words can be used for practicing the conversation. If no bracketed numbers appear, all the words in the lesson can be used.)

   The following steps are recommended for Model Conversation Practice:

   a. Preview: Have students look at the model illustration and discuss who they think the speakers are and where the conversation takes place.
   b. The teacher presents the model or plays the audio one or more times and checks students' understanding of the situation and the vocabulary.
   c. Students repeat each line of the conversation chorally and individually.
   d. Students practice the model in pairs.
   e. A pair of students presents a conversation based on the model, but using a different word from the vocabulary list.
   f. In pairs, students practice several conversations based on the model, using different words on the page.
   g. Pairs present their conversations to the class.

5. **Additional Conversation Practice:** Many lessons provide two additional skeletal dialogs for further conversation practice with the vocabulary. (These can be found in the yellow-shaded area at the bottom of the page.) Have students practice and present these conversations using any words they wish. Before they practice the additional conversations, you may want to have students listen to the sample additional conversations on the Audio Program.

6. **Spelling Practice:** Have students practice spelling the words as a class, in pairs, or in small groups. Say a word, and have students spell it aloud or write it. Or, using the transparency, point to an item and have students write the word.

7. **Themes for Discussion, Composition, Journals, and Portfolios:** Each lesson of *Word by Word* provides one or more questions for discussion and composition. (These can be found in a blue-shaded area at the bottom of the page.) Have students respond to the questions as a class, in pairs, or in small groups. Or, have students write their responses at home, share their written work with other students, and discuss as a class, in pairs, or in small groups.

   Students may enjoy keeping a journal of their written work. If time permits, you may want to write a response in each student's journal, sharing your own opinions and experiences as well as reacting to what the student has written. If you are keeping portfolios of students' work, these compositions serve as excellent examples of students' progress in learning English.

8. **Communication Activities:** The *Word by Word* Teacher's Guide and Lesson Planner with CD-ROM provides a wealth of games, tasks, brainstorming, discussion, movement, drawing, miming, role-playing, and other activities designed to take advantage of students' different learning styles and particular abilities and strengths. For each lesson, choose one or more of these activities to reinforce students' vocabulary learning in a way that is stimulating, creative, and enjoyable.

***WORD BY WORD*** aims to offer students a communicative, meaningful, and lively way of practicing English vocabulary. In conveying to you the substance of our program, we hope that we have also conveyed the spirit: that learning vocabulary can be genuinely interactive . . . relevant to our students' lives . . . responsive to students' differing strengths and learning styles . . . and fun!

*Steven J. Molinsky*
*Bill Bliss*

# 個人情報

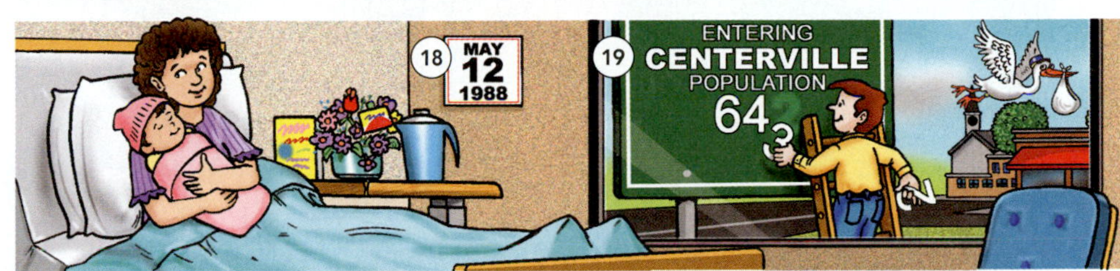

**Registration Form**

Name: Gloria (First) P. (Middle Initial) Sánchez (Last)

Address: 95 (Number) Garden Street (Street) 3G (Apartment Number)
Los Angeles (City) CA (State) 90036 (Zip Code)

Telephone 323-524-3278 Cell Phone 323-695-1864

E-Mail Address gloria97@ail.com SSN 227-93-6185 Sex M__ F X

Date of Birth 5/12/88 Place of Birth Centerville, Texas

| | | |
|---|---|---|
| 名前 | **1** | name |
| 名 | **2** | first name |
| ミドルネームのイニシャル | **3** | middle initial |
| 名字／姓 | **4** | last name/family name/surname |
| 住所 | **5** | address |
| 番地 | **6** | street number |
| 通り（町） | **7** | street |
| 部屋番号 | **8** | apartment number |
| 市 | **9** | city |
| 州 | **10** | state |
| 郵便番号 | **11** | zip code |
| 市外局番 | **12** | area code |
| 電話番号 | **13** | telephone number/phone number |
| 携帯電話番号 | **14** | cell phone number |
| メールアドレス | **15** | e-mail address |
| 社会保障番号 | **16** | social security number |
| 性別 | **17** | sex |
| 誕生日 | **18** | date of birth |
| 誕生地 | **19** | place of birth |

A. What's your **name**?
B. Gloria P. Sánchez.

A. What's your ________?
B. .............
A. Did you say .............?
B. Yes. That's right.

A. What's your last name?
B. .............
A. How do you spell that?
B. .............

Tell about yourself:
My name is .............
My address is .............
My telephone number is .............

Now interview a friend.

# FAMILY MEMBERS I

## 家族 1

夫 **1** husband
妻 **2** wife

**両親 parents**
父 **3** father
母 **4** mother

**子供 children**
娘 **5** daughter
息子 **6** son
赤ん坊 **7** baby

**兄弟／姉妹 siblings**
姉／妹 **8** sister
兄／弟 **9** brother

**祖父母 grandparents**
祖母 **10** grandmother
祖父 **11** grandfather

**孫 grandchildren**
孫娘 **12** granddaughter
孫息子 **13** grandson

A. Who is he?
B. He's my **husband**.
A. What's his name?
B. His name is *Jack*.

A. Who is she?
B. She's my **wife**.
A. What's her name?
B. Her name is *Nancy*.

A. I'd like to introduce my ________.
B. Nice to meet you.
C. Nice to meet you, too.

A. What's your ________'s name?
B. His/Her name is ..............

Who are the people in your family?
What are their names?

Tell about photos of family members.

# FAMILY MEMBERS II

家族２

Helen  Walter

Jack  Nancy  Frank  Linda

Jennifer  Timmy  Alan

| | | |
|---|---|---|
| おじ | **1** | uncle |
| おば | **2** | aunt |
| めい | **3** | niece |
| おい | **4** | nephew |
| いとこ | **5** | cousin |
| 義母 | **6** | mother-in-law |
| 義父 | **7** | father-in-law |
| 義理の息子 | **8** | son-in-law |
| 義理の娘 | **9** | daughter-in-law |
| 義理の兄／義理の弟 | **10** | brother-in-law |
| 義理の姉／義理の妹 | **11** | sister-in-law |

1. Jack is Alan's ____.
2. Nancy is Alan's ____.
3. Jennifer is Frank and Linda's ____.
4. Timmy is Frank and Linda's ____.
5. Alan is Jennifer and Timmy's ____.
6. Helen is Jack's ____.
7. Walter is Jack's ____.
8. Jack is Helen and Walter's ____.
9. Linda is Helen and Walter's ____.
10. Frank is Jack's ____.
11. Linda is Jack's ____.

A. Who is he/she?
B. He's/She's my ________.
A. What's his/her name?
B. His/Her name is ________.

A. Let me introduce my ________.
B. I'm glad to meet you.
C. Nice meeting you, too.

Tell about your relatives:
What are their names?
Where do they live?

Draw your family tree and tell about it.

# THE CLASSROOM

## 教室

| | | |
|---|---|---|
| 先生 | **1** | teacher |
| 助手 | **2** | teacher's aide |
| 生徒 | **3** | student |
| 机 | **4** | desk |
| いす | **5** | seat / chair |
| テーブル | **6** | table |
| コンピュータ | **7** | computer |
| オーバーヘッド・プロジェクター | **8** | overhead projector |
| スクリーン | **9** | screen |
| 黒板 | **10** | chalkboard / board |
| 時計 | **11** | clock |
| 地図 | **12** | map |
| 掲示板 | **13** | bulletin board |
| スピーカー | **14** | P.A. system / loudspeaker |
| ホワイドボード／ボード | **15** | whiteboard / board |
| 地球儀 | **16** | globe |
| 本棚 | **17** | bookcase / bookshelf |
| 教卓 | **18** | teacher's desk |
| ゴミ箱 | **19** | wastebasket |

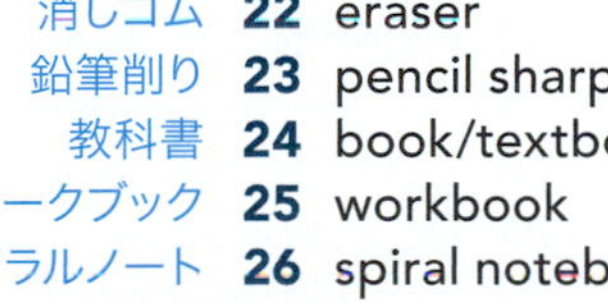

| | | |
|---|---|---|
| ペン **20** pen | バインダー **27** binder/notebook | マーカー **34** marker |
| 鉛筆 **21** pencil | ノート用紙 **28** notebook paper | 画びょう **35** thumbtack |
| 消しゴム **22** eraser | 方眼紙 **29** graph paper | キーボード **36** keyboard |
| 鉛筆削り **23** pencil sharpener | ものさし **30** ruler | モニター **37** monitor |
| 教科書 **24** book/textbook | 電卓 **31** calculator | マウス **38** mouse |
| ワークブック **25** workbook | チョーク **32** chalk | プリンタ **39** printer |
| スパイラルノート **26** spiral notebook | 黒板消し **33** eraser | |

A. Where's the **teacher**?
B. The **teacher** is *next to* the **board**.

A. Where's the **globe**?
B. The **globe** is *on* the **bookcase**.

A. Is there a/an _____ in your classroom?*
B. Yes. There's a/an _____ next to/on the _____.

A. Is there a/an _____ in your classroom?*
B. No, there isn't.

Describe your classroom. (There's a/an .............)

* *With 28, 29, 32 use:* Is there _____ in your classroom?

# CLASSROOM ACTIONS

## 教室での動作

名前を言いなさい。 **1** Say your name.
もう一度名前を言いなさい。 **2** Repeat your name.
名前のスペリングを言いなさい。 **3** Spell your name.
プリント体で名前を書きなさい。 **4** Print your name.
筆記体で名前を書きなさい。 **5** Sign your name.
立ちなさい。 **6** Stand up.
黒板のところへ行きなさい。 **7** Go to the board.
黒板に書きなさい。 **8** Write on the board.
黒板を消しなさい。 **9** Erase the board.
席に着きなさい。 **10** Sit down./Take your seat.
本を開けなさい。 **11** Open your book.
10ページを読みなさい。 **12** Read page ten.
10ページを勉強しなさい。 **13** Study page ten.
本を閉じなさい。 **14** Close your book.
本を片づけなさい。 **15** Put away your book.
手をあげなさい。 **16** Raise your hand.

質問しなさい。 **17** Ask a question.
質問を聞きなさい。 **18** Listen to the question.
質問に答えなさい。 **19** Answer the question.
答えを聞きなさい。 **20** Listen to the answer.
宿題をしなさい。 **21** Do your homework.
宿題を持ってきなさい。 **22** Bring in your homework.
答えあわせをしなさい。 **23** Go over the answers.
間違いを直しなさい。 **24** Correct your mistakes.
宿題を提出しなさい。 **25** Hand in your homework.
いっしょに本を見なさい。 **26** Share a book.
問題(質問)について話し合いなさい。 **27** Discuss the question.
お互いに助け合いなさい。 **28** Help each other.
いっしょにやりなさい。 **29** Work together.
クラスで発表しなさい。 **30** Share with the class.

辞書を引きなさい。 **31** Look in the dictionary.
単語を(辞書で)調べなさい。 **32** Look up a word.
その単語を発音しなさい。 **33** Pronounce the word.
意味を読みなさい。 **34** Read the definition.
その単語を写しなさい。 **35** Copy the word.
自分だけでやりなさい。 **36** Work alone./ Do your own work.
パートナーといっしょにやりなさい。 **37** Work with a partner.
小さなグループに分かれなさい。 **38** Break up into small groups.
グループで作業しなさい。 **39** Work in a group.
クラス全員でやりなさい。 **40** Work as a class.
ブラインドを下ろしなさい。 **41** Lower the shades.
明かりを消しなさい。 **42** Turn off the lights.
スクリーンを見なさい。 **43** Look at the screen.
メモを取りなさい。 **44** Take notes.
明かりをつけなさい。 **45** Turn on the lights.
紙を1枚取り出しなさい。 **46** Take out a piece of paper.

テストを配りなさい。 **47** Pass out the tests.
問いに答えなさい。 **48** Answer the questions.
答えを確かめなさい。 **49** Check your answers.
テストを集めなさい。 **50** Collect the tests.
正しい答えを選びなさい。 **51** Choose the correct answer.
正しい答えを丸で囲みなさい。 **52** Circle the correct answer.
空欄を埋めなさい。 **53** Fill in the blank.
答えの記号(番号)を塗りつぶしなさい。 **54** Mark the answer sheet./ Bubble the answer.
語句を結びつけなさい。 **55** Match the words.
その単語に下線を引きなさい。 **56** Underline the word.
その単語をXで消しなさい。 **57** Cross out the word.
正しい単語に直しなさい。 **58** Unscramble the word.
正しい語順に並べなさい。 **59** Put the words in order.
別の紙に書きなさい。 **60** Write on a separate sheet of paper.

You're the teacher! Give instructions to your students!

# PREPOSITIONS

## 場所を表す前置詞 (句)

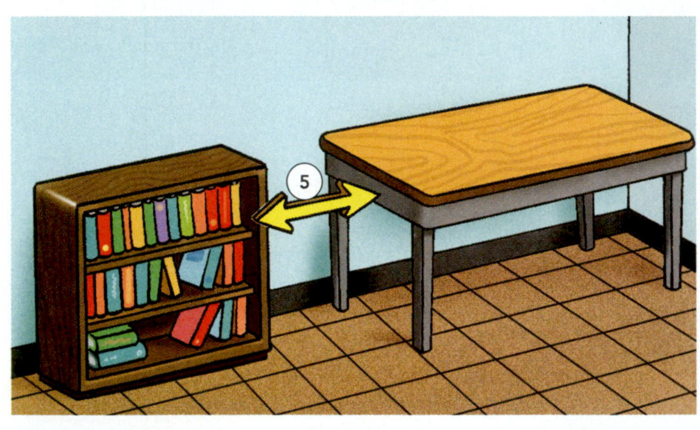


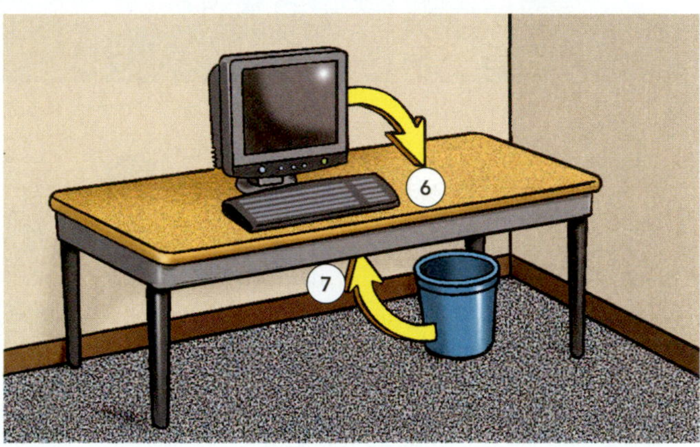

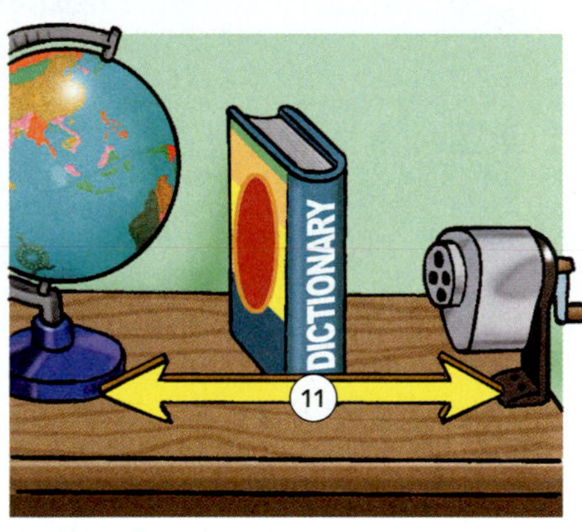


～の上に **1** above
～の下に **2** below

～の前に **3** in front of
～の後ろに **4** behind

～の隣に **5** next to

～の上に **6** on
～の下に **7** under

～の左に **8** to the left of
～の右に **9** to the right of

～の中に **10** in

～の間に **11** between

[1–10]
A. Where's the *clock*?
B. The *clock* is **above** the *bulletin board*.

[11]
A. Where's the *dictionary*?
B. The *dictionary* is **between** the *globe* and the *pencil sharpener*.

Tell about the classroom on page 4. Use the prepositions in this lesson.

Tell about your classroom.

# 日常生活の動作 1

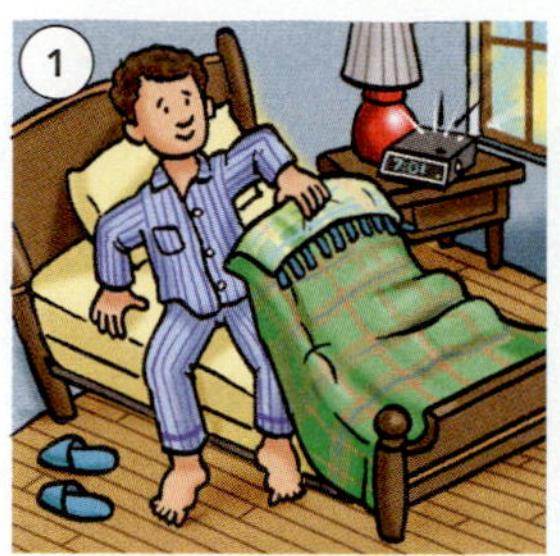

起床する **1** get up
シャワーを浴びる **2** take a shower
歯を磨く **3** brush *my** teeth
ひげを剃る **4** shave
洋服に着替える **5** get dressed
顔を洗う **6** wash *my** face
化粧する **7** put on makeup
髪をブラシでとかす **8** brush *my** hair
髪をくしでとかす **9** comb *my** hair
ベッドを整える **10** make the bed

* my, his, her, our, your, their

服を脱ぐ **11** get undressed
風呂に入る **12** take a bath
床につく **13** go to bed
寝る **14** sleep
朝食を作る **15** make breakfast
昼食を作る **16** make lunch
夕食を作る **17** cook/make dinner
朝食を食べる **18** eat/have breakfast
昼食を食べる **19** eat/have lunch
夕食を食べる **20** eat/have dinner

A. What do you do every day?
B. I **get up**, I **take a shower**, and I **brush my teeth**.

A. What does he do every day?
B. He ________s, he ________s, and he ________s.

A. What does she do every day?
B. She ________s, she ________s, and she________s.

What do you do every day? Make a list.

Interview some friends and tell about their everyday activities.

# 日常生活の動作 2

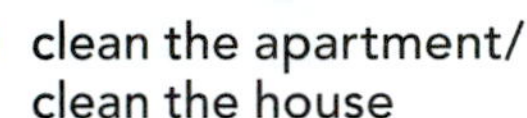

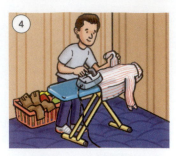

| | | |
|---|---|---|
| 家の掃除をする | **1** | clean the apartment/ clean the house |
| 皿を洗う | **2** | wash the dishes |
| 洗濯する | **3** | do the laundry |
| アイロンをかける | **4** | iron |
| 赤ちゃんに食事をさせる | **5** | feed the baby |
| ネコにえさを与える | **6** | feed the cat |
| 犬を散歩させる | **7** | walk the dog |
| 勉強する | **8** | study |
| 仕事に行く | **9** | go to work |
| 学校に行く | **10** | go to school |
| 車で仕事に行く | **11** | drive to work |
| バスで学校に行く | **12** | take the bus to school |
| 仕事をする | **13** | work |
| 会社（仕事場）を出る | **14** | leave work |
| 買い物に行く | **15** | go to the store |
| 帰宅する | **16** | come home/get home |

A. Hello. What are you doing?
B. I'm **clean**ing the **apartment**.

A. Hello, ............. This is .............
What are you doing?
B. I'm ________ing. How about you?
A. I'm ________ing.

A. Are you going to ________ soon?
B. Yes. I'm going to ________ in a little while.

What are you going to do tomorrow? Make a list of everything you are going to do.

# レジャー活動

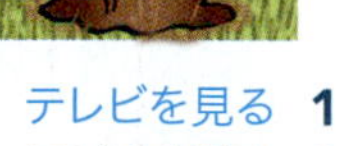

| | | |
|---|---|---|
| テレビを見る | **1** | watch TV |
| ラジオを聴く | **2** | listen to the radio |
| 音楽を聴く | **3** | listen to music |
| 読書する | **4** | read a book |
| 新聞を読む | **5** | read the newspaper |
| 遊ぶ | **6** | play |
| トランプをする | **7** | play cards |
| バスケットボールをする | **8** | play basketball |

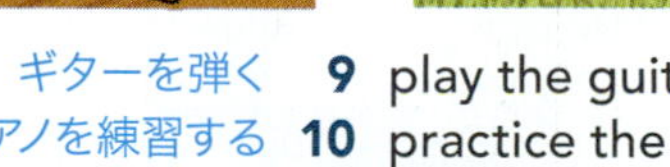

| | | |
|---|---|---|
| ギターを弾く | **9** | play the guitar |
| ピアノを練習する | **10** | practice the piano |
| 運動する | **11** | exercise |
| 泳ぐ | **12** | swim |
| 花を植える | **13** | plant flowers |
| コンピュータを使う | **14** | use the computer |
| 手紙を書く | **15** | write a letter |
| のんびりする | **16** | relax |

A. Hi. What are you doing?
B. I'm **watch**ing **TV**.

A. Hi, .............. Are you ________ing?
B. No, I'm not. I'm ________ing.

A. What's your (husband/wife/son/daughter/. . .) doing?
B. He's/She's ________ing.

What leisure activities do you like to do?

What do your family members and friends like to do?

# 日常会話

## Greeting People 出会ったときのあいさつ

## Leave Taking 別れるときのあいさつ

こんにちは。 **1** Hello. / Hi.
おはよう(ございます)。 **2** Good morning.
こんにちは。 **3** Good afternoon.
こんばんは。 **4** Good evening.
お元気ですか。 **5** How are you? / How are you doing?
はい、元気です。 **6** Fine. / Fine, thanks. / Okay.

どうしていますか。 **7** What's new? / What's new with you?
変わりありません。 **8** Not much. / Not too much.
さようなら。(バイバイ。) **9** Good-bye. / Bye.
おやすみ(なさい)。 **10** Good night.
ではまた。 **11** See you later. / See you soon.

## Introducing Yourself and Others 自己紹介する

## Getting Someone's Attention
注意を引く

## Expressing Gratitude
感謝の気持ちを伝える

## Saying You Don't Understand
自分にはわからないことを相手に伝える

## Calling Someone on the Telephone
電話で話したい相手を出してもらう

| | | |
|---|---|---|
| こんにちは。私は 〜 です。 | **12** | Hello. My name is .........../<br>Hi. I'm .......... |
| どうぞよろしく。 | **13** | Nice to meet you. |
| こちらこそ。 | **14** | Nice to meet you, too. |
| こちらは 〜 さんです。 | **15** | I'd like to introduce .........../<br>This is .......... |
| 失礼します。 | **16** | Excuse me. |
| 質問してもよいですか。 | **17** | May I ask a question? |
| (どうも)ありがとう。 | **18** | Thank you. / Thanks. |
| どういたしまして。 | **19** | You're welcome. |
| わかりません。/<br>すみません。わかりません。 | **20** | I don't understand. /<br>Sorry. I don't understand. |
| もう一度言ってください。 | **21** | Can you please repeat that?/<br>Can you please say that again? |
| こんにちは。私は 〜 です。<br>〜 さんはいらっしゃいますか。 | **22** | Hello. This is ..........<br>May I please speak to .........? |
| はい。少しお待ちください。 | **23** | Yes. Hold on a moment. |
| あいにく 〜 は今こちらに<br>おりません。 | **24** | I'm sorry. ......... isn't<br>here right now. |

Practice conversations with other students. Use all the expressions on pages 12 and 13.

# 天候

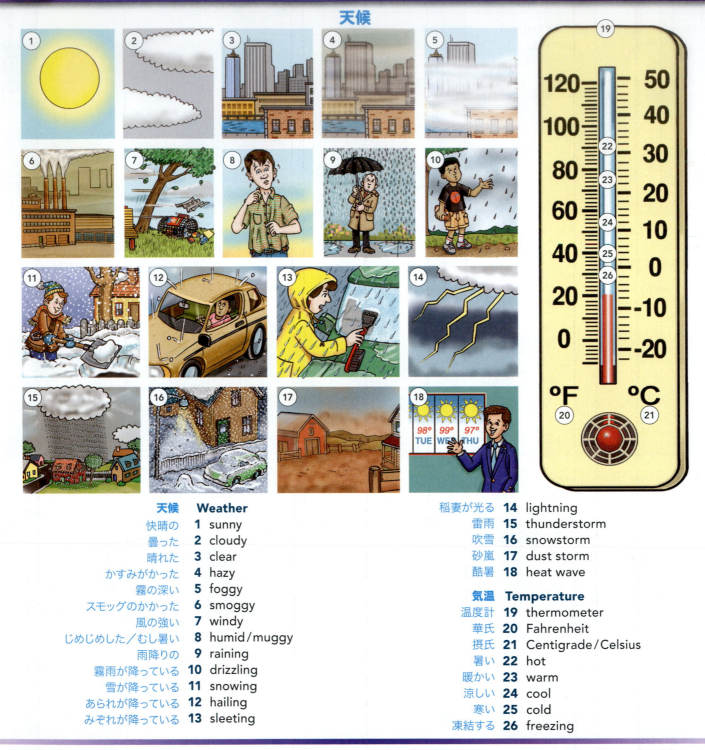

## 天候 Weather

| | | |
|---|---|---|
| 快晴の | 1 | sunny |
| 曇った | 2 | cloudy |
| 晴れた | 3 | clear |
| かすみがかった | 4 | hazy |
| 霧の深い | 5 | foggy |
| スモッグのかかった | 6 | smoggy |
| 風の強い | 7 | windy |
| じめじめした／むし暑い | 8 | humid/muggy |
| 雨降りの | 9 | raining |
| 霧雨が降っている | 10 | drizzling |
| 雪が降っている | 11 | snowing |
| あられが降っている | 12 | hailing |
| みぞれが降っている | 13 | sleeting |
| 稲妻が光る | 14 | lightning |
| 雷雨 | 15 | thunderstorm |
| 吹雪 | 16 | snowstorm |
| 砂嵐 | 17 | dust storm |
| 酷暑 | 18 | heat wave |

## 気温 Temperature

| | | |
|---|---|---|
| 温度計 | 19 | thermometer |
| 華氏 | 20 | Fahrenheit |
| 摂氏 | 21 | Centigrade/Celsius |
| 暑い | 22 | hot |
| 暖かい | 23 | warm |
| 涼しい | 24 | cool |
| 寒い | 25 | cold |
| 凍結する | 26 | freezing |

[1–13]
A. What's the weather like?
B. It's ________.

[14–18]
A. What's the weather forecast?
B. There's going to be __[14]__/ a __[15–18]__.

[20–26]
A. How's the weather?
B. It's __[22–26]__.
A. What's the temperature?
B. It's . . . degrees __[20–21]__.

What's the weather like today? What's the temperature?

What's the weather forecast for tomorrow?

数

## Cardinal Numbers 基数

| | | | | | | | |
|---|---|---|---|---|---|---|---|
| **0** | zero | **11** | eleven | **21** | twenty-one | **101** | one hundred (and) one |
| **1** | one | **12** | twelve | **22** | twenty-two | **102** | one hundred (and) two |
| **2** | two | **13** | thirteen | **30** | thirty | **1,000** | one thousand （千） |
| **3** | three | **14** | fourteen | **40** | forty | **10,000** | ten thousand （一万） |
| **4** | four | **15** | fifteen | **50** | fifty | **100,000** | one hundred thousand （十万） |
| **5** | five | **16** | sixteen | **60** | sixty | **1,000,000** | one million （百万） |
| **6** | six | **17** | seventeen | **70** | seventy | **1,000,000,000** | one billion （十億） |
| **7** | seven | **18** | eighteen | **80** | eighty | | |
| **8** | eight | **19** | nineteen | **90** | ninety | | |
| **9** | nine | **20** | twenty | **100** | one hundred （百） | | |
| **10** | ten | | | | | | |

A. How old are you?
B. I'm ______ years old.

A. How many people are there in your family?
B. ______.

## Ordinal Numbers 序数

| | | | | | | | |
|---|---|---|---|---|---|---|---|
| **1st** | first | **11th** | eleventh | **21st** | twenty-first | **101st** | one hundred (and) first |
| **2nd** | second | **12th** | twelfth | **22nd** | twenty-second | **102nd** | one hundred (and) second |
| **3rd** | third | **13th** | thirteenth | **30th** | thirtieth | **1,000th** | one thousandth |
| **4th** | fourth | **14th** | fourteenth | **40th** | fortieth | **10,000th** | ten thousandth |
| **5th** | fifth | **15th** | fifteenth | **50th** | fiftieth | **100,000th** | one hundred thousandth |
| **6th** | sixth | **16th** | sixteenth | **60th** | sixtieth | **1,000,000th** | one millionth |
| **7th** | seventh | **17th** | seventeenth | **70th** | seventieth | **1,000,000,000th** | one billionth |
| **8th** | eighth | **18th** | eighteenth | **80th** | eightieth | | |
| **9th** | ninth | **19th** | nineteenth | **90th** | ninetieth | | |
| **10th** | tenth | **20th** | twentieth | **100th** | one hundredth | | |

A. What floor do you live on?
B. I live on the ______ floor.

A. Is this your first trip to our country?
B. No. It's my ______ trip.

How many students are there in your class?

How many people are there in your country?

What were the names of your teachers in elementary school? (My *first*-grade teacher was Ms./Mrs./Mr. . . .)

# TIME

时刻

*two* o'clock

*two* fifteen/ a quarter after *two*

*two* thirty/ half past *two*

*two* forty-five/ a quarter to *three*

*two* oh five

*two* twenty/ twenty after *two*

*two* forty/ twenty to *three*

*two* fifty-five/ five to *three*

A. What time is it?
B. It's ______.

A. What time does the movie begin?
B. At ______.

*two* A.M.

*two* P.M.

noon/ twelve noon

midnight/ twelve midnight

A. When does the train leave?
B. At ______.

A. What time will we arrive?
B. At ______.

Tell about your daily schedule:
What do you do? When?
(I get up at ______. I .............)

Do you usually have enough time to do things, or do you "run out of time"? Tell about it.

Tell about the use of time in different cultures or countries you know:
Do people arrive on time for work? appointments? parties?
Do trains and buses operate exactly on schedule?
Do movies and sports events begin on time?
Do workplaces use time clocks or timesheets to record employees' work hours?

# 貨幣

## Coins 硬貨

| Name | Value | Written as: | |
|---|---|---|---|
| 1 penny | one cent | 1¢ | $ .01 |
| 2 nickel | five cents | 5¢ | $ .05 |
| 3 dime | ten cents | 10¢ | $ .10 |
| 4 quarter | twenty-five cents | 25¢ | $ .25 |
| 5 half dollar | fifty cents | 50¢ | $ .50 |
| 6 silver dollar | one dollar | | $1.00 |

A. How much is a **penny** worth?
B. A **penny** is worth **one cent**.

A. *Soda* costs *ninety-five cents*. Do you have enough change?
B. Yes. I have a/two/three ______(s) and . . . . . . .

## Currency 通貨紙幣

| Name | We sometimes say: | Value | Written as: |
|---|---|---|---|
| 7 (one-) dollar bill | a one | one dollar | $ 1.00 |
| 8 five-dollar bill | a five | five dollars | $ 5.00 |
| 9 ten-dollar bill | a ten | ten dollars | $ 10.00 |
| 10 twenty-dollar bill | a twenty | twenty dollars | $ 20.00 |
| 11 fifty-dollar bill | a fifty | fifty dollars | $ 50.00 |
| 12 (one-) hundred dollar bill | a hundred | one hundred dollars | $100.00 |

A. I'm going to the supermarket. Do you have any cash?
B. I have a **twenty-dollar bill**.
A. **Twenty dollars** is enough. Thanks.

A. Can you change **a five-dollar bill/a five**?
B. Yes. I have ***five* one-dollar bills/ *five* ones.**

| Written as: | We say: |
|---|---|
| $1.30 | a dollar and thirty cents<br>a dollar thirty |
| $2.50 | two dollars and fifty cents<br>two fifty |
| $56.49 | fifty-six dollars and forty-nine cents<br>fifty-six forty-nine |

Tell about some things you usually buy. What do they cost?

Name and describe the coins and currency in your country. What are they worth in U.S. dollars?

# カレンダー

| | | |
|---|---|---|
| 年 | **1** | year |
| 月 | **2** | month |
| 週 | **3** | week |
| 日 | **4** | day |
| 週末 | **5** | weekend |

**曜日 Days of the Week**

| | | |
|---|---|---|
| 日曜日 | **6** | Sunday |
| 月曜日 | **7** | Monday |
| 火曜日 | **8** | Tuesday |
| 水曜日 | **9** | Wednesday |
| 木曜日 | **10** | Thursday |
| 金曜日 | **11** | Friday |
| 土曜日 | **12** | Saturday |

**1年の月 Months of the Year**

| | | |
|---|---|---|
| 1月 | **13** | January |
| 2月 | **14** | February |
| 3月 | **15** | March |
| 4月 | **16** | April |
| 5月 | **17** | May |
| 6月 | **18** | June |
| 7月 | **19** | July |
| 8月 | **20** | August |
| 9月 | **21** | September |
| 10月 | **22** | October |
| 11月 | **23** | November |
| 12月 | **24** | December |

| | | |
|---|---|---|
| 2012年1月3日 | **25** | January 3, 2012<br>January third, two thousand twelve |
| 誕生日 | **26** | birthday |
| 記念日 | **27** | anniversary |
| 予約 | **28** | appointment |

A. What year is it?
B. It's ________.

[13–24]
A. What month is it?
B. It's ________.

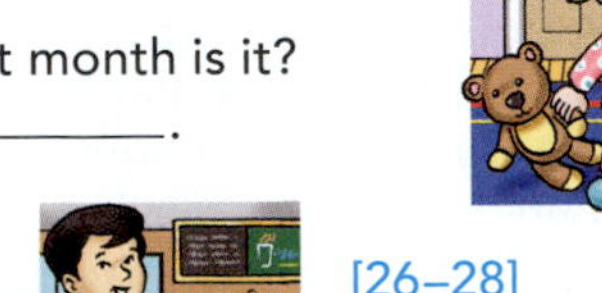

[6–12]
A. What day is it?
B. It's ________.

A. What's today's date?
B. It's ________.

[26–28]
A. When is your ________?
B. It's on ________.

Which days of the week do you go to work/school?
(I go to work/school on ________.)

What do you do on the weekend?

What is your date of birth?
(I was born on ....*month day, year*.....)

What's your favorite day of the week? Why?

What's your favorite month of the year? Why?

# 時と季節

| | | |
|---|---|---|
| 昨日 | 1 | yesterday |
| 今日 | 2 | today |
| 明日 | 3 | tomorrow |
| 朝／午前 | 4 | morning |
| 午後 | 5 | afternoon |
| 夕方 | 6 | evening |
| 夜 | 7 | night |
| 昨日の朝 | 8 | yesterday morning |
| 昨日の午後 | 9 | yesterday afternoon |
| 昨日の夕方 | 10 | yesterday evening |
| 昨晩 | 11 | last night |
| 今朝 | 12 | this morning |
| 今日の午後 | 13 | this afternoon |
| 今日の夕方 | 14 | this evening |
| 今晩 | 15 | tonight |
| 明日の朝 | 16 | tomorrow morning |
| 明日の午後 | 17 | tomorrow afternoon |
| 明日の夕方 | 18 | tomorrow evening |
| 明日の夜 | 19 | tomorrow night |
| 先週 | 20 | last week |
| 今週 | 21 | this week |
| 来週 | 22 | next week |
| 週に1回 | 23 | once a week |
| 週に2回 | 24 | twice a week |
| 週に3回 | 25 | three times a week |
| 毎日 | 26 | every day |

**季節 Seasons**

| | | |
|---|---|---|
| 春 | 27 | spring |
| 夏 | 28 | summer |
| 秋 | 29 | fall/autumn |
| 冬 | 30 | winter |

What did you do yesterday morning/afternoon/evening? What did you do last night?

What are you going to do tomorrow morning/afternoon/evening/night?

What did you do last week?

What are your plans for next week?

How many times a week do you have English class?/go to the supermarket?/exercise?

What's your favorite season? Why?

# TYPES OF HOUSING AND COMMUNITIES

## 住居形態と地域社会

| | | |
|---|---|---|
| アパート／マンション | **1** | apartment building |
| 一戸建て住宅 | **2** | house |
| 二世帯用住宅 | **3** | duplex/two-family house |
| 都市住宅 | **4** | townhouse/townhome |
| (分譲)マンション | **5** | condominium/condo |
| 寮 | **6** | dormitory/dorm |
| トレーラハウス／移動住宅 | **7** | mobile home |
| 老人ホーム | **8** | nursing home |
| 避難所／保護施設 | **9** | shelter |
| 農場 | **10** | farm |
| 牧場 | **11** | ranch |
| ハウスボート(家船) | **12** | houseboat |
| 都市 | **13** | the city |
| 郊外 | **14** | the suburbs |
| 田舎 | **15** | the country |
| 町／村 | **16** | a town/village |

A. Where do you live?

B. I live in a/an [1–9]. / on a [10–12]. / in [13–16].

[1–12]
A. Town Taxi Company.
B. Hello. Please send a taxi to ....(address).....
A. Is that a house or an apartment building?
B. It's a/an ________.
A. All right. We'll be there right away.

[1–12]
A. This is the Emergency Operator.
B. Please send an ambulance to ....(address).....
A. Is that a private home?
B. It's a/an ________.
A. What's your name and telephone number?
B. ............................

Tell about people you know and where they live.

Discuss:
Who lives in dormitories?
Who lives in nursing homes?
Who lives in shelters?
Why?

# THE LIVING ROOM

## リビング/居間

| | | |
|---|---|---|
| 本棚/書棚 | 1 | bookcase |
| 写真 | 2 | picture/photograph |
| 絵 | 3 | painting |
| マントル(炉棚) | 4 | mantel |
| 暖炉 | 5 | fireplace |
| 暖炉ガード | 6 | fireplace screen |
| DVDプレーヤー | 7 | DVD player |
| テレビ | 8 | television/TV |
| ビデオデッキ | 9 | VCR/video cassette recorder |
| 壁 | 10 | wall |
| 天井 | 11 | ceiling |
| カーテン | 12 | drapes |
| 窓 | 13 | window |
| 2人掛けソファ | 14 | loveseat |
| 壁面ユニット家具 | 15 | wall unit |
| スピーカー | 16 | speaker |
| ステレオ | 17 | stereo system |
| マガジンラック | 18 | magazine holder |
| クッション | 19 | (throw) pillow |
| ソファ | 20 | sofa/couch |
| (観葉)植物 | 21 | plant |
| センターテーブル | 22 | coffee table |
| じゅうたん | 23 | rug |
| ランプ | 24 | lamp |
| ランプのかさ | 25 | lampshade |
| サイドテーブル | 26 | end table |
| 床 | 27 | floor |
| フロアランプ | 28 | floor lamp |
| ひじ掛けいす | 29 | armchair |

A. Where are you?
B. I'm in the living room.
A. What are you doing?
B. I'm dusting* the **bookcase**.

* dusting/cleaning

A. You have a very nice living room!
B. Thank you.
A. Your ________ is/are beautiful!
B. Thank you for saying so.

A. Uh-oh! I just spilled coffee on your ________!
B. That's okay. Don't worry about it.

Tell about your living room.
(In my living room there's .............)

# THE DINING ROOM

## 食堂

| | | |
|---|---|---|
| 食卓 | 1 | (dining room) table |
| いす | 2 | (dining room) chair |
| サイドテーブル | 3 | buffet |
| トレイ／盆 | 4 | tray |
| ティーポット | 5 | teapot |
| コーヒーポット | 6 | coffee pot |
| 砂糖入れ | 7 | sugar bowl |
| クリーム入れ | 8 | creamer |
| 水さし | 9 | pitcher |
| シャンデリア | 10 | chandelier |
| 食器棚 | 11 | china cabinet |
| 陶磁器 | 12 | china |
| サラダボウル | 13 | salad bowl |
| サービングボウル | 14 | serving bowl |
| サービングディッシュ | 15 | serving dish |
| 花瓶 | 16 | vase |
| ろうそく | 17 | candle |
| 燭台 | 18 | candlestick |
| 大皿 | 19 | platter |
| バター入れ | 20 | butter dish |
| 食卓用食塩入れ | 21 | salt shaker |
| 食卓用こしょう入れ | 22 | pepper shaker |
| テーブルクロス | 23 | tablecloth |
| ナプキン | 24 | napkin |
| フォーク | 25 | fork |
| 取り皿 | 26 | plate |
| ナイフ | 27 | knife |
| スプーン | 28 | spoon |
| ボウル | 29 | bowl |
| マグカップ | 30 | mug |
| コップ | 31 | glass |
| カップ | 32 | cup |
| 受け皿 | 33 | saucer |

A. This **dining room table** is very nice.
B. Thank you. It was a gift from my *grandmother*.*

*grandmother/grandfather/aunt/uncle/. . .

[In a store]

A. May I help you?
B. Yes, please. Do you have ________s?*
A. Yes. ________s* are right over there.
B. Thank you.

**With 12, use the singular.*

[At home]

A. Look at this old ________ I just bought!
B. Where did you buy it?
A. At a yard sale. How do you like it?
B. It's VERY unusual!

Tell about your dining room.
(In my dining room there's ..............)

# 寝室

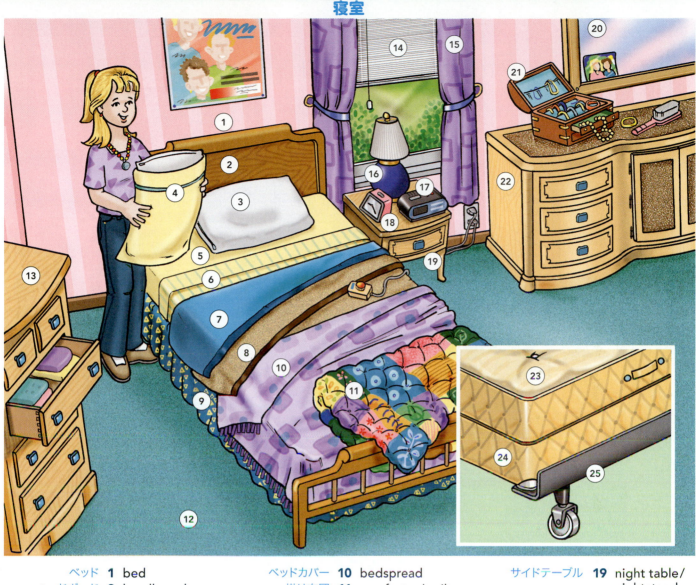

| | | |
|---|---|---|
| ベッド **1** bed | ベッドカバー **10** bedspread | サイドテーブル **19** night table/nightstand |
| ヘッドボード **2** headboard | 掛け布団 **11** comforter/quilt | 鏡 **20** mirror |
| 枕 **3** pillow | じゅうたん **12** carpet | 宝石入れ **21** jewelry box |
| 枕カバー **4** pillowcase | たんす **13** chest (of drawers) | ドレッサー **22** dresser/bureau |
| シーツ **5** fitted sheet | ブラインド **14** blinds | マットレス **23** mattress |
| 上掛けシーツ **6** (flat) sheet | カーテン **15** curtains | ボックススプリング **24** box spring |
| 毛布 **7** blanket | ランプ **16** lamp | ベッドの枠 **25** bed frame |
| 電気毛布 **8** electric blanket | 目覚まし時計 **17** alarm clock | |
| ダストラッフル（ひだ付きの埃よけ） **9** dust ruffle | ラジオ付き時計 **18** clock radio | |

A. Ooh! Look at that big bug!
B. Where?
A. It's on the **bed**!
B. I'LL get it.

[In a store]

A. Excuse me. I'm looking for a/an ________.*
B. We have some very nice ________s, and they're all on sale this week!
A. Oh, good!

* *With 14 & 15, use:* Excuse me. I'm looking for _____.

[In a bedroom]

A. Oh, no! I just lost my contact lens!
B. Where?
A. I think it's on the ________.
B. I'll help you look.

Tell about your bedroom. (In my bedroom there's .............)

# THE KITCHEN

## 台所

| | | |
|---|---|---|
| 冷蔵庫 | **1** | refrigerator |
| 冷凍庫 | **2** | freezer |
| ごみ箱 | **3** | garbage pail |
| 電動泡立て器 | **4** | (electric) mixer |
| 戸棚 | **5** | cabinet |
| キッチンペーパーホルダー | **6** | paper towel holder |
| キャニスター | **7** | canister |
| 調理台 | **8** | (kitchen) counter |
| 食器洗い機用洗剤 | **9** | dishwasher detergent |
| 台所用洗剤 | **10** | dishwashing liquid |
| 蛇口 | **11** | faucet |
| 流し | **12** | (kitchen) sink |
| 食器洗い機 | **13** | dishwasher |
| ディスポーザー（ごみ処理機） | **14** | (garbage) disposal |
| ふきん | **15** | dish towel |
| 食器用水切り | **16** | dish rack/ dish drainer |
| スパイスラック | **17** | spice rack |
| (電動)缶切り | **18** | (electric) can opener |
| ミキサー | **19** | blender |
| オーブントースター | **20** | toaster oven |
| 電子レンジ | **21** | microwave (oven) |
| なべつかみ | **22** | potholder |
| やかん | **23** | tea kettle |
| レンジ | **24** | stove/range |
| バーナー | **25** | burner |
| オーブン | **26** | oven |
| トースター | **27** | toaster |
| コーヒーメーカー | **28** | coffeemaker |
| ごみ圧縮機 | **29** | trash compactor |
| まな板 | **30** | cutting board |
| 料理の本 | **31** | cookbook |
| フードプロセッサー | **32** | food processor |
| いす | **33** | kitchen chair |
| テーブル | **34** | kitchen table |
| ランチョンマット | **35** | placemat |

A. I think we need a new **refrigerator**.
B. I think you're right.

[In a store]

A. Excuse me. Are your ________s still on sale?
B. Yes, they are. They're twenty percent off.

[In a kitchen]

A. When did you get this/these new ________(s)?
B. I got it/them last week.

Tell about your kitchen.
(In my kitchen there's ..............)

# 赤ちゃんの部屋

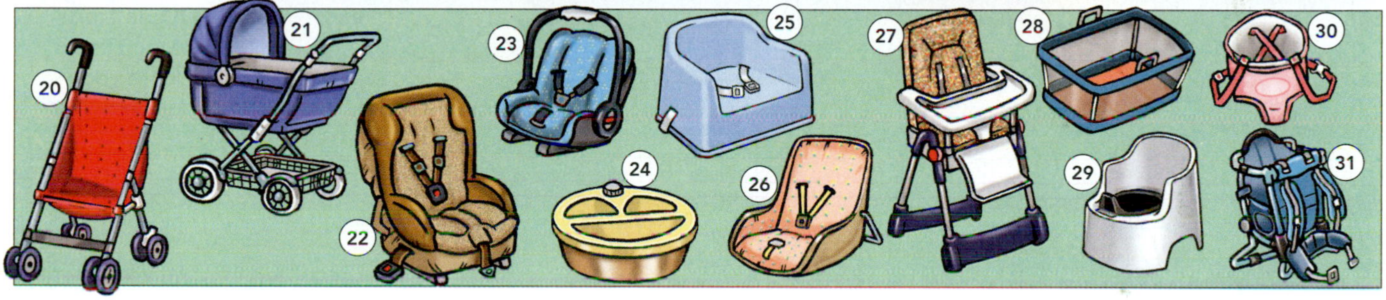

| | | |
|---|---|---|
| テディベア | 1 | teddy bear |
| ベビーモニター／インターホン | 2 | baby monitor/ intercom |
| たんす | 3 | chest (of drawers) |
| ベビーベッド | 4 | crib |
| 保護パッド／ベッドの枠 | 5 | crib bumper/ bumper pad |
| モビール | 6 | mobile |
| おむつ交換台 | 7 | changing table |
| ロンパース | 8 | stretch suit |
| (おむつ交換用)マット | 9 | changing pad |
| おむつバケツ | 10 | diaper pail |
| 常夜灯 | 11 | night light |
| おもちゃ箱 | 12 | toy chest |
| ぬいぐるみ | 13 | stuffed animal |
| 人形 | 14 | doll |
| ブランコ | 15 | swing |
| ベビーサークル | 16 | playpen |
| ガラガラ | 17 | rattle |
| 歩行器 | 18 | walker |
| ゆりかご | 19 | cradle |
| ベビーカー | 20 | stroller |
| 乳母車 | 21 | baby carriage |
| チャイルドシート | 22 | car seat/ safety seat |
| ベビーキャリー | 23 | baby carrier |
| 離乳食の保温器 | 24 | food warmer |
| ブースターシート | 25 | booster seat |
| ベビーシート | 26 | baby seat |
| ハイチェア | 27 | high chair |
| (持ち運びできる)ベビーベッド | 28 | portable crib |
| おまる | 29 | potty |
| だっこひも | 30 | baby frontpack |
| バックパック式キャリア | 31 | baby backpack |

A. Thank you for the **teddy bear**. It's a very nice gift.
B. You're welcome. Tell me, when are you due?
A. In a few more weeks.

A. That's a very nice ________.
Where did you get it?
B. It was a gift from ..............

A. Do you have everything you need before the baby comes?
B. Almost everything. We're still looking for a/an ________ and a/an ________.

Tell about your country:
What things do people buy for a new baby?
Does a new baby sleep in a separate room, as in the United States?

# THE BATHROOM

## バスルーム（浴室・トイレ・洗面所）

| | | |
|---|---|---|
| くずかご | 1 | wastebasket |
| 化粧台 | 2 | vanity |
| 石けん | 3 | soap |
| 石けん皿 | 4 | soap dish |
| 液体石けん入れ | 5 | soap dispenser |
| 洗面台 | 6 | (bathroom) sink |
| 蛇口 | 7 | faucet |
| 薬用品棚 | 8 | medicine cabinet |
| 鏡 | 9 | mirror |
| コップ | 10 | cup |
| 歯ブラシ | 11 | toothbrush |
| 歯ブラシ立て | 12 | toothbrush holder |
| 電動歯ブラシ | 13 | electric toothbrush |
| ドライヤー | 14 | hair dryer |
| 棚 | 15 | shelf |
| 洗濯かご | 16 | hamper |
| 換気扇 | 17 | fan |
| バスタオル | 18 | bath towel |
| 手ふきタオル | 19 | hand towel |
| 浴用タオル | 20 | washcloth/facecloth |
| タオル掛け | 21 | towel rack |
| プランジャー（排水管掃除用） | 22 | plunger |
| トイレブラシ | 23 | toilet brush |
| トイレットペーパー | 24 | toilet paper |
| 芳香剤 | 25 | air freshener |
| 便器 | 26 | toilet |
| 便座 | 27 | toilet seat |
| シャワー | 28 | shower |
| シャワーヘッド | 29 | shower head |
| シャワーカーテン | 30 | shower curtain |
| 浴槽 | 31 | bathtub/tub |
| 滑り止めマット | 32 | rubber mat |
| 排水溝 | 33 | drain |
| スポンジ | 34 | sponge |
| バスマット | 35 | bath mat |
| 体重計 | 36 | scale |

A. Where's the **hair dryer**?
B. It's *on* the **vanity**.

A. Where's the **soap**?
B. It's *in* the **soap dish**.

A. Where's the **plunger**?
B. It's *next to* the **toilet brush**.

A. [Knock. Knock.] Did I leave my glasses in there?
B. Yes. They're on/in/next to the ______.

A. *Bobby*? You didn't clean up the bathroom! There's toothpaste on the ______, and there's powder all over the ______!
B. Sorry. I'll clean it up right away.

Tell about your bathroom.
(In my bathroom there's ............)

# 家の外観

## 前庭 Front Yard

- 街灯柱 **1** lamppost
- 郵便受け **2** mailbox
- 玄関口 **3** front walk
- 玄関口の階段 **4** front steps
- ポーチ **5** (front) porch
- 防風ドア **6** storm door
- 玄関ドア **7** front door
- 呼び鈴 **8** doorbell
- 玄関灯 **9** (front) light
- 窓 **10** window
- 網戸 **11** (window) screen
- 雨戸 **12** shutter
- 屋根 **13** roof
- 車庫 **14** garage
- 車庫ドア **15** garage door
- ドライブウェイ（私設車道） **16** driveway

## 裏庭 Backyard

- 庭いす **17** lawn chair
- 芝刈り機 **18** lawnmower
- 物置 **19** tool shed
- 網戸 **20** screen door
- 裏口 **21** back door
- ドアの取っ手 **22** door knob
- デッキ／ベランダ **23** deck
- バーベキューグリル **24** barbecue/ (outdoor) grill
- テラス **25** patio
- 雨どい **26** gutter
- 竪樋（たてとい） **27** drainpipe
- 衛星放送アンテナ **28** satellite dish
- テレビアンテナ **29** TV antenna
- 煙突 **30** chimney
- 勝手口 **31** side door
- フェンス **32** fence

A. When are you going to repair the **lamppost**?
B. I'm going to repair it next Saturday.

[On the telephone]
A. Harry's Home Repairs.
B. Hello. Do you fix ________s?
A. No, we don't.
B. Oh, okay. Thank you.

[At work on Monday morning]
A. What did you do this weekend?
B. Nothing much. I repaired my ________ and my ________.

Do you like to repair things?
What things can you repair yourself?
What things can't you repair? Who repairs them?

# THE APARTMENT BUILDING

## アパートメント

**アパートを探す** **Looking for an Apartment**

- アパートの広告／三行広告 **1** apartment ads/classified ads
- アパート物件リスト **2** apartment listings
- 空き部屋の看板 **3** vacancy sign

**賃貸契約にサインする** **Signing a Lease**

- 借家人 **4** tenant
- 家主 **5** landlord
- 賃貸契約書 **6** lease
- 保証金 **7** security deposit

**引っ越し（入居）** **Moving In**

- 引っ越しトラック **8** moving truck/moving van
- 近所の人 **9** neighbor
- ビル管理人 **10** building manager
- ドアマン（玄関番） **11** doorman
- 鍵 **12** key
- 錠 **13** lock
- 1階 **14** first floor
- 2階 **15** second floor
- 3階 **16** third floor
- 4階 **17** fourth floor
- 屋根 **18** roof
- 非常階段 **19** fire escape
- 地下駐車場 **20** parking garage
- バルコニー **21** balcony
- 中庭 **22** courtyard
- 駐車場 **23** parking lot
- 駐車スペース **24** parking space
- プール **25** swimming pool
- 気泡風呂 **26** whirlpool
- ゴミ入れ **27** trash bin
- エアコン（空調設備） **28** air conditioner

**玄関ホール/ロビー Lobby**

インターホン/スピーカー **29** intercom/speaker
ブザー **30** buzzer
郵便受け **31** mailbox
エレベーター **32** elevator
階段 **33** stairway

**玄関 Doorway**

のぞき穴 **34** peephole
ドアチェーン **35** (door) chain
本締錠 **36** dead-bolt lock
煙感知器 **37** smoke detector

**廊下 Hallway**

非常階段 **38** fire exit/emergency stairway
火災報知器 **39** fire alarm
スプリンクラー **40** sprinkler system
管理人 **41** superintendent
ダストシュート **42** garbage chute/trash chute

**地階 Basement**

倉庫 **43** storage room
収納ロッカー **44** storage locker
洗濯室 **45** laundry room
セキュリティゲート **46** security gate

[19–46]
A. Is there a **fire escape**?
B. Yes, there is. Do you want to see the apartment?
A. Yes, I do.

[19–46]
[Renting an apartment]
A. Let me show you around.
B. Okay.
A. This is the ______, and here's the ______.
B. I see.

[19–46]
[On the telephone]
A. Mom and Dad? I found an apartment.
B. Good. Tell us about it.
A. It has a/an ______ and a/an ______.
B. That's nice. Does it have a/an ______?
A. Yes, it does.

Do you or someone you know live in an apartment building? Tell about it.

# 住居の問題と修理

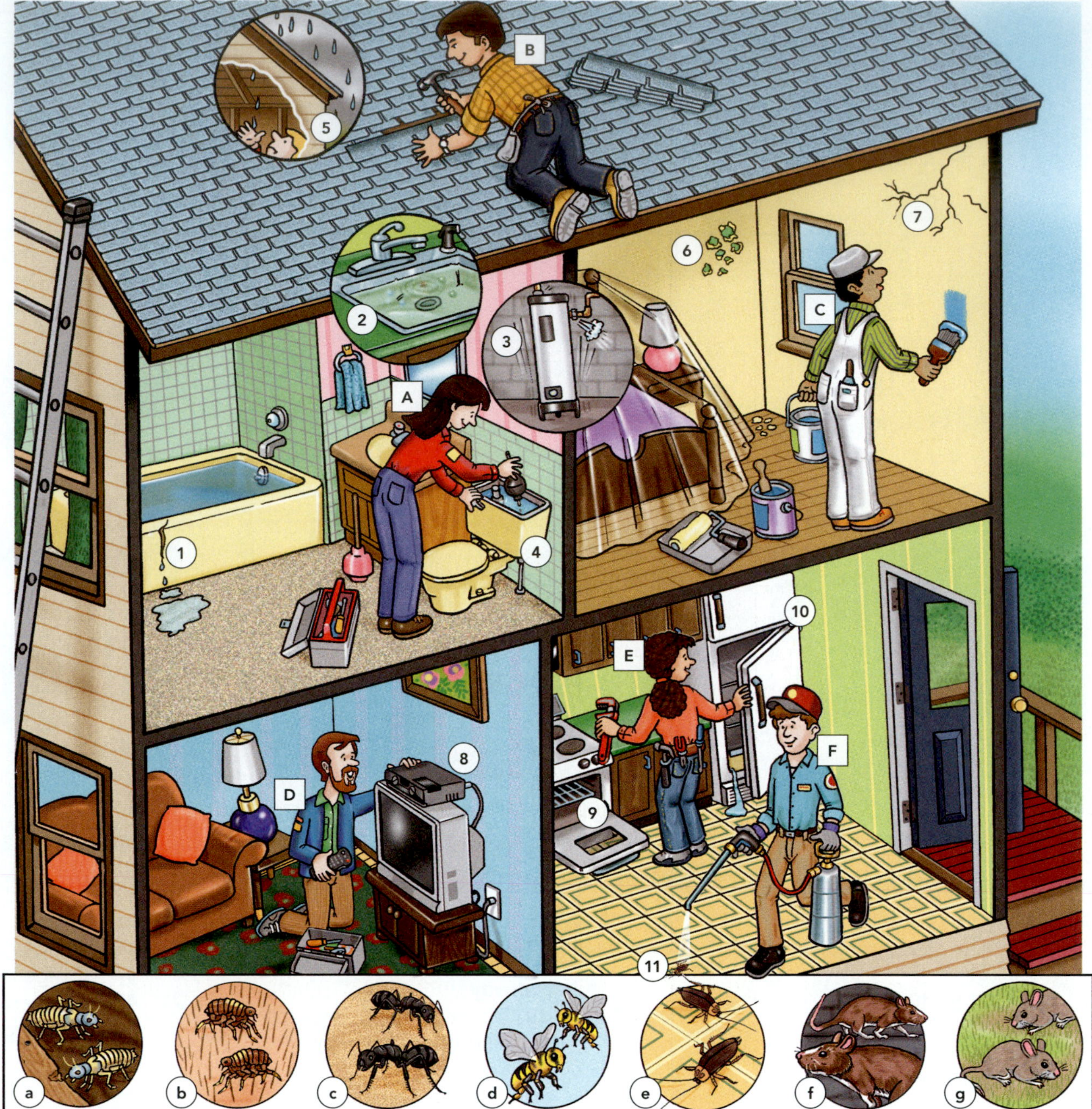


配管工 **A plumber**
浴槽がもれています。 **1** The bathtub is leaking.
流しが詰まっています。 **2** The sink is clogged.
湯沸かし器が故障しています。 **3** The hot water heater isn't working.
トイレが壊れています。 **4** The toilet is broken.

屋根職人 **B roofer**
屋根が雨漏りしています。 **5** The roof is leaking.

ペンキ屋 **C (house) painter**
ペンキがはがれています。 **6** The paint is peeling.
壁にひびが入っています。 **7** The wall is cracked.

ケーブルテレビ会社 **D cable TV company**
ケーブルテレビがつきません。 **8** The cable TV isn't working.

家電製品の修理屋 **E appliance repairperson**
レンジが壊れています。 **9** The stove isn't working.
冷蔵庫が壊れています。 **10** The refrigerator is broken.

害虫駆除業者 **F exterminator/ pest control specialist**
台所に ____ がいます。 **11** There are ____ in the kitchen.

- シロアリ **a** termites
- ノミ **b** fleas
- アリ **c** ants
- ハチ **d** bees
- ゴキブリ **e** cockroaches
- ドブネズミ **f** rats
- ネズミ **g** mice

錠前屋 **G locksmith**
錠が壊れています。 **12** The lock is broken.

電気工 **H electrician**
玄関灯がつきません。 **13** The front light doesn't go on.
呼び鈴が鳴りません。 **14** The doorbell doesn't ring.
居間が停電しています。 **15** The power is out in the living room.

煙突掃除夫 **I chimneysweep**
煙突が汚れています。 **16** The chimney is dirty.

便利屋 **J home repairperson/"handyman"**
洗面所のタイルがゆるんでいます。 **17** The tiles in the bathroom are loose.

大工 **K carpenter**
ステップが壊れています。 **18** The steps are broken.
ドアが開きません。 **19** The door doesn't open.

暖房/エアコンサービス **L heating and air conditioning service**
暖房システムが壊れています。 **20** The heating system is broken.
エアコンがつきません。 **21** The air conditioning isn't working.

A. What's the matter?
B. ___[1–21]___.
A. I think we should call a/an ___[A–L]___.

[1–21]
A. I'm having a problem in my apartment/house.
B. What's the problem?
A. ________.

[A–L]
A. Can you recommend a good ________?
B. Yes. You should call ..............

What do you do when there are problems in your home? Do you fix things yourself, or do you call someone?

# CLEANING YOUR HOME

## 家の掃除

床を掃く **A** sweep the floor
掃除機をかける **B** vacuum
床をモップがけする **C** mop the floor
窓を拭く **D** wash the windows
はたきをかける **E** dust
床にワックスをかける **F** wax the floor
家具をみがく **G** polish the furniture
洗面所を掃除する **H** clean the bathroom
ゴミを出す **I** take out the garbage

ほうき **1** broom
ちりとり **2** dustpan
小ほうき **3** whisk broom
じゅうたん掃除機 **4** carpet sweeper
掃除機 **5** vacuum (cleaner)
掃除機付属品 **6** vacuum cleaner attachments
掃除機用ゴミバッグ **7** vacuum cleaner bag
ハンドクリーナー **8** hand vacuum
ダストモップ **9** (dust) mop/(dry) mop
スポンジモップ **10** (sponge) mop
モップ **11** (wet) mop
ペーパータオル **12** paper towels
窓用洗剤 **13** window cleaner
アンモニア **14** ammonia
ぞうきん **15** dust cloth
はたき **16** feather duster
ワックス **17** floor wax
家具用洗剤／家具みがき **18** furniture polish
クレンザー **19** cleanser
たわし **20** scrub brush
スポンジ **21** sponge
バケツ **22** bucket/pail
ごみバケツ **23** trash can/garbage can
リサイクル用品入れ **24** recycling bin

[A–I]
A. What are you doing?
B. I'm **sweep**ing **the floor**.

[1–24]
A. I can't find the **broom**.
B. Look over there!

[1–12, 15, 16, 20–24]
A. Excuse me. Do you sell ________(s)?
B. Yes. They're at the back of the store.
A. Thanks.

[13, 14, 17–19]
A. Excuse me. Do you sell ________?
B. Yes. It's at the back of the store.
A. Thanks.

What household cleaning chores do people do in your home? What things do they use?

# 家庭用品

| | | |
|---|---|---|
| ヤード尺 | 1 | yardstick |
| ハエたたき | 2 | fly swatter |
| プランジャー／排水管掃除器 | 3 | plunger |
| 懐中電灯 | 4 | flashlight |
| 延長コード | 5 | extension cord |
| 巻き尺 | 6 | tape measure |
| 脚立 | 7 | step ladder |
| ねずみとり | 8 | mousetrap |
| マスキングテープ | 9 | masking tape |
| 絶縁テープ | 10 | electrical tape |
| ガムテープ | 11 | duct tape |
| 電池 | 12 | batteries |
| 電球 | 13 | lightbulbs/bulbs |
| ヒューズ | 14 | fuses |
| 機械油 | 15 | oil |
| 接着剤 | 16 | glue |
| 軍手／作業手袋 | 17 | work gloves |
| 殺虫剤 | 18 | bug spray/insect spray |
| ゴキブリ用殺虫剤 | 19 | roach killer |
| 紙やすり／サンドペーパー | 20 | sandpaper |
| ペンキ | 21 | paint |
| シンナー | 22 | paint thinner |
| ペンキブラシ／ペンキ用の刷毛 | 23 | paintbrush/brush |
| ペンキ皿 | 24 | paint pan |
| ペンキローラー | 25 | paint roller |
| 塗料吹き付け機 | 26 | spray gun |

A. I can't find the **yardstick**!
B. Look in the utility cabinet.
A. I did.
B. Oh! Wait a minute! I lent the **yardstick** to the neighbors.

[1–8, 23–26]
A. I'm going to the hardware store.
Can you think of anything we need?
B. Yes. We need a/an ________.
A. Oh, that's right.

[9–22]
A. I'm going to the hardware store.
Can you think of anything we need?
B. Yes. We need ________.
A. Oh, that's right.

What home supplies do you have? How and when do you use each one?

# TOOLS AND HARDWARE

## 道具と金物

| | | |
|---|---|---|
| ハンマー／金づち | 1 | hammer |
| 木槌 | 2 | mallet |
| 斧 | 3 | ax |
| のこぎり | 4 | saw/handsaw |
| 金のこ | 5 | hacksaw |
| 水準器 | 6 | level |
| ドライバー／ねじ回し | 7 | screwdriver |
| プラスドライバー | 8 | Phillips screwdriver |
| スパナ | 9 | wrench |
| モンキーレンチ／パイプレンチ | 10 | monkey wrench/ pipe wrench |
| のみ | 11 | chisel |
| はぎとり器 | 12 | scraper |
| ワイヤーストリッパー | 13 | wire stripper |
| 手回しドリル | 14 | hand drill |
| 万力 | 15 | vise |
| ペンチ | 16 | pliers |
| 道具箱 | 17 | toolbox |
| かんな | 18 | plane |
| 電気ドリル | 19 | electric drill |
| ドリルの刃 | 20 | (drill) bit |
| 電動丸のこ／電動のこ | 21 | circular saw/ power saw |
| 電動紙やすり | 22 | power sander |
| リューター | 23 | router |
| 針金 | 24 | wire |
| くぎ | 25 | nail |
| ワッシャー／座金 | 26 | washer |
| ナット | 27 | nut |
| 木ねじ | 28 | wood screw |
| 小ねじ | 29 | machine screw |
| ボルト | 30 | bolt |

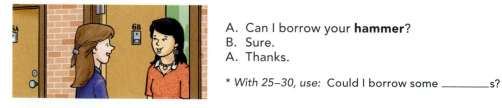

A. Can I borrow your **hammer**?
B. Sure.
A. Thanks.

* *With 25–30, use:* Could I borrow some ________s?

[1–15, 17–24]
A. Where's the ________?
B. It's on/next to/near/over/under the ________.

[16, 25–30]
A. Where are the ________s?
B. They're on/next to/near/over/under the ________.

Do you like to work with tools? What tools do you have in your home?

# GARDENING TOOLS AND ACTIONS

## ガーデニング道具と作業

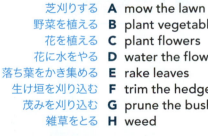

| | | | | | | | |
|---|---|---|---|---|---|---|---|
| 芝刈りする | **A** mow the lawn | ラインカッター | **3** line trimmer | じょうろ | **13** watering can |
| 野菜を植える | **B** plant vegetables | シャベル | **4** shovel | くま手 | **14** rake |
| 花を植える | **C** plant flowers | 野菜の種 | **5** vegetable seeds | ブロワー | **15** leaf blower |
| 花に水をやる | **D** water the flowers | くわ | **6** hoe | 庭用ゴミ袋 | **16** yard waste bag |
| 落ち葉をかき集める | **E** rake leaves | 移植ごて | **7** trowel | 植木ばさみ／刈り込みバサミ | **17** (hedge) clippers |
| 生け垣を刈り込む | **F** trim the hedge | 手押し車 | **8** wheelbarrow | ヘッジトリマー | **18** hedge trimmer |
| 茂みを刈り込む | **G** prune the bushes | 肥料 | **9** fertilizer | 剪定鋏 | **19** pruning shears |
| 雑草をとる | **H** weed | ホース | **10** (garden) hose | 草抜き | **20** weeder |
| 芝刈り機 | **1** lawnmower | ノズル | **11** nozzle | | |
| ガソリン缶 | **2** gas can | スプリンクラー | **12** sprinkler | | |

[A–H]
A. Hi! Are you busy?
B. Yes. I'm **mow**ing **the lawn**.

[1–20]
A. What are you looking for?
B. The **lawnmower**.

[A–H]
A. What are you going to do tomorrow?
B. I'm going to ________.

[1–20]
A. Can I borrow your ________?
B. Sure.

Do you ever work with any of these tools? Which ones? What do you do with them?

## 街の風景1

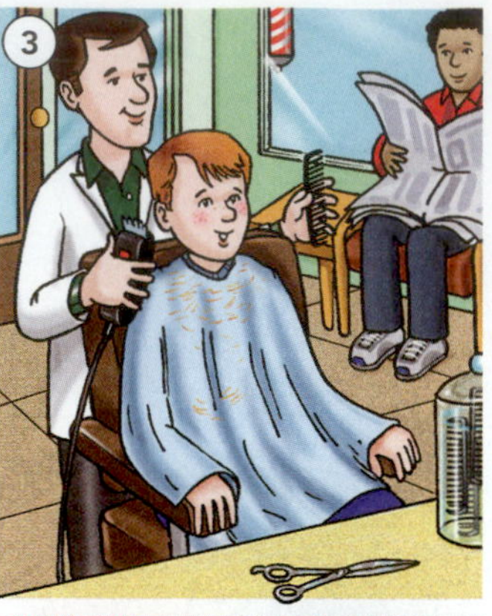

パン屋 **1** bakery
銀行 **2** bank
床屋 **3** barber shop
本屋 **4** book store
バス発着所 **5** bus station
キャンディショップ **6** candy store

車販売代理店 **7** car dealership
カード屋 **8** card store
託児所 **9** child-care center / day-care center
クリーニング店 **10** cleaners / dry cleaners

診療所 **11** clinic
衣料品店 **12** clothing store
喫茶店 **13** coffee shop
コンピュータ販売店／OA店 **14** computer store
コンビニエンスストア **15** convenience store
コピーセンター **16** copy center

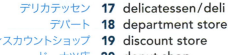

| | | |
|---|---|---|
| デリカテッセン | **17** | delicatessen/deli |
| デパート | **18** | department store |
| ディスカウントショップ | **19** | discount store |
| ドーナツ店 | **20** | donut shop |
| 薬局 | **21** | drug store/ pharmacy |
| 電器店 | **22** | electronics store |
| メガネ屋 | **23** | eye-care center/ optician |
| ファーストフード店 | **24** | fast-food restaurant |
| 花屋 | **25** | flower shop/ florist |
| 家具屋 | **26** | furniture store |
| ガソリンスタンド | **27** | gas station/ service station |
| 食料雑貨店 | **28** | grocery store |

A. Where are you going?
B. I'm going to the **bakery**.

A. Hi! How are you today?
B. Fine. Where are you going?
A. To the _______. How about you?
B. I'm going to the _______.

A. Oh, no! I can't find my wallet/purse!
B. Did you leave it at the _______?
A. Maybe I did.

Which of these places are in your neighborhood?
(In my neighborhood there's a/an .............)

## 街の風景 2

美容院 **1** hair salon
金物屋 **2** hardware store
スポーツクラブ／スポーツジム **3** health club
病院 **4** hospital
ホテル **5** hotel

アイスクリーム店 **6** ice cream shop
宝石店 **7** jewelry store
コインランドリー **8** laundromat
図書館 **9** library
マタニティー用品店 **10** maternity shop
モーテル **11** motel

映画館 **12** movie theater
レコード・CD店 **13** music store
ネイルサロン **14** nail salon
公園 **15** park
ペットショップ **16** pet shop/pet store

写真屋 **17** photo shop
ピザ屋 **18** pizza shop
郵便局 **19** post office
レストラン **20** restaurant

学校 **21** school
靴屋 **22** shoe store
ショッピングモール **23** (shopping) mall
スーパーマーケット **24** supermarket

おもちゃ屋 **25** toy store
駅 **26** train station
旅行代理店 **27** travel agency
ビデオショップ **28** video store

A. Where's the **hair salon**?
B. It's right over there.

A. Is there a/an _______ nearby?
B. Yes. There's a/an _______ around the corner.
A. Thanks.

A. Excuse me. Where's the _______?
B. It's down the street, next to the _______.
A. Thank you.

Which of these places are in your neighborhood?
(In my neighborhood there's a/an ............)

# 市街

| | | |
|---|---|---|
| 裁判所 | 1 | courthouse |
| タクシー | 2 | taxi/cab/taxicab |
| タクシー乗り場 | 3 | taxi stand |
| タクシー運転手 | 4 | taxi driver/cab driver |
| 消火栓 | 5 | fire hydrant |
| くず入れ | 6 | trash container |
| 市庁舎 | 7 | city hall |
| 火災報知器 | 8 | fire alarm box |
| ポスト | 9 | mailbox |
| 下水道 | 10 | sewer |
| 警察署 | 11 | police station |
| 拘置所 | 12 | jail |
| 歩道 | 13 | sidewalk |
| 車道／通り | 14 | street |
| 街灯 | 15 | street light |
| 駐車場 | 16 | parking lot |
| (駐車違反を取り締まる)婦人警官 | 17 | meter maid |
| パーキングメーター | 18 | parking meter |
| 清掃車 | 19 | garbage truck |
| 地下鉄 | 20 | subway |
| 地下鉄の駅 | 21 | subway station |

新聞スタンド **22** newsstand
信号 **23** traffic light / traffic signal
交差点 **24** intersection
警官 **25** police officer
横断歩道 **26** crosswalk
歩行者 **27** pedestrian
アイスクリーム販売車 **28** ice cream truck

縁石 **29** curb
屋内駐車場 **30** parking garage
消防署 **31** fire station
バス停 **32** bus stop
バス **33** bus
バス運転手 **34** bus driver
オフィスビル **35** office building

公衆電話 **36** public telephone
街路標識 **37** street sign
マンホール **38** manhole
オートバイ **39** motorcycle
露店商 **40** street vendor
ドライブスルー窓口 **41** drive-through window

A. Where's the _______?
B. On/In/Next to/Between/Across from/ In front of/Behind/Under/Over the _______.

[An Election Speech]

If I am elected mayor, I'll take care of all the problems in our city. We need to do something about our _______s. We also need to do something about our _______s. And look at our _______s! We REALLY need to do something about THEM! We need a new mayor who can solve these problems. If I am elected mayor, we'll be proud of our _______s, _______s, and _______s again! Vote for me!

Go to an intersection in your city or town. What do you see? Make a list. Then tell about it.

# PEOPLE AND PHYSICAL DESCRIPTIONS

## 人と身体的特徴

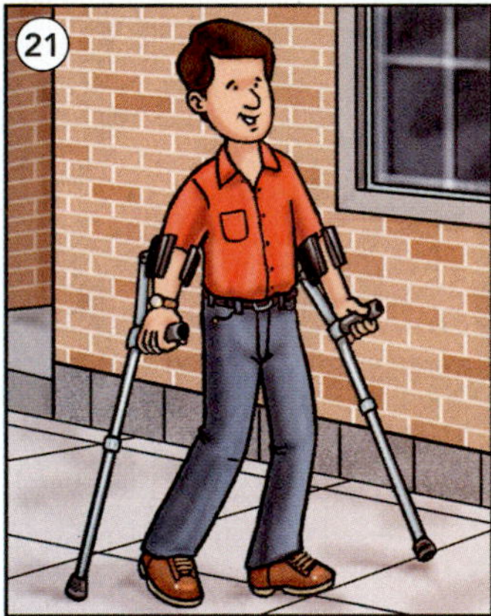

**子供・子供 (複数)** **1 child-children**
赤ちゃん／乳児 **2** baby/infant
幼児 **3** toddler
男の子 **4** boy
女の子 **5** girl
ティーンエージャー **6** teenager

**大人** **7 adult**
男の人・男の人 (複数) **8** man–men
女の人・女の人 (複数) **9** woman–women
老人 **10** senior citizen/ elderly person

**年** **age**
若い **11** young
中年の **12** middle-aged
年とった **13** old/elderly

**身長** **height**
背が高い **14** tall
中背の **15** average height
背が低い **16** short

**体重** **weight**
太った **17** heavy
中肉の **18** average weight
細い／痩せている **19** thin/slim
妊娠している **20** pregnant

身体の不自由な **21** physically challenged
目の不自由な **22** vision impaired
耳の不自由な **23** hearing impaired

**髪の毛・ひげに関する表現 Describing Hair**

長い／ロングヘアの **24** long
セミロング **25** shoulder length
短い／ショートヘアの **26** short

ストレートの／直毛の **27** straight
ウェーブがかかった **28** wavy
巻き毛の／カーリーヘアの **29** curly

黒い **30** black
茶色い **31** brown
ブロンドの **32** blond
赤毛の **33** red
白髪の **34** gray

禿げた **35** bald
あごひげ **36** beard
口ひげ **37** mustache

A. Tell me about *your brother.*
B. *He's a tall heavy boy* with *short curly brown* hair.

A. What does *your new boss* look like?
B. *She's average height*, and *she* has *long straight black* hair.

A. Can you describe *the person*?
B. *He's a tall thin middle-aged man.*
A. Anything else?
B. Yes. *He's bald*, and *he* has *a mustache*.

A. Can you describe *your grandmother*?
B. *She's a short thin elderly person* with *long wavy gray* hair.
A. Anything else?
B. Yes. *She's hearing impaired.*

Tell about yourself.

Tell about people in your family.

Tell about your favorite actor or actress or other famous person.

# 人や物に関する表現

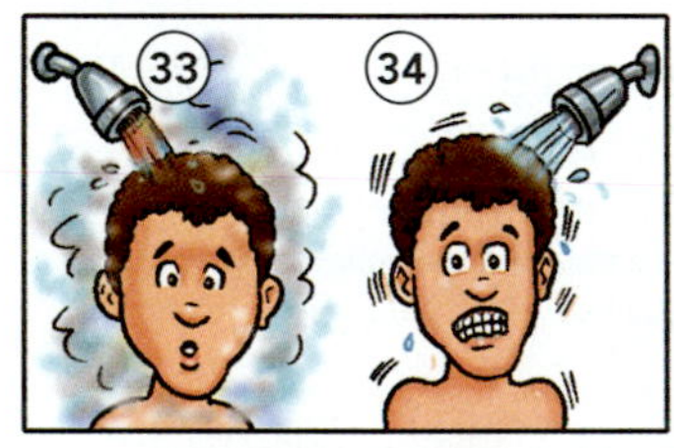

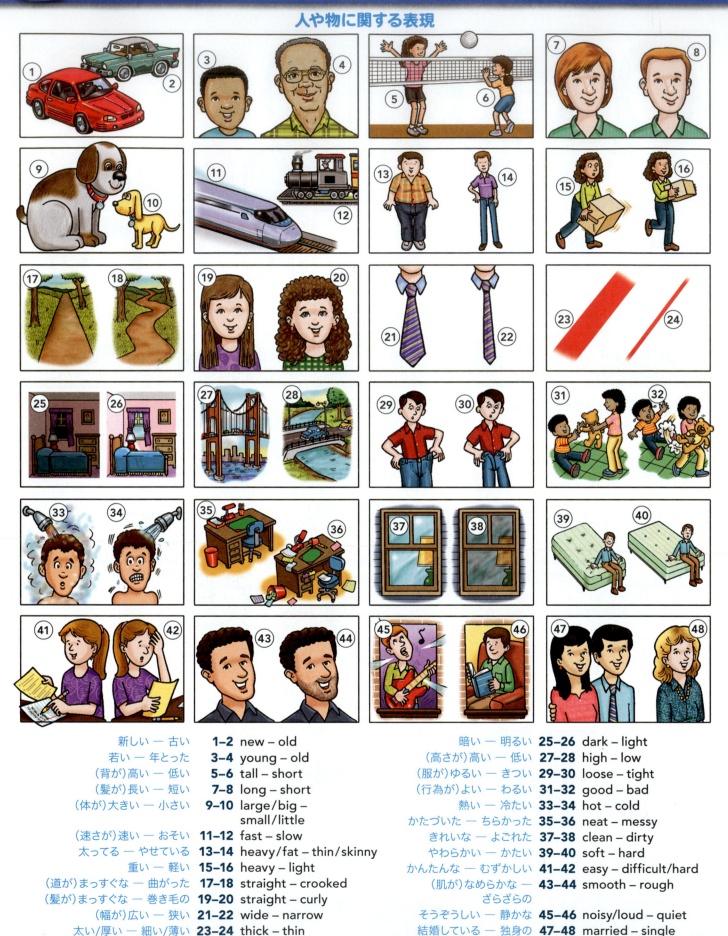

新しい — 古い **1–2** new – old
若い — 年とった **3–4** young – old
(背が)高い — 低い **5–6** tall – short
(髪が)長い — 短い **7–8** long – short
(体が)大きい — 小さい **9–10** large/big – small/little
(速さが)速い — おそい **11–12** fast – slow
太ってる — やせている **13–14** heavy/fat – thin/skinny
重い — 軽い **15–16** heavy – light
(道が)まっすぐな — 曲がった **17–18** straight – crooked
(髪が)まっすぐな — 巻き毛の **19–20** straight – curly
(幅が)広い — 狭い **21–22** wide – narrow
太い/厚い — 細い/薄い **23–24** thick – thin

暗い — 明るい **25–26** dark – light
(高さが)高い — 低い **27–28** high – low
(服が)ゆるい — きつい **29–30** loose – tight
(行為が)よい — わるい **31–32** good – bad
熱い — 冷たい **33–34** hot – cold
かたづいた — ちらかった **35–36** neat – messy
きれいな — よごれた **37–38** clean – dirty
やわらかい — かたい **39–40** soft – hard
かんたんな — むずかしい **41–42** easy – difficult/hard
(肌が)なめらかな — ざらざらの **43–44** smooth – rough
そうぞうしい — 静かな **45–46** noisy/loud – quiet
結婚している — 独身の **47–48** married – single

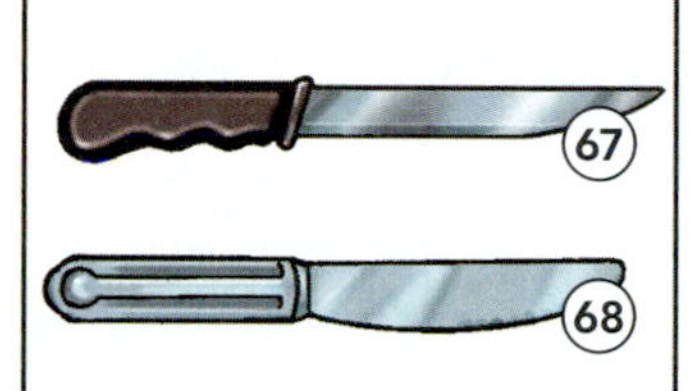

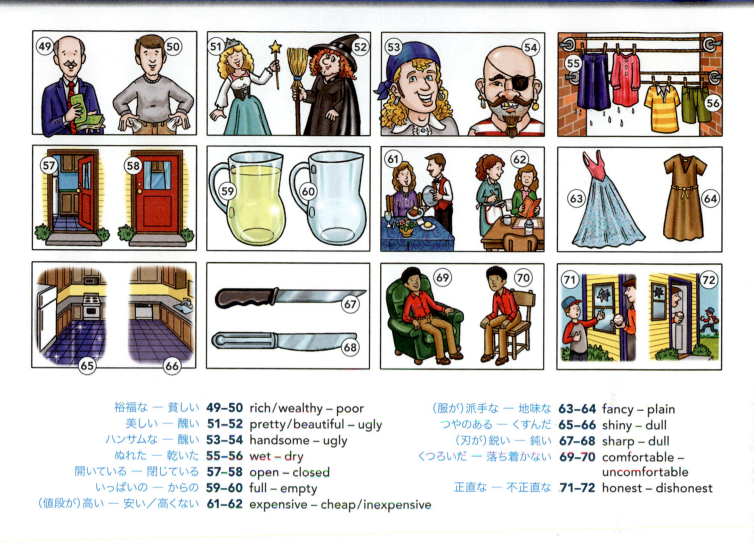

裕福な — 貧しい **49–50** rich/wealthy – poor
美しい — 醜い **51–52** pretty/beautiful – ugly
ハンサムな — 醜い **53–54** handsome – ugly
ぬれた — 乾いた **55–56** wet – dry
開いている — 閉じている **57–58** open – closed
いっぱいの — からの **59–60** full – empty
(値段が)高い — 安い/高くない **61–62** expensive – cheap/inexpensive
(服が)派手な — 地味な **63–64** fancy – plain
つやのある — くすんだ **65–66** shiny – dull
(刃が)鋭い — 鈍い **67–68** sharp – dull
くつろいだ — 落ち着かない **69–70** comfortable – uncomfortable
正直な — 不正直な **71–72** honest – dishonest

[1–2]
A. Is your car **new**?
B. No. It's **old**.

1–2 Is your car ______?
3–4 Is he ______?
5–6 Is your sister ______?
7–8 Is his hair ______?
9–10 Is their dog ______?
11–12 Is the train ______?
13–14 Is your friend ______?
15–16 Is the box ______?
17–18 Is the road ______?
19–20 Is her hair ______?
21–22 Is the tie ______?
23–24 Is the line ______?
25–26 Is the room ______?
27–28 Is the bridge ______?
29–30 Are the pants ______?
31–32 Are your neighbor's children ______?
33–34 Is the water ______?
35–36 Is your desk ______?
37–38 Are the windows ______?
39–40 Is the mattress ______?
41–42 Is the homework ______?
43–44 Is your skin ______?
45–46 Is your neighbor ______?
47–48 Is your sister ______?
49–50 Is your uncle ______?
51–52 Is the witch ______?
53–54 Is the pirate ______?
55–56 Are the clothes ______?
57–58 Is the door ______?
59–60 Is the pitcher ______?
61–62 Is that restaurant ______?
63–64 Is the dress ______?
65–66 Is your kitchen floor ______?
67–68 Is the knife ______?
69–70 Is the chair ______?
71–72 Is he ______?

A. Tell me about your ..........
B. He's/She's/It's/They're ______.

A. Do you have a/an ______ .........?
B. No. I have a/an ______ .........

Describe yourself.
Describe a person you know.
Describe some things in your home.
Describe some things in your community.

# 体調と感情に関する表現

疲れた **1** tired
眠い **2** sleepy
疲れきった **3** exhausted
病気の **4** sick/ill
暑い **5** hot
寒い **6** cold

おなかがすいた **7** hungry
のどがかわいた **8** thirsty
おなかがいっぱいの **9** full
うれしい **10** happy
悲しい **11** sad/unhappy

みじめな **12** miserable
興奮している **13** excited
がっかりした **14** disappointed
気が動転している **15** upset
いらいらした **16** annoyed

- 怒った **17** angry/mad
- 激怒した **18** furious
- うんざりした／あきれた **19** disgusted
- (思うようにならず) いらいらした **20** frustrated
- びっくりした **21** surprised
- ショックを受けた **22** shocked
- 寂しい **23** lonely
- ホームシックになっている **24** homesick
- 落ち着かない **25** nervous
- 心配した **26** worried
- こわがっている **27** scared/afraid
- あきた／退屈している **28** bored
- 誇らしい／誇りに思っている **29** proud
- ばつの悪い／恥ずかしい **30** embarrassed
- うらやましい **31** jealous
- 混乱した／途方にくれた **32** confused

A. You look ________.
B. I am. I'm VERY ________.

A. Are you ________?
B. No. Why do you ask? Do I LOOK ________?
A. Yes. You do.

What makes you happy? sad? mad?

What do you do when you feel nervous? annoyed?

Do you ever feel embarrassed? When?

# FRUITS

果物

| | | |
|---|---|---|
| リンゴ **1** apple | イチジク **12** fig | オレンジ **22** orange |
| モモ **2** peach | ココナツ **13** coconut | ミカン **23** tangerine |
| 洋ナシ **3** pear | アボカド **14** avocado | ブドウ **24** grapes |
| バナナ **4** banana | カンタロープメロン **15** cantaloupe | サクランボ **25** cherries |
| プランテーン **5** plantain | ハニーデューメロン **16** honeydew (melon) | プルーン **26** prunes |
| スモモ／プラム **6** plum | スイカ **17** watermelon | ナツメヤシ **27** dates |
| アンズ **7** apricot | パイナップル **18** pineapple | 干しブドウ **28** raisins |
| ネクタリン **8** nectarine | グレープフルーツ **19** grapefruit | ナッツ **29** nuts |
| キウイ **9** kiwi | レモン **20** lemon | ラズベリー／木イチゴ **30** raspberries |
| パパイヤ **10** papaya | ライム **21** lime | ブルーベリー **31** blueberries |
| マンゴー **11** mango | | イチゴ **32** strawberries |

[1–23]
A. This **apple** is delicious! Where did you get it?
B. At *Sam's Supermarket*.

[24–32]
A. These **grapes** are delicious! Where did you get them?
B. At *Franny's Fruit Stand*.

A. I'm hungry. Do we have any fruit?
B. Yes. We have ________s* and ________s.*

* *With 15–19, use:* We have ______ and ______.

A. Do we have any more ________s?†
B. No. I'll get some more when I go to the supermarket.

† *With 15–19 use:* Do we have any more ______?

What are your favorite fruits? Which fruits don't you like?

Which of these fruits grow where you live?

Name and describe other fruits you know.

# 野菜

| | | |
|---|---|---|
| セロリ | **1** | celery |
| トウモロコシ | **2** | corn |
| ブロッコリー | **3** | broccoli |
| カリフラワー | **4** | cauliflower |
| ホウレンソウ | **5** | spinach |
| パセリ | **6** | parsley |
| アスパラガス | **7** | asparagus |
| ナス | **8** | eggplant |
| レタス | **9** | lettuce |
| キャベツ | **10** | cabbage |
| パクチョイ | **11** | bok choy |
| ズッキーニ | **12** | zucchini |
| 西洋カボチャ(どんぐり形) | **13** | acorn squash |
| バターナットカボチャ | **14** | butternut squash |
| ニンニク | **15** | garlic |
| エンドウ豆 | **16** | pea |
| インゲン | **17** | string bean/ green bean |
| リマ豆 | **18** | lima bean |
| 黒豆 | **19** | black bean |
| キドニービーン | **20** | kidney bean |
| 芽キャベツ | **21** | brussels sprout |
| キュウリ | **22** | cucumber |
| トマト | **23** | tomato |
| ニンジン | **24** | carrot |
| ラディッシュ | **25** | radish |
| マッシュルーム | **26** | mushroom |
| アーティチョーク | **27** | artichoke |
| ジャガイモ | **28** | potato |
| サツマイモ | **29** | sweet potato |
| ヤム芋 | **30** | yam |
| ピーマン | **31** | green pepper/ sweet pepper |
| 赤ピーマン | **32** | red pepper |
| ハラペーニョ | **33** | jalapeño (pepper) |
| トウガラシ | **34** | chili pepper |
| ビーツ | **35** | beet |
| 玉ネギ | **36** | onion |
| シャーロット/ラッキョウ | **37** | scallion/ green onion |
| カブ | **38** | turnip |

A. What do we need from the supermarket?
B. We need **celery*** and **peas**.†

* 1–15 † 16–38

A. How do you like the __[1–15]__/__[16–38]__s?
B. It's/They're delicious.

A. *Bobby*? Finish your vegetables!
B. But you KNOW I hate __[1–15]__/__[16–38]__s!
A. I know. But it's/they're good for you!

Which vegetables do you like?
Which vegetables don't you like?

Which of these vegetables grow where you live?

Name and describe other vegetables you know.

# 肉類・シーフード

**肉類 Meat**

| | | |
|---|---|---|
| ステーキ用牛肉 | **1** | steak |
| 牛ひき肉 | **2** | ground beef |
| シチュー用牛肉 | **3** | stewing beef |
| ローストビーフ | **4** | roast beef |
| あばら肉／リブ | **5** | ribs |
| 子羊の脚肉 | **6** | leg of lamb |
| ラムチョップ | **7** | lamb chops |
| センマイ | **8** | tripe |
| レバー | **9** | liver |
| 豚肉 | **10** | pork |
| ポークチョップ | **11** | pork chops |
| ソーセージ | **12** | sausages |
| ハム | **13** | ham |
| ベーコン | **14** | bacon |

**鶏肉 Poultry**

| | | |
|---|---|---|
| 鶏肉 | **15** | chicken |
| 鶏のむね肉 | **16** | chicken breasts |
| 鶏の脚肉／鶏の骨付もも肉／ドラムスティック | **17** | chicken legs/ drumsticks |
| 鶏の手羽肉 | **18** | chicken wings |
| 鶏のもも肉 | **19** | chicken thighs |
| 七面鳥肉 | **20** | turkey |
| 鴨肉 | **21** | duck |

**シーフード Seafood**

**魚 FISH**

| | | |
|---|---|---|
| サケ | **22** | salmon |
| オヒョウ | **23** | halibut |
| タラ | **24** | haddock |
| カレイ | **25** | flounder |
| マス | **26** | trout |
| ナマズ | **27** | catfish |
| シタビラメ | **28** | filet of sole |

**貝・甲殻類 SHELLFISH**

| | | |
|---|---|---|
| 小エビ | **29** | shrimp |
| ホタテ貝 | **30** | scallops |
| カニ | **31** | crabs |
| ハマグリ | **32** | clams |
| ムール貝 | **33** | mussels |
| カキ | **34** | oysters |
| ロブスター | **35** | lobster |

A. I'm going to the supermarket. What do we need?
B. Please get some **steak**.
A. **Steak**? All right.

A. Excuse me. Where can I find ________?
B. Look in the ________ Section.
A. Thank you.

A. This/These ________ looks/ look very fresh!
B. Let's get some for dinner.

Do you eat meat, poultry, or seafood?
Which of these foods do you like?

Which of these foods are popular in your country?

## 乳製品・ジュース・その他の飲み物

### 乳製品 Dairy Products

- 牛乳 1 milk
- 低脂肪牛乳 2 low-fat milk
- スキムミルク 3 skim milk
- チョコレートミルク 4 chocolate milk
- オレンジジュース※ 5 orange juice
- チーズ 6 cheese
- バター 7 butter
- マーガリン 8 margarine
- サワークリーム 9 sour cream
- クリームチーズ 10 cream cheese
- カッテージチーズ 11 cottage cheese
- ヨーグルト 12 yogurt
- 豆腐※ 13 tofu
- 卵 14 eggs

### ジュース Juices

- リンゴジュース 15 apple juice
- パイナップルジュース 16 pineapple juice
- グレープフルーツジュース 17 grapefruit juice
- トマトジュース 18 tomato juice
- グレープジュース 19 grape juice
- フルーツパンチ 20 fruit punch
- 紙パック入りジュース 21 juice paks
- 粉末ジュース 22 powdered drink mix

### 飲み物 Beverages

- 炭酸飲料 23 soda
- 低カロリー炭酸飲料 24 diet soda
- ミネラルウォーター 25 bottled water

### コーヒー・紅茶 Coffee and Tea

- コーヒー 26 coffee
- カフェイン抜きコーヒー 27 decaffeinated coffee/decaf
- インスタントコーヒー 28 instant coffee
- 紅茶 29 tea
- ハーブティー 30 herbal tea
- ココア 31 cocoa/hot chocolate mix

※これらは乳製品ではありませんが、同じ棚に並んでいることがあります。

A. I'm going to the supermarket to get some **milk**. Do we need anything else?
B. Yes. Please get some **apple juice**.

A. Excuse me. Where can I find ________?
B. Look in the ________ Section.
A. Thanks.

A. Look! ________ is/are on sale this week!
B. Let's get some!

Which of these foods do you like?

Which of these foods are good for you?

Which brands of these foods do you buy?

# DELI, FROZEN FOODS, AND SNACK FOODS

## 惣菜・冷凍食品・スナック

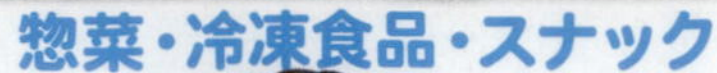

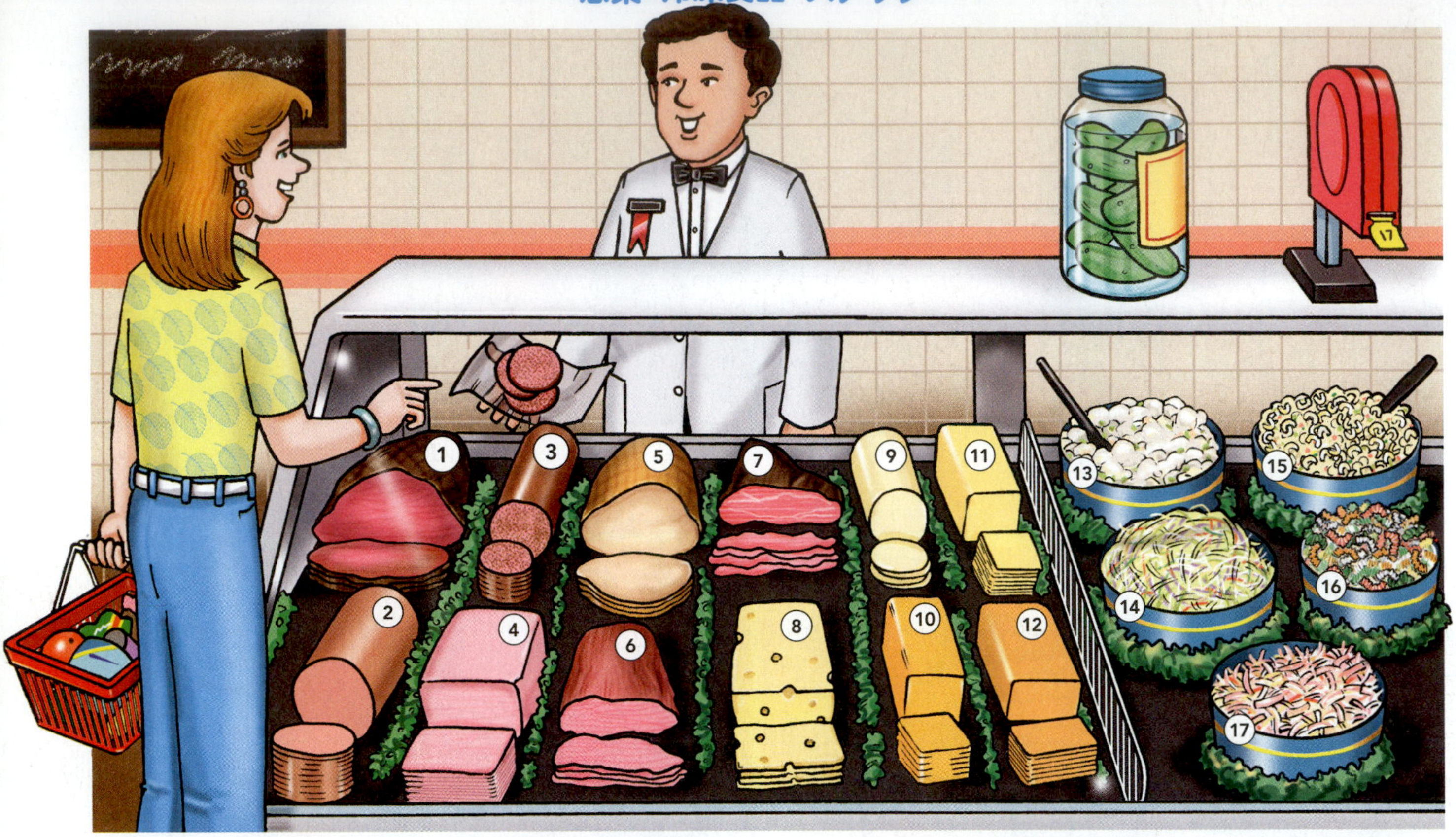

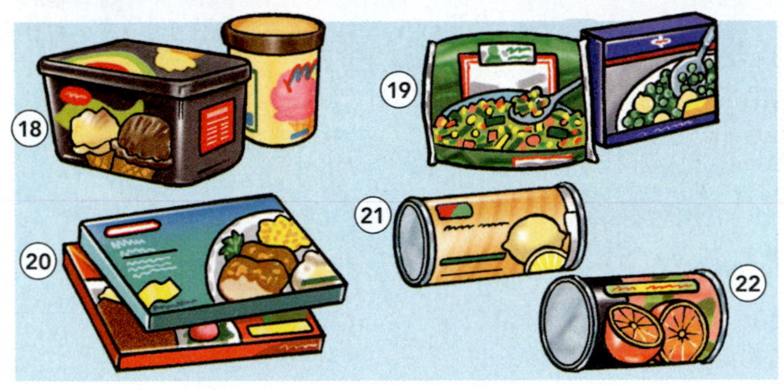

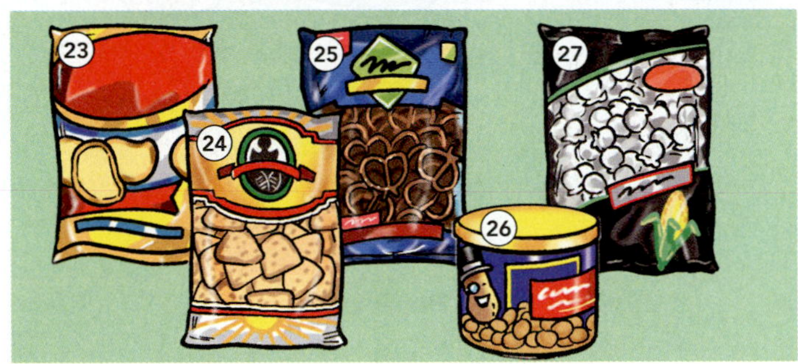

**惣菜 Deli**

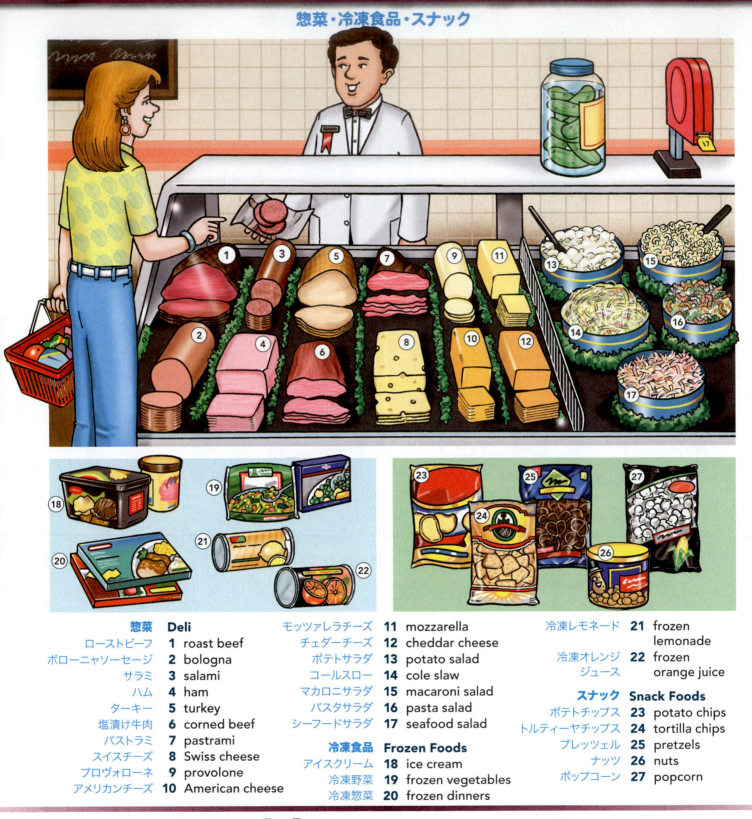

ローストビーフ 1 roast beef
ボローニャソーセージ 2 bologna
サラミ 3 salami
ハム 4 ham
ターキー 5 turkey
塩漬け牛肉 6 corned beef
パストラミ 7 pastrami
スイスチーズ 8 Swiss cheese
プロヴォローネ 9 provolone
アメリカンチーズ 10 American cheese
モッツァレラチーズ 11 mozzarella
チェダーチーズ 12 cheddar cheese
ポテトサラダ 13 potato salad
コールスロー 14 cole slaw
マカロニサラダ 15 macaroni salad
パスタサラダ 16 pasta salad
シーフードサラダ 17 seafood salad

**冷凍食品 Frozen Foods**

アイスクリーム 18 ice cream
冷凍野菜 19 frozen vegetables
冷凍惣菜 20 frozen dinners
冷凍レモネード 21 frozen lemonade
冷凍オレンジジュース 22 frozen orange juice

**スナック Snack Foods**

ポテトチップス 23 potato chips
トルティーヤチップス 24 tortilla chips
プレッツェル 25 pretzels
ナッツ 26 nuts
ポップコーン 27 popcorn

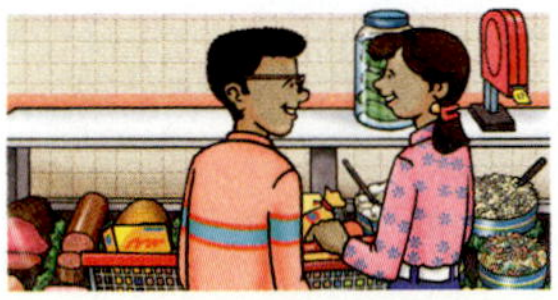

A. Should we get some **roast beef**?
B. Good idea. And let's get some **potato salad**.

[1–17]
A. May I help you?
B. Yes, please. I'd like some ________.

[1–27]
A. Excuse me. Where is/are ________?
B. It's/They're in the ________ Section.

What kinds of snack foods are popular in your country?

Are frozen foods common in your country? What kinds of foods are in the Frozen Foods Section?

# 食料品

## 箱入り食品 Packaged Goods

- シリアル 1 cereal
- クッキー 2 cookies
- クラッカー 3 crackers
- マカロニ 4 macaroni
- めん類 5 noodles
- スパゲティー 6 spaghetti
- 米 7 rice

## 缶詰 Canned Goods

- スープ 8 soup
- ツナの缶詰 9 tuna (fish)
- 野菜の缶詰 10 (canned) vegetables
- フルーツの缶詰 11 (canned) fruit

## ジャム・ゼリー Jams and Jellies

- ジャム 12 jam
- ゼリー状のジャム 13 jelly
- ピーナッツバター 14 peanut butter

## 調味料 Condiments

- ケチャップ 15 ketchup
- からし 16 mustard
- (ピクルスなどの) つけ合わせ 17 relish
- ピクルス 18 pickles
- オリーブ 19 olives
- 塩 20 salt
- こしょう 21 pepper
- 香辛料 22 spices
- しょう油 23 soy sauce
- マヨネーズ 24 mayonnaise
- 料理用油 25 (cooking) oil
- オリーブ油 26 olive oil
- サルサ 27 salsa
- 酢 28 vinegar
- ドレッシング 29 salad dressing

## パン・ケーキ類 Baked Goods

- 食パン 30 bread
- ロールパン 31 rolls
- イングリッシュマフィン 32 English muffins
- ピタパン 33 pita bread
- ケーキ 34 cake

## 製菓材 Baking Products

- 小麦粉 35 flour
- 砂糖 36 sugar
- ケーキミックス 37 cake mix

A. I got **cereal** and **soup**. What else is on the shopping list?
B. **Ketchup** and **bread**.

A. Excuse me. I'm looking for ______.
B. It's/They're next to the ______.

A. Pardon me. I'm looking for ______.
B. It's/They're between the ______ and the ______.

Which of these foods do you like?

Which brands of these foods do you buy?

# 家庭用品・ベビー用品・ペットフード

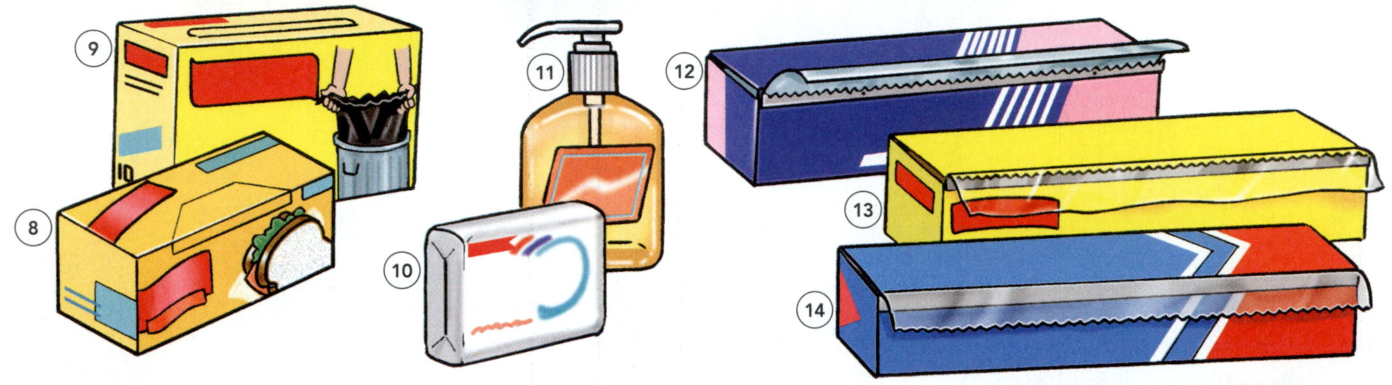

**紙製品 Paper Products**
- ペーパーナプキン 1 napkins
- 紙コップ 2 paper cups
- ティッシュペーパー 3 tissues
- ストロー 4 straws
- 紙皿 5 paper plates
- ペーパータオル 6 paper towels
- トイレットペーパー 7 toilet paper

**家庭用品 Household Items**
- サンドイッチ用袋 8 sandwich bags
- ゴミ袋 9 trash bags
- 石けん 10 soap
- 液体石けん 11 liquid soap
- アルミホイル 12 aluminum foil
- ラップ 13 plastic wrap
- パラフィン紙 14 waxed paper

**ベビー用品 Baby Products**
- ベビーシリアル 15 baby cereal
- ベビーフード 16 baby food
- 粉ミルク 17 formula
- おしり拭き 18 wipes
- 紙おむつ 19 (disposable) diapers

**ペットフード Pet Food**
- キャットフード 20 cat food
- ドッグフード 21 dog food

A. Excuse me. Where can I find **napkins**?
B. **Napkins**? Look in Aisle 4.

[7, 10–17, 20, 21]
A. We forgot to get ________!
B. I'll get it. Where is it?
A. It's in Aisle ________.

[1–6, 8, 9, 18, 19]
A. We forgot to get ________!
B. I'll get them. Where are they?
A. They're in Aisle ________.

What do you need from the supermarket? Make a complete shopping list!

# スーパーマーケット

| | | |
|---|---|---|
| 通路 | 1 | aisle |
| 買物客 | 2 | shopper/customer |
| 店内用かご | 3 | shopping basket |
| レジの列 | 4 | checkout line |
| レジ台 | 5 | checkout counter |
| ベルトコンベア | 6 | conveyor belt |
| レジ | 7 | cash register |
| ショッピングカート | 8 | shopping cart |
| ガム | 9 | (chewing) gum |
| チョコレート／キャンディーバー | 10 | candy |
| クーポン券 | 11 | coupons |
| レジ係 | 12 | cashier |
| 紙袋 | 13 | paper bag |
| 袋詰め係 | 14 | bagger/packer |
| エクスプレスレジ（買物量の少ない人用のレジ） | 15 | express checkout (line) |
| タブロイド判新聞 | 16 | tabloid (newspaper) |
| 雑誌 | 17 | magazine |
| スキャナ | 18 | scanner |
| ポリ袋 | 19 | plastic bag |
| 農産物 | 20 | produce |
| 責任者 | 21 | manager |
| 店員 | 22 | clerk |
| はかり | 23 | scale |
| アルミ缶回収機 | 24 | can-return machine |
| ボトル回収機 | 25 | bottle-return machine |

[1–8, 11–19, 21–25]
A. This is a gigantic supermarket!
B. It is! Look at all the **aisle**s!

[9, 10, 20]
A. This is a gigantic supermarket!
B. It is. Look at all the **produce**!

Where do you usually shop for food? Do you go to a supermarket, or do you go to a small grocery store? Describe the place where you shop.

Describe the differences between U.S. supermarkets and food stores in your country.

# CONTAINERS AND QUANTITIES

## 容器と量

- 袋 **1** bag
- びん／本 **2** bottle
- 箱 **3** box
- 房／束 **4** bunch
- 缶 **5** can
- (牛乳など)パック **6** carton
- (容器入り食品)個 **7** container
- ダース(12個) **8** dozen*

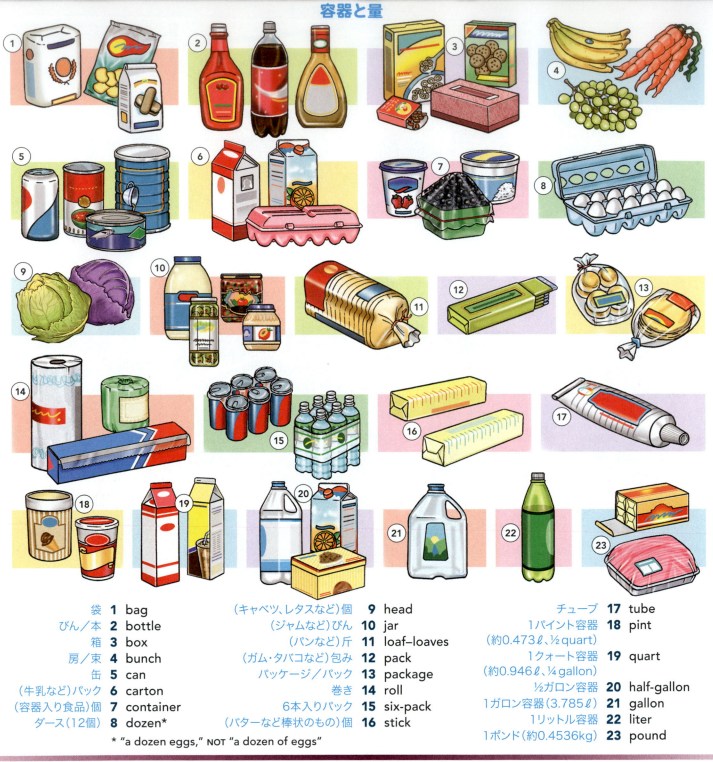

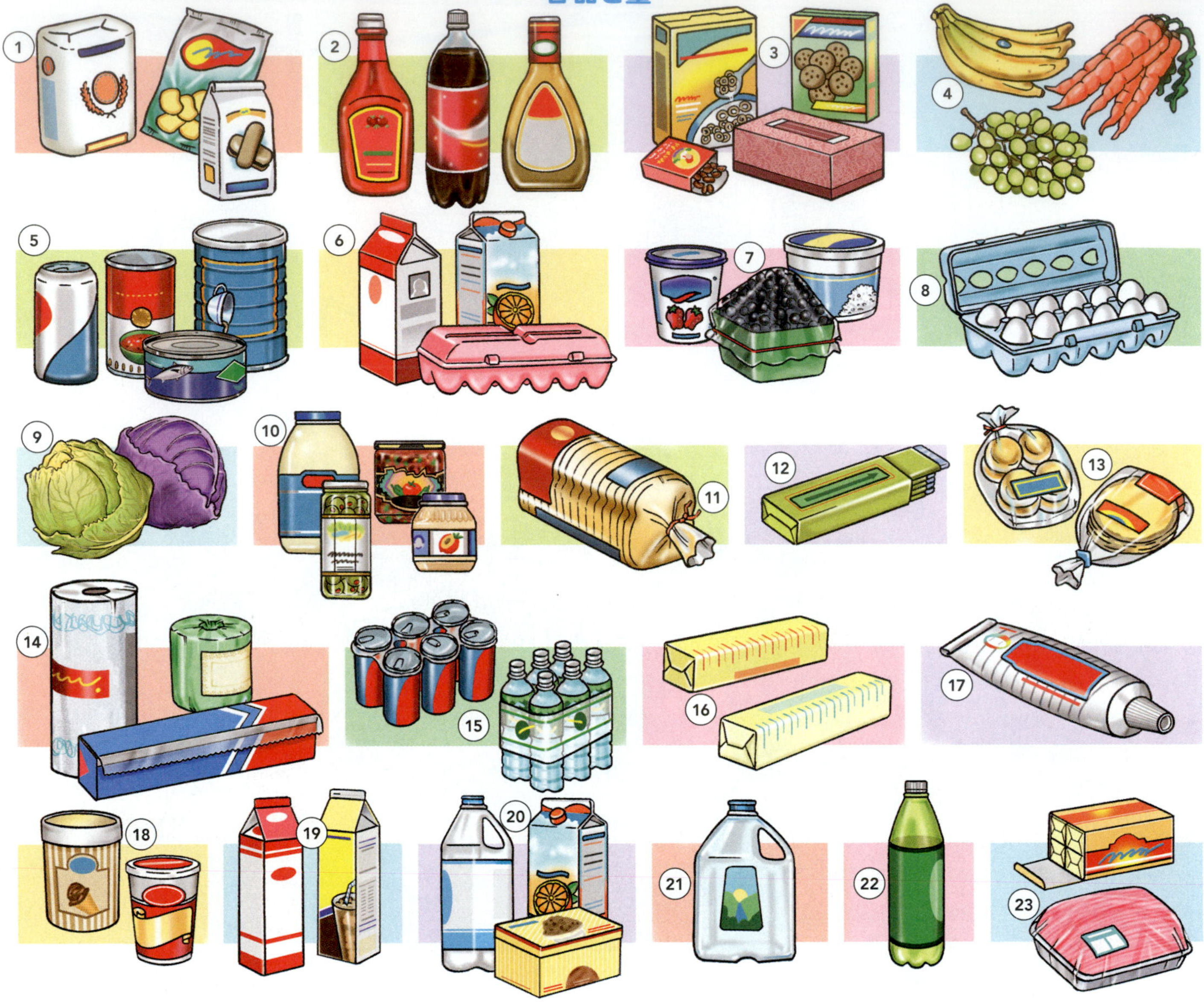

* "a dozen eggs," NOT "a dozen of eggs"

- (キャベツ、レタスなど)個 **9** head
- (ジャムなど)びん **10** jar
- (パンなど)斤 **11** loaf–loaves
- (ガム・タバコなど)包み **12** pack
- パッケージ／パック **13** package
- 巻き **14** roll
- 6本入りパック **15** six-pack
- (バターなど棒状のもの)個 **16** stick

- チューブ **17** tube
- 1パイント容器(約0.473ℓ、½quart) **18** pint
- 1クォート容器(約0.946ℓ、¼gallon) **19** quart
- ½ガロン容器 **20** half-gallon
- 1ガロン容器(3.785ℓ) **21** gallon
- 1リットル容器 **22** liter
- 1ポンド(約0.4536kg) **23** pound

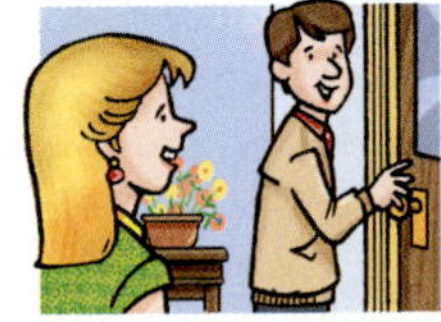

A. Please get a **bag** of *flour* when you go to the supermarket.
B. A **bag** of *flour*? Okay.

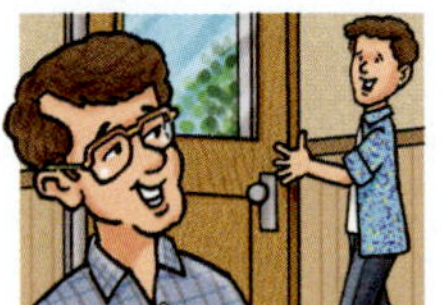

A. Please get two **bottles** of *ketchup* when you go to the supermarket.
B. Two **bottles** of *ketchup*? Okay.

[At home]
A. What did you get at the supermarket?
B. I got ______, ______, and ______.

[In a supermarket]
A. Is this the express checkout line?
B. Yes, it is. Do you have more than eight items?
A. No. I only have ______, ______, and ______.

Open your kitchen cabinets and refrigerator. Make a list of all the things you find.

What do you do with empty bottles, jars, and cans? Do you recycle them, reuse them, or throw them away?

# 計量の単位

小さじ teaspoon
tsp.

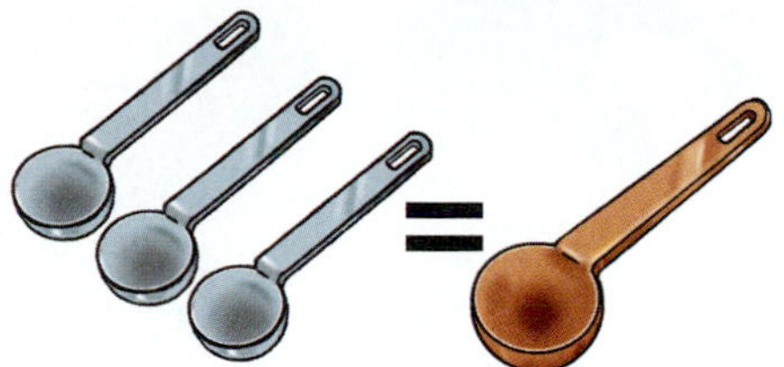

大さじ tablespoon
Tbsp.

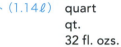

オンス 1 (fluid) ounce
1 fl. oz.

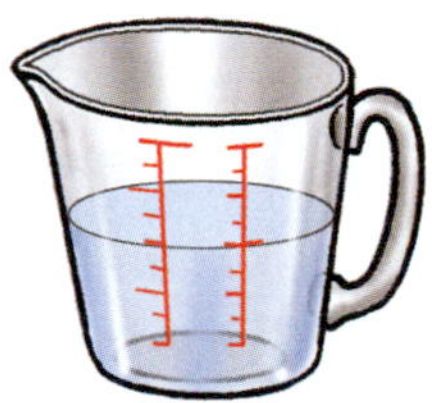

カップ cup
c.
8 fl. ozs.

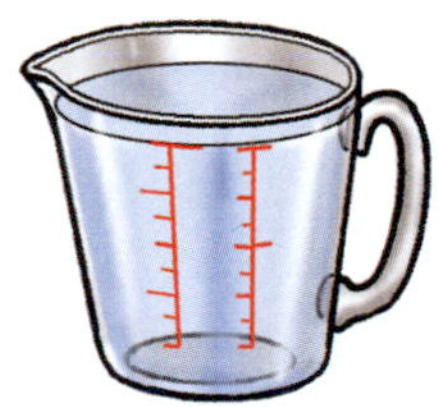

パイント pint
pt.
16 fl. ozs.

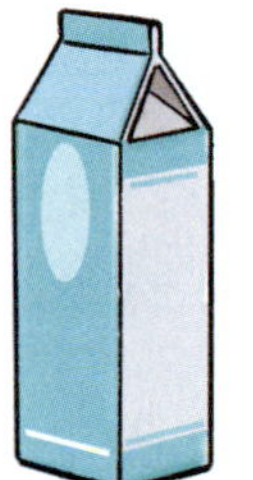

クォート（1.14ℓ） quart
qt.
32 fl. ozs.

ガロン（3.78531ℓ） gallon
gal.
128 fl. ozs.

A. How much water should I put in?
B. The recipe says to add one _______ of water.

A. This fruit punch is delicious! What's in it?
B. Two _______s of apple juice, three _______ of orange juice, and a _______ of grape juice.

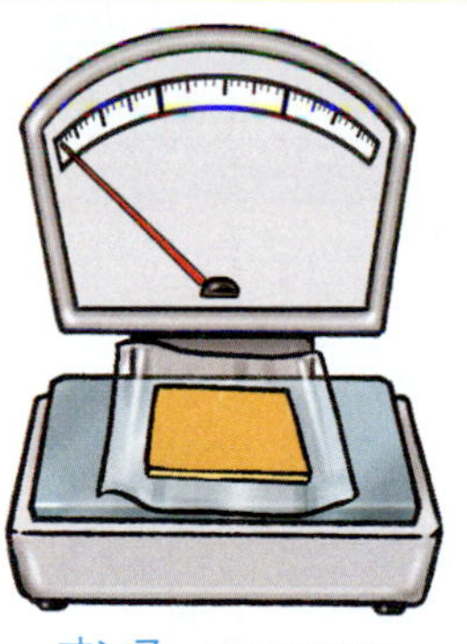

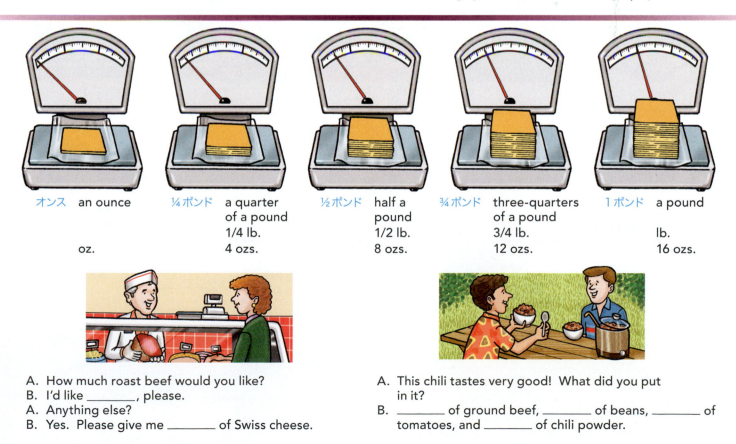

オンス an ounce
oz.

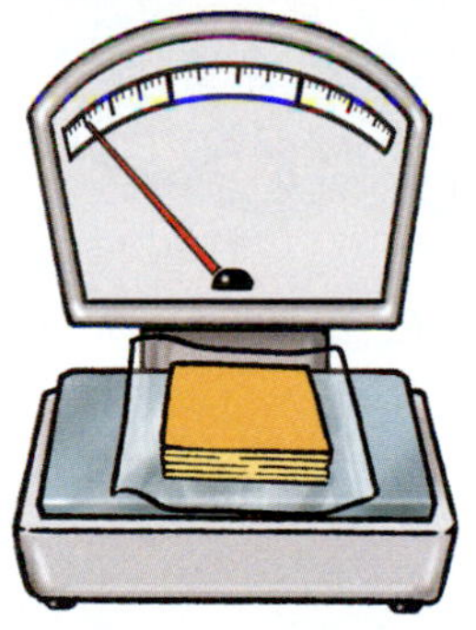

¼ポンド a quarter of a pound
1/4 lb.
4 ozs.

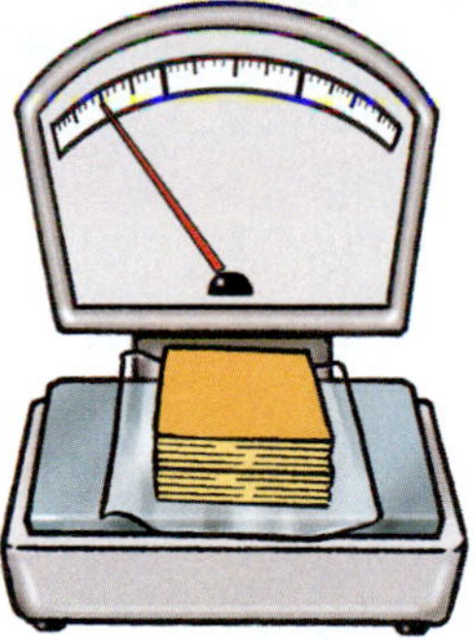

½ポンド half a pound
1/2 lb.
8 ozs.

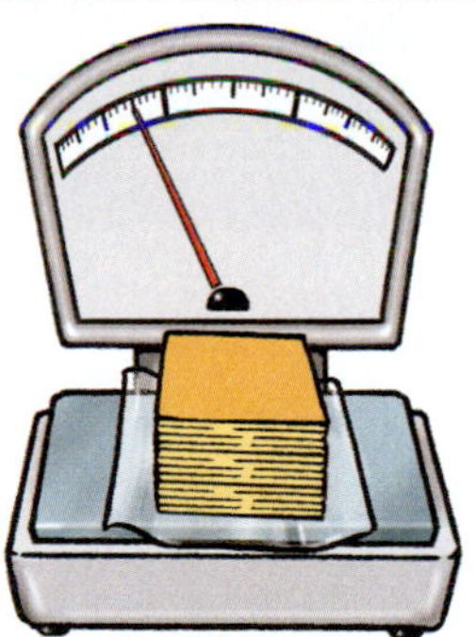

¾ポンド three-quarters of a pound
3/4 lb.
12 ozs.

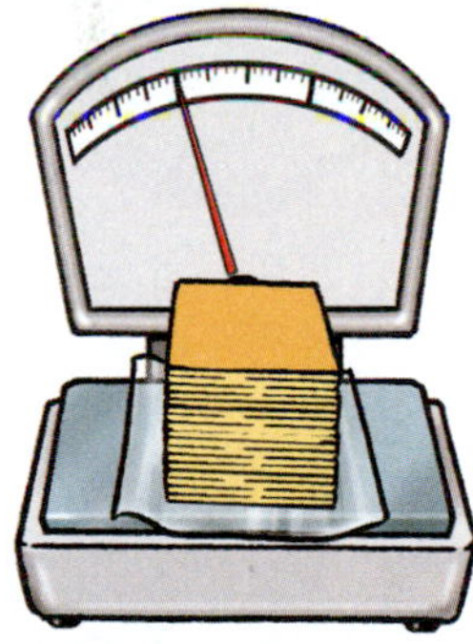

1ポンド a pound
lb.
16 ozs.

A. How much roast beef would you like?
B. I'd like _______, please.
A. Anything else?
B. Yes. Please give me _______ of Swiss cheese.

A. This chili tastes very good! What did you put in it?
B. _______ of ground beef, _______ of beans, _______ of tomatoes, and _______ of chili powder.

# FOOD PREPARATION AND RECIPES

## 料理の下準備と調理

| | | |
|---|---|---|
| 切る | 1 | cut (up) |
| きざむ | 2 | chop (up) |
| 薄く切る | 3 | slice |
| すりおろす | 4 | grate |
| 皮をむく | 5 | peel |
| 割る | 6 | break |
| かき混ぜる | 7 | beat |
| かきまわす | 8 | stir |
| 注ぐ | 9 | pour |
| 加える | 10 | add |
| ～と～を合わせる | 11 | combine _____ and _____ |
| ～と～を混ぜ合わせる | 12 | mix _____ and _____ |
| ～を～に入れる | 13 | put _____ in _____ |
| 加熱して料理する | 14 | cook |
| オーブンで焼く | 15 | bake |
| ゆでる | 16 | boil |
| 直火で焼く | 17 | broil |
| 蒸す | 18 | steam |
| いためる／揚げる | 19 | fry |
| 軽くいためる | 20 | saute |
| ぐつぐつ煮る | 21 | simmer |
| ローストする／あぶり焼きにする | 22 | roast |
| バーベキューする／網焼きする | 23 | barbecue/grill |
| 強火で手早くいためる | 24 | stir-fry |
| 電子レンジで調理する | 25 | microwave |

A. Can I help you?
B. Yes. Please **cut up** the vegetables.

[1–25]
A. What are you doing?
B. I'm ________ing the .............

[14–25]
A. How long should I ________ the .............?
B. ________ the ............. for ............. minutes/seconds.

What's your favorite recipe? Give instructions and use the units of measure on page 57. For example:

Mix a cup of flour and two tablespoons of sugar.
Add half a pound of butter.
Bake at 350° (degrees) for twenty minutes.

# KITCHEN UTENSILS AND COOKWARE

## 台所用品と調理器具

| | | |
|---|---|---|
| アイスクリームサーバー | **1** | ice cream scoop |
| 缶切り | **2** | can opener |
| せん抜き | **3** | bottle opener |
| 皮むき | **4** | (vegetable) peeler |
| 泡立て器 | **5** | (egg) beater |
| ふた | **6** | lid/cover/top |
| なべ | **7** | pot |
| フライパン | **8** | frying pan/skillet |
| 二重なべ | **9** | double boiler |
| 中華なべ | **10** | wok |
| 玉じゃくし | **11** | ladle |
| 万能こし器 | **12** | strainer |
| フライ返し | **13** | spatula |
| 蒸し器 | **14** | steamer |
| 包丁／ナイフ | **15** | knife |
| にんにくつぶし | **16** | garlic press |
| おろし器 | **17** | grater |
| キャセロール | **18** | casserole dish |
| ローストパン | **19** | roasting pan |
| ロースト用ラック | **20** | roasting rack |
| スライサー | **21** | carving knife |
| 片手鍋 | **22** | saucepan |
| 水切り | **23** | colander |
| キッチンタイマー | **24** | kitchen timer |
| めん棒 | **25** | rolling pin |
| パイ皿 | **26** | pie plate |
| 果物ナイフ | **27** | paring knife |
| クッキーシート | **28** | cookie sheet |
| クッキー抜き型 | **29** | cookie cutter |
| ボウル | **30** | (mixing) bowl |
| 泡立て器 | **31** | whisk |
| 計量カップ | **32** | measuring cup |
| 計量スプーン | **33** | measuring spoon |
| ケーキ型 | **34** | cake pan |
| 木べら | **35** | wooden spoon |

A. Could I possibly borrow your **ice cream scoop**?
B. Sure. I'll be happy to lend you my **ice cream scoop**.
A. Thanks.

A. What are you looking for?
B. I can't find the ________.
A. Look in that drawer/in that cabinet/ on the counter/next to the ________/ ..............

[A Commercial]

Come to *Kitchen World*! We have everything you need for your kitchen, from ________s and ________s, to ________s and ________s. Are you looking for a new ________? Is it time to throw out your old ________? Come to *Kitchen World* today! We have everything you need!

What kitchen utensils and cookware do you have in your kitchen?

Which things do you use very often?

Which things do you rarely use?

# FAST FOOD

## ファーストフード

| | | |
|---|---|---|
| ハンバーガー | 1 | hamburger |
| チーズバーガー | 2 | cheeseburger |
| ホットドッグ | 3 | hot dog |
| フィッシュサンド | 4 | fish sandwich |
| チキンサンド | 5 | chicken sandwich |
| フライドチキン | 6 | fried chicken |
| フライドポテト | 7 | french fries |
| ナチョス | 8 | nachos |
| タコス | 9 | taco |
| ブリトー | 10 | burrito |
| (一)切れのピザ | 11 | slice of pizza |
| (一)杯のチリコンカルネ | 12 | bowl of chili |
| サラダ | 13 | salad |
| アイスクリーム | 14 | ice cream |
| フローズンヨーグルト | 15 | frozen yogurt |
| ミルクシェイク | 16 | milkshake |
| 炭酸飲料 | 17 | soda |
| ふた | 18 | lids |
| 紙コップ | 19 | paper cups |
| ストロー | 20 | straws |
| ナプキン | 21 | napkins |
| プラスチックのスプーン、フォーク、ナイフ類 | 22 | plastic utensils |
| ケチャップ | 23 | ketchup |
| マスタード | 24 | mustard |
| マヨネーズ | 25 | mayonnaise |
| (ピクルスなどの)つけ合わせ | 26 | relish |
| ドレッシング | 27 | salad dressing |

A. May I help you?
B. Yes. I'd like a/an [1–5, 9–17] / an order of [6–8].

A. Excuse me. We're almost out of [18–27].
B. I'll get some more from the supply room. Thanks for telling me.

Do you go to fast-food restaurants? Which ones? How often? What do you order?

Are there fast-food restaurants in your country? Are they popular? What foods do they have?

# 軽食

| | | |
|---|---|---|
| ドーナツ | 1 | donut |
| マフィン | 2 | muffin |
| ベーグル | 3 | bagel |
| パン | 4 | bun |
| ペストリー | 5 | danish/pastry |
| ビスケット／スコーン | 6 | biscuit |
| クロワッサン | 7 | croissant |
| 卵 | 8 | eggs |
| ホットケーキ | 9 | pancakes |
| ワッフル | 10 | waffles |
| トースト | 11 | toast |
| ベーコン | 12 | bacon |
| ソーセージ | 13 | sausages |
| ホームフライ | 14 | home fries |
| コーヒー | 15 | coffee |
| カフェイン抜きコーヒー | 16 | decaf coffee |
| 紅茶 | 17 | tea |
| アイスティー | 18 | iced tea |
| レモネード | 19 | lemonade |
| ココア | 20 | hot chocolate |
| 牛乳 | 21 | milk |
| ツナサンドイッチ | 22 | tuna fish sandwich |
| 卵サンドイッチ | 23 | egg salad sandwich |
| チキンサラダサンド | 24 | chicken salad sandwich |
| ハムとチーズのサンドイッチ | 25 | ham and cheese sandwich |
| 塩漬けビーフのサンドイッチ | 26 | corned beef sandwich |
| BLT(ベーコン・レタス・トマト)のサンドイッチ | 27 | BLT/bacon, lettuce, and tomato sandwich |
| ローストビーフサンドイッチ | 28 | roast beef sandwich |
| 精白パン | 29 | white bread |
| 全粒粉パン | 30 | whole wheat bread |
| ピタパン | 31 | pita bread |
| (粗製の)ライ麦パン／パンパーニッケル | 32 | pumpernickel |
| ライ麦パン | 33 | rye bread |
| ロールパン | 34 | a roll |
| コッペパン | 35 | a submarine roll |

A. May I help you?
B. Yes. I'd like a __[1–7]__/an order of __[8–14]__, please.
A. Anything to drink?
B. Yes. I'll have a small/medium-size/large/extra-large __[15–21]__.

A. I'd like a __[22–28]__ on __[29–35]__, please.
B. What do you want on it?
A. Lettuce/tomato/mayonnaise/mustard/. . .

Do you like these foods? Which ones? Where do you get them? How often do you have them?

# レストラン

| | | |
|---|---|---|
| 客を案内する | **A** | seat the customers |
| 水を注ぐ | **B** | pour the water |
| オーダーを取る | **C** | take the order |
| 配膳する | **D** | serve the meal |
| ウェイトレス | **1** | hostess |
| ウェイター | **2** | host |
| 食事する人／客 | **3** | diner/patron/customer |
| 仕切り席 | **4** | booth |
| テーブル | **5** | table |
| 子供用いす | **6** | high chair |
| 子供用補助いす | **7** | booster seat |
| メニュー | **8** | menu |
| ブレッドバスケット | **9** | bread basket |
| ウェイターの助手 | **10** | busperson |
| ウェイトレス／給仕 | **11** | waitress/server |
| ウェイター／給仕 | **12** | waiter/server |
| サラダバー | **13** | salad bar |
| ダイニングルーム | **14** | dining room |
| キッチン | **15** | kitchen |
| シェフ／コック | **16** | chef |

[4–9]
A. Would you like a **booth**?
B. Yes, please.

[10–12]
A. Hello. My name is *Julie*, and I'll be your **waitress** this evening.
B. Hello.

[1, 2, 13–16]
A. This restaurant has a wonderful **salad bar**.
B. I agree.

テーブルを片付ける **E** clear the table
支払う **F** pay the check
チップを置く **G** leave a tip
テーブルの用意をする **H** set the table

皿洗い場 **17** dishroom
皿洗い係 **18** dishwasher
トレイ／盆 **19** tray
デザートカート **20** dessert cart
勘定書 **21** check
チップ **22** tip
サラダ皿 **23** salad plate
パン皿 **24** bread-and-butter plate
ディナー皿 **25** dinner plate

スープ皿 **26** soup bowl
水用グラス **27** water glass
ワイングラス **28** wine glass
カップ **29** cup
受け皿 **30** saucer
ナプキン **31** napkin

**銀食器 silverware**

サラダフォーク **32** salad fork
フォーク **33** dinner fork
ナイフ **34** knife
ティースプーン **35** teaspoon
スープスプーン **36** soup spoon
バターナイフ **37** butter knife

[A–H]
A. Please ________.
B. All right. I'll ________ right away.

[23–37]
A. Excuse me. Where does the ________ go?
B. It goes { to the left of the ________. / to the right of the ________. / on the ________. / between the ________ and the ________. }

[1, 2, 10–12, 16, 18]
A. Do you have any job openings?
B. Yes. We're looking for a ________.

[23–37]
A. Excuse me. I dropped my ________.
B. That's okay. I'll get you another ________ from the kitchen.

Tell about a restaurant you know. Describe the place and the people. (Is the restaurant large or small? How many tables are there? How many people work there? Is there a salad bar? . . . )

| | | |
|---|---|---|
| フルーツカクテル | **1** | fruit cup/ fruit cocktail |
| トマトジュース | **2** | tomato juice |
| 小エビのカクテル | **3** | shrimp cocktail |
| 鳥の手羽焼 | **4** | chicken wings |
| ナチョス | **5** | nachos |
| ポテトスキン | **6** | potato skins |
| グリーンサラダ | **7** | tossed salad/ garden salad |
| ギリシャ風サラダ | **8** | Greek salad |
| ホウレンソウサラダ | **9** | spinach salad |
| アンティパスト | **10** | antipasto (plate) |
| シーザーサラダ | **11** | Caesar salad |
| ミートローフ | **12** | meatloaf |
| ローストビーフ/プライムリブ | **13** | roast beef/ prime rib |
| チキン焼き | **14** | baked chicken |
| 焼き魚 | **15** | broiled fish |
| スパゲティミートボール | **16** | spaghetti and meatballs |
| 仔牛のカツレツ | **17** | veal cutlet |
| ベークドポテト | **18** | a baked potato |
| マッシュポテト | **19** | mashed potatoes |
| フライドポテト | **20** | french fries |
| 米 | **21** | rice |
| 麺類 | **22** | noodles |
| ミックスベジタブル | **23** | mixed vegetables |
| チョコレートケーキ | **24** | chocolate cake |
| アップルパイ | **25** | apple pie |
| アイスクリーム | **26** | ice cream |
| (フルーツ)ゼリー | **27** | jello |
| プリン | **28** | pudding |
| アイスクリームサンデー | **29** | ice cream sundae |

[Ordering dinner]

A. May I take your order?
B. Yes, please. For the appetizer, I'd like the __[1–6]__.
A. And what kind of salad would you like?
B. I'll have the __[7–11]__.
A. And for the main course?
B. I'd like the __[12–17]__, please.
A. What side dish would you like with that?
B. Hmm. I think I'll have __[18–23]__.

[Ordering dessert]

A. Would you care for some dessert?
B. Yes. I'll have __[24–28]__/an __[29]__.

Tell about the food at a restaurant you know. What's on the menu?

What are some typical foods on the menus of restaurants in your country?

# 色

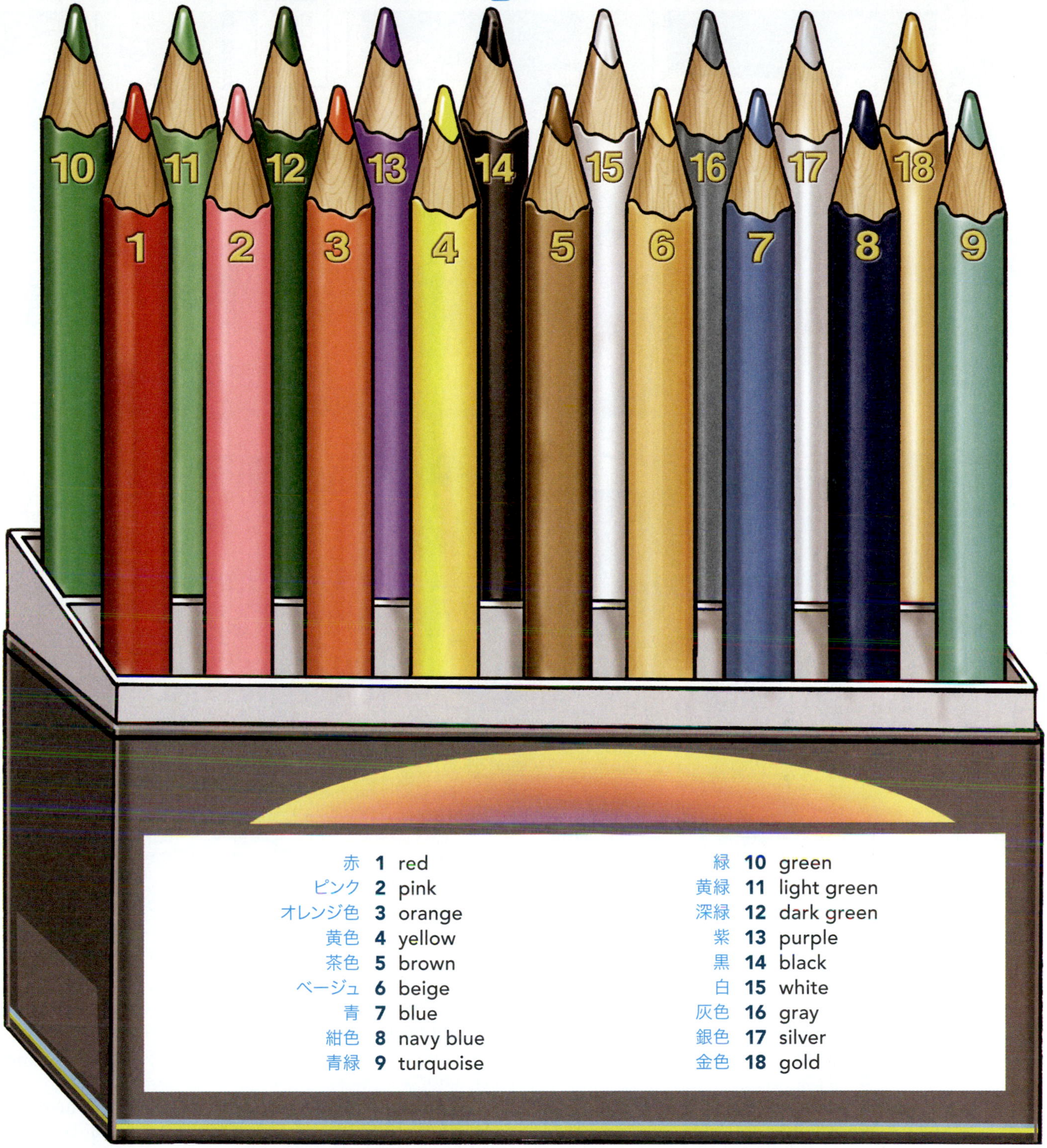

| | | | | | |
|---|---|---|---|---|---|
| 赤 | 1 | red | 緑 | 10 | green |
| ピンク | 2 | pink | 黄緑 | 11 | light green |
| オレンジ色 | 3 | orange | 深緑 | 12 | dark green |
| 黄色 | 4 | yellow | 紫 | 13 | purple |
| 茶色 | 5 | brown | 黒 | 14 | black |
| ベージュ | 6 | beige | 白 | 15 | white |
| 青 | 7 | blue | 灰色 | 16 | gray |
| 紺色 | 8 | navy blue | 銀色 | 17 | silver |
| 青緑 | 9 | turquoise | 金色 | 18 | gold |

A. What's your favorite color?
B. **Red**.

A. I like your ________ shirt.
You look very good in ________.
B. Thank you. ________ is my favorite color.

A. My TV is broken.
B. What's the matter with it?
A. People's faces are ________, the sky is ________, and the grass is ________!

Do you know the flags of different countries? What are the colors of flags you know?

What color makes you happy? What color makes you sad? Why?

# CLOTHING

## 衣類

| | | |
|---|---|---|
| ブラウス | 1 | blouse |
| スカート | 2 | skirt |
| シャツ | 3 | shirt |
| ズボン／スラックス | 4 | pants/slacks |
| カジュアルシャツ | 5 | sport shirt |
| ジーンズ | 6 | jeans |
| ポロシャツ／ニットシャツ | 7 | knit shirt/jersey |
| ワンピース | 8 | dress |
| セーター | 9 | sweater |
| ジャケット | 10 | jacket |
| スポーツコート／カジュアルジャケット／ジャケット | 11 | sport coat/sport jacket/jacket |
| スーツ／背広 | 12 | suit |
| 三つ揃いの背広 | 13 | three-piece suit |
| ネクタイ | 14 | tie/necktie |
| 制服 | 15 | uniform |
| Tシャツ | 16 | T-shirt |
| ショートパンツ（半ズボン） | 17 | shorts |
| マタニティドレス | 18 | maternity dress |
| ジャンプスーツ | 19 | jumpsuit |
| ベスト | 20 | vest |
| ジャンパースカート | 21 | jumper |
| ブレザー | 22 | blazer |
| チュニック | 23 | tunic |
| スパッツ／カルソン | 24 | leggings |
| オーバーオール | 25 | overalls |
| タートルネック（のセーター） | 26 | turtleneck |
| タキシード | 27 | tuxedo |
| 蝶ネクタイ | 28 | bow tie |
| イブニングドレス | 29 | (evening) gown |

A. I think I'll wear my new **blouse** today.
B. Good idea!

A. I really like your ________.
B. Thank you.
A. Where did you get it/them?
B. At ..............

A. Oh, no! I just ripped my ________!
B. What a shame!

What clothing items in this lesson do you wear?

What color clothing do you like to wear?

What do you wear at work or at school? at parties? at weddings?

# 上着類

| | | |
|---|---|---|
| コート | 1 | coat |
| オーバーコート | 2 | overcoat |
| (縁のある)帽子 | 3 | hat |
| ジャケット | 4 | jacket |
| マフラー | 5 | scarf/muffler |
| ニットジャケット | 6 | sweater jacket |
| タイツ | 7 | tights |
| (縁のない)帽子 | 8 | cap |
| レザージャケット | 9 | leather jacket |
| 野球帽 | 10 | baseball cap |
| ウインドブレーカー | 11 | windbreaker |
| レインコート | 12 | raincoat |
| レインハット | 13 | rain hat |
| トレンチコート | 14 | trench coat |
| 傘 | 15 | umbrella |
| ポンチョ | 16 | poncho |
| レインコート | 17 | rain jacket |
| 長靴 | 18 | rain boots |
| スキー帽 | 19 | ski hat |
| スキー用ジャケット | 20 | ski jacket |
| 手袋 | 21 | gloves |
| スキーマスク | 22 | ski mask |
| ダウンジャケット | 23 | down jacket |
| ミトン | 24 | mittens |
| パーカー | 25 | parka |
| サングラス | 26 | sunglasses |
| 耳当て | 27 | ear muffs |
| ダウンベスト | 28 | down vest |

A. What's the weather like today?
B. It's cool/cold/raining/snowing.
A. I think I'll wear my ______.

[1–6, 8–17, 19, 20, 22, 23, 25, 28]
A. May I help you?
B. Yes, please. I'm looking for a/an ______.

[7, 18, 21, 24, 26, 27]
A. May I help you?
B. Yes, please. I'm looking for ______.

What do you wear outside when the weather is cool?/when it's raining?/when it's very cold?

# パジャマ・下着類

| | | |
|---|---|---|
| パジャマ | 1 | pajamas |
| ネグリジェ／ナイトガウン | 2 | nightgown |
| シャツねまき | 3 | nightshirt |
| バスローブ | 4 | bathrobe/robe |
| スリッパ | 5 | slippers |
| ブランケット スリーパー／つなぎのパジャマ | 6 | blanket sleeper |
| Tシャツ／肌着 | 7 | undershirt/T-shirt |
| ブリーフ | 8 | (jockey) shorts/ underpants/briefs |
| トランクス | 9 | boxer shorts/ boxers |
| サポーター | 10 | athletic supporter/ jockstrap |
| ももひき | 11 | long underwear/ long johns |
| くつ下 | 12 | socks |
| (ビキニ型)ショーツ | 13 | (bikini) panties |
| ショーツ／パンツ | 14 | briefs/ underpants |
| ブラジャー | 15 | bra |
| キャミソール | 16 | camisole |
| ペチコート | 17 | half slip |
| シュミーズ／スリップ | 18 | (full) slip |
| ストッキング | 19 | stockings |
| パンティーストッキング | 20 | pantyhose |
| タイツ | 21 | tights |
| ハイソックス | 22 | knee-highs |
| ハイソックス | 23 | knee socks |

A. I can't find my new ________.
B. Did you look in the bureau/dresser/closet?
A. Yes, I did.
B. Then it's/they're probably in the wash.

What sleepwear items do you wear? What sleepwear items do people in your family wear?

# スポーツウェア・靴

タンクトップ **1** tank top
ジョギングパンツ **2** running shorts
スエットバンド **3** sweatband
ジョギングスーツ／ウォームアップスーツ **4** jogging suit/running suit/warm-up suit
Tシャツ **5** T-shirt
バイクパンツ **6** lycra shorts/bike shorts
スエットシャツ／トレーナー **7** sweatshirt
スエットパンツ **8** sweatpants
外衣 **9** cover-up
水着 **10** swimsuit/bathing suit
水着／水泳パンツ **11** swimming trunks/swimsuit/bathing suit
レオタード **12** leotard
靴 **13** shoes
ハイヒール **14** (high) heels
パンプス **15** pumps
ローファー **16** loafers
アスレチックシューズ／スニーカー **17** sneakers/athletic shoes
テニスシューズ **18** tennis shoes
ジョギングシューズ **19** running shoes
ハイカットバスケットシューズ **20** high-tops/high-top sneakers
サンダル **21** sandals
ビーチサンダル **22** thongs/flip-flops
ブーツ **23** boots
ワークブーツ **24** work boots
登山靴 **25** hiking boots
カウボーイブーツ **26** cowboy boots
モカシン **27** moccasins

[1–12]
A. Excuse me. I found this/these ______ in the dryer. Is it/Are they yours?
B. Yes. It's/They're mine. Thank you.

[13–27]
A. Are those new ______?
B. Yes, they are.
A. They're very nice.
B. Thanks.

Do you exercise? What do you do? What kind of clothing do you wear when you exercise?

What kind of shoes do you wear when you go to work or to school? when you exercise? when you relax at home? when you go out with friends or family members?

# 宝石・アクセサリー

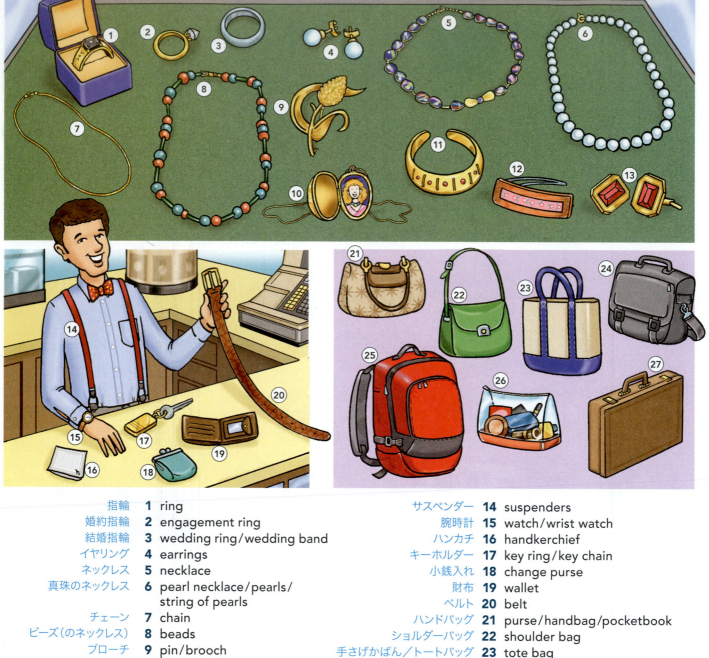

| | | | |
|---|---|---|---|
| 指輪 | **1** | ring | |
| 婚約指輪 | **2** | engagement ring | |
| 結婚指輪 | **3** | wedding ring/wedding band | |
| イヤリング | **4** | earrings | |
| ネックレス | **5** | necklace | |
| 真珠のネックレス | **6** | pearl necklace/pearls/ string of pearls | |
| チェーン | **7** | chain | |
| ビーズ(のネックレス) | **8** | beads | |
| ブローチ | **9** | pin/brooch | |
| ロケット | **10** | locket | |
| ブレスレット | **11** | bracelet | |
| 髪止め飾りピン | **12** | barrette | |
| カフスボタン | **13** | cuff links | |
| サスペンダー | **14** | suspenders | |
| 腕時計 | **15** | watch/wrist watch | |
| ハンカチ | **16** | handkerchief | |
| キーホルダー | **17** | key ring/key chain | |
| 小銭入れ | **18** | change purse | |
| 財布 | **19** | wallet | |
| ベルト | **20** | belt | |
| ハンドバッグ | **21** | purse/handbag/pocketbook | |
| ショルダーバッグ | **22** | shoulder bag | |
| 手さげかばん/トートバッグ | **23** | tote bag | |
| ブックバッグ | **24** | book bag | |
| リュックサック/デイパック | **25** | backpack | |
| コスメポーチ | **26** | makeup bag | |
| 書類かばん/ブリーフケース | **27** | briefcase | |

A. Oh, no! I think I lost my **ring**!
B. I'll help you look for it.

A. Oh, no! I think I lost my **earrings**!
B. I'll help you look for them.

[In a store]
A. Excuse me. Is this/Are these ________ on sale this week?
B. Yes. It's/They're half price.

[On the street]
A. Help! Police! Stop that man/woman!
B. What happened?!
A. He/She just stole my ________ and my ________!

Do you like to wear jewelry? What jewelry do you have?

In your country, what do men, women, and children use to carry their things?

# DESCRIBING CLOTHING

## 衣類に関する表現

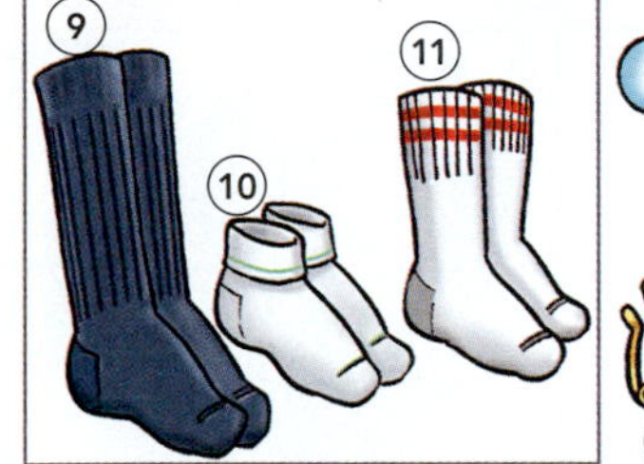

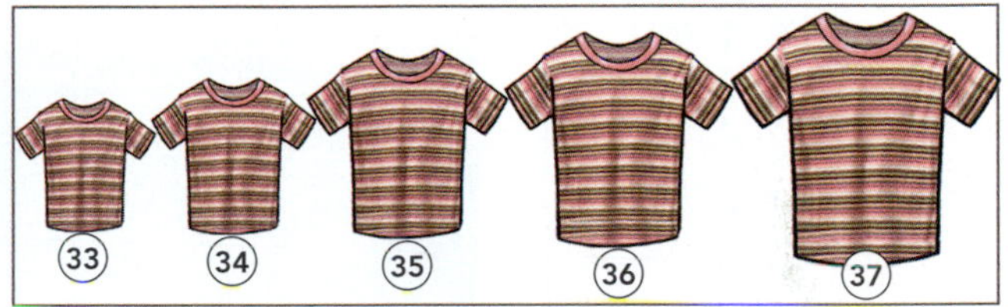


### 衣類の種類 Types of Clothing

- 長袖シャツ **1** long-sleeved shirt
- 半袖シャツ **2** short-sleeved shirt
- ノースリーブ **3** sleeveless shirt
- タートルネックシャツ **4** turtleneck (shirt)

- Vネックセーター **5** V-neck sweater
- カーディガン **6** cardigan sweater
- クルーネックセーター **7** crewneck sweater
- タートルネックセーター **8** turtleneck sweater

- ハイソックス **9** knee-high socks
- スニーカーソックス／アンクルソックス **10** ankle socks
- クルーソックス **11** crew socks

- ピアス **12** pierced earrings
- イヤリング **13** clip-on earrings

### 素材の種類 Types of Material

- コーデュロイ(パンツ) **14** corduroy *pants*
- レザー(ブーツ) **15** leather *boots*
- ナイロン(ストッキング) **16** nylon *stockings*
- コットン(Tシャツ) **17** cotton *T-shirt*
- デニム(ジャケット) **18** denim *jacket*
- フランネル(シャツ) **19** flannel *shirt*
- ポリエステル(シャツ) **20** polyester *blouse*
- リンネル(ドレス) **21** linen *dress*
- シルク(スカーフ) **22** silk *scarf*
- ウール(セーター) **23** wool *sweater*
- 麦わら(帽子) **24** straw *hat*

### 模様 Patterns

- しま模様の **25** striped
- 市松模様の **26** checked
- 格子柄の **27** plaid
- 水玉模様の **28** polka-dotted
- 模様のついた／プリント柄の **29** patterned/print
- 花模様の **30** flowered/floral
- ペイズリー模様の **31** paisley
- (青い)無地の **32** solid *blue*

### サイズ Sizes

- XSサイズ **33** extra-small
- Sサイズ **34** small
- Mサイズ **35** medium
- Lサイズ **36** large
- XLサイズ **37** extra-large

[1–24]
A. May I help you?
B. Yes, please. I'm looking for a *shirt*.*
A. What kind?
B. I'm looking for a *long-sleeved shirt*.

* *With 9–16:* I'm looking for ______.

[25–32]
A. How do you like this ______ tie/shirt/skirt?
B. Actually, I prefer that ______ one.

[33–37]
A. What size are you looking for?
B. ______.

Describe your favorite clothing items. For each item, tell about the color, the type of material, the size, and the pattern.

# CLOTHING PROBLEMS AND ALTERATIONS

## 衣類に関する問題・直し

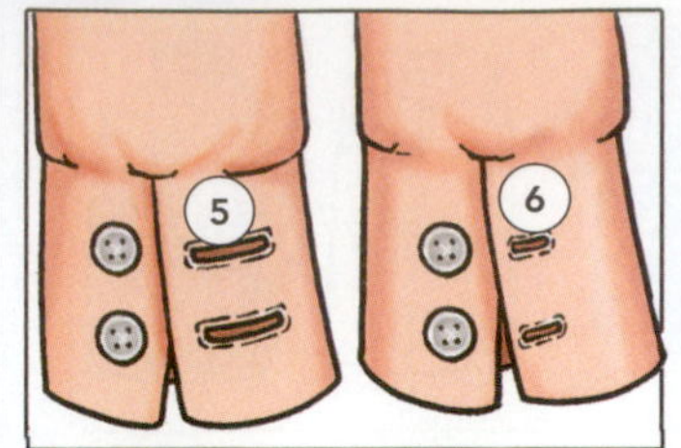

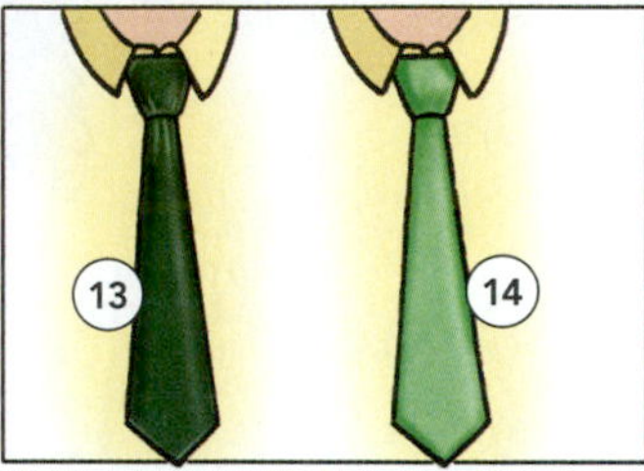
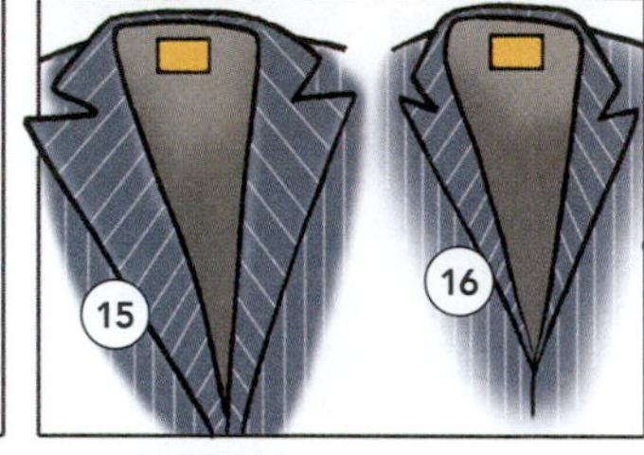
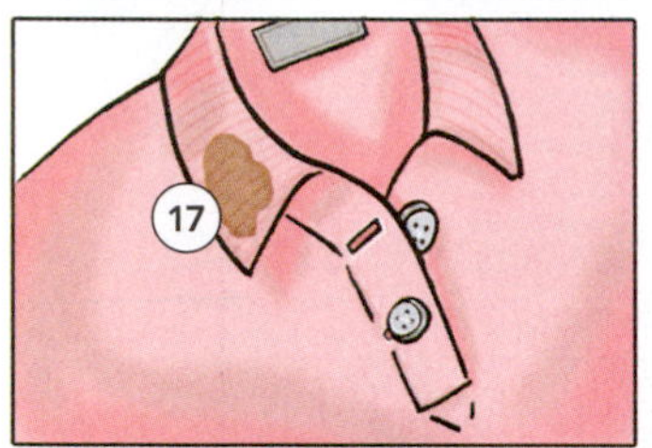

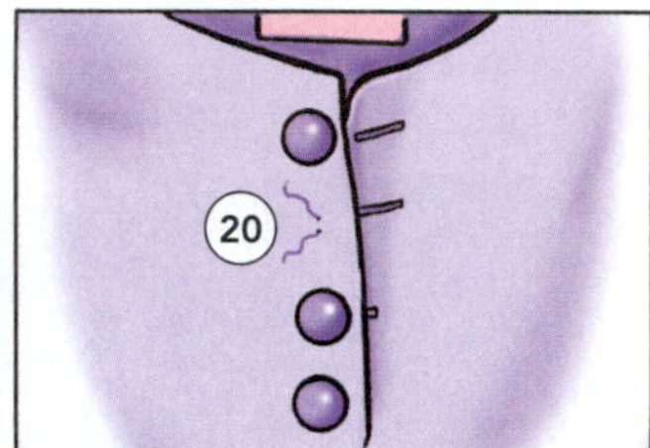
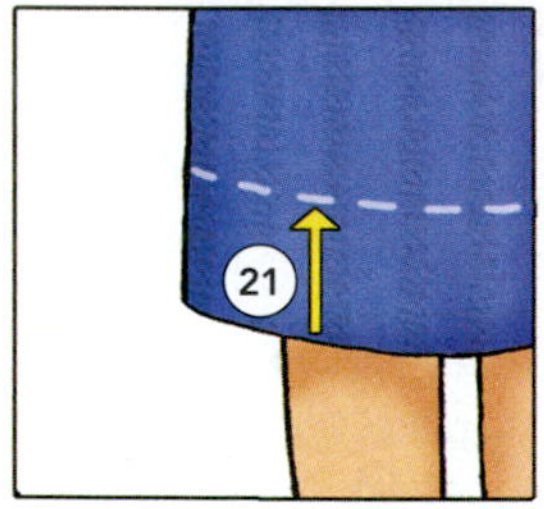
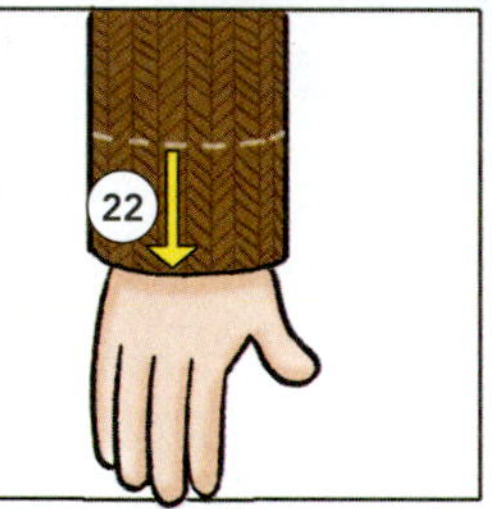

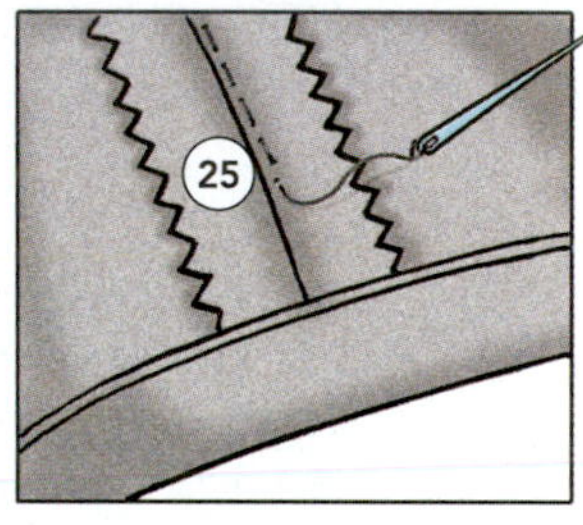

長い — 短い **1–2** long – short
きつい — ゆるい **3–4** tight – loose/baggy
大きい — 小さい **5–6** large/big – small
高い — 低い **7–8** high – low
はでな — 地味な **9–10** fancy – plain
厚手の — 薄手の **11–12** heavy – light
(色が)暗い — 明るい **13–14** dark – light
広い — 狭い **15–16** wide – narrow

しみの付いた(襟) **17** stained *collar*
破けた(ポケット) **18** ripped/torn *pocket*
壊れた(ファスナー) **19** broken *zipper*
なくなった(ボタン) **20** missing *button*
(スカートの)丈を詰める **21** shorten the *skirt*
(袖を)出す **22** lengthen the *sleeves*
(ジャケットの)幅を詰める **23** take in the *jacket*
(パンツの)幅を出す **24** let out the *pants*
(縫い代を)かがる **25** fix/repair the *seam*

[1–2]
A. Are the sleeves too **long**?
B. No. They're too **short**.

1–2 Are the sleeves too ________?
3–4 Are the pants too ________?
5–6 Are the buttonholes too ________?
7–8 Are the heels too ________?

9–10 Are the buttons too ________?
11–12 Is the coat too ________?
13–14 Is the color too ________?
15–16 Are the lapels too ________?

[17–20]
A. What's the matter with it?
B. It has a **stained** *collar*.

[21–25]
A. Please **shorten** the *skirt*.
B. **Shorten** the *skirt*? Okay.

Tell about the differences between clothing people wear now and clothing people wore a long time ago.

# LAUNDRY

## 洗濯物

洗濯物の種分け **A** sort the laundry
洗濯機に洗濯物を入れる **B** load the washer
洗濯機をからにする **C** unload the washer
乾燥機に洗濯物を入れる **D** load the dryer
物干しひもに洗濯物を干す **E** hang clothes on the clothesline
アイロンをかける **F** iron
洗濯物をたたむ **G** fold the laundry
衣類を掛ける **H** hang up clothing
整理する **I** put things away

洗濯物 **1** laundry
色の薄い衣類 **2** light clothing
色の濃い衣類 **3** dark clothing
洗濯かご **4** laundry basket
洗濯物袋 **5** laundry bag
洗濯機 **6** washer/washing machine
洗濯洗剤 **7** laundry detergent
柔軟剤 **8** fabric softener

漂白剤 **9** bleach
ぬれた洗濯物 **10** wet clothing
乾燥機 **11** dryer
糸くずフィルター **12** lint trap
静電気とり **13** static cling remover
物干しひも **14** clothesline
洗濯バサミ **15** clothespin
アイロン **16** iron
アイロン台 **17** ironing board
しわのよった衣類 **18** wrinkled clothing
アイロンのかかった衣類 **19** ironed clothing
スプレー糊 **20** spray starch
清潔な衣類 **21** clean clothing
戸棚／クロゼット **22** closet
ハンガー **23** hanger
引き出し **24** drawer
棚 **25** shelf-shelves

[A–I]
A. What are you doing?
B. I'm _______ing.

[4–6, 11, 14–17, 23]
A. Excuse me. Do you sell _______s?
B. Yes. They're at the back of the store.
A. Thank you.

[7–9, 13, 20]
A. Excuse me. Do you sell _______?
B. Yes. It's at the back of the store.
A. Thank you.

Who does the laundry in your home? What things does this person use?

# THE DEPARTMENT STORE

## デパート

| | | |
|---|---|---|
| 売場案内 | **1** | (store) directory |
| 宝石売場 | **2** | Jewelry Counter |
| 香水売場 | **3** | Perfume Counter |
| エスカレーター | **4** | escalator |
| エレベーター | **5** | elevator |
| 紳士服売場 | **6** | Men's Clothing Department |
| 商品受取所 | **7** | customer pickup area |
| 婦人服売場 | **8** | Women's Clothing Department |
| 子供服売場 | **9** | Children's Clothing Department |
| 家庭用品売場 | **10** | Housewares Department |
| 家具売場 | **11** | Furniture Department/ Home Furnishings Department |
| 家庭用電化製品売場 | **12** | Household Appliances Department |
| テレビ・音響製品売場 | **13** | Electronics Department |
| お客様サービスカウンター | **14** | Customer Assistance Counter/ Customer Service Counter |
| 男子トイレ | **15** | men's room |
| 女子トイレ | **16** | ladies' room |
| 水飲み場 | **17** | water fountain |
| スナック（軽食）スタンド | **18** | snack bar |
| 贈答品包装カウンター | **19** | Gift Wrap Counter |

A. Excuse me. Where's the **store directory**?
B. It's over there, next to the **Jewelry Counter**.
A. Thanks.
B. You're welcome.

A. Excuse me. Do you sell *ties**?
B. Yes. You can find *ties** in the __[6, 8–13]__ /at the __[2, 3]__ on the first/second/third/fourth floor.
A. Thank you.

*ties/bracelets/dresses/toasters/. . .

Describe a department store you know. Tell what is on each floor.

# SHOPPING

## ショッピング

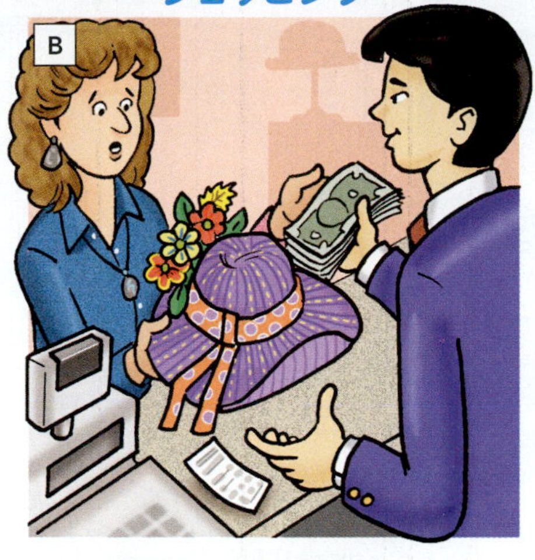

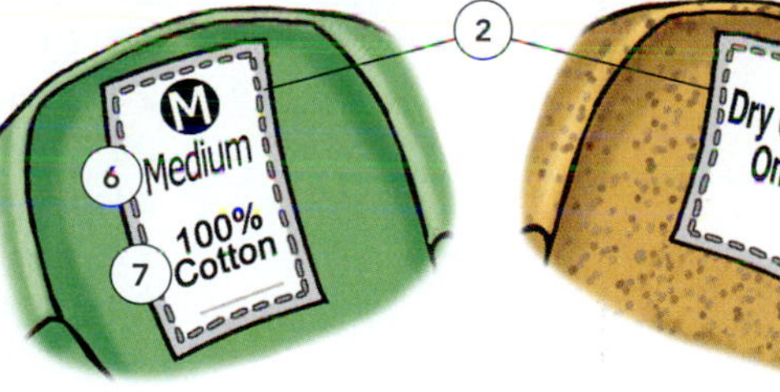

| | | | | | | | |
|---|---|---|---|---|---|---|---|
| 買う | **A** buy | 特売表示 | **1** sale sign | 取り扱い表示 | **8** care instructions |
| 返品する | **B** return | ラベル | **2** label | 通常価格 | **9** regular price |
| 交換する | **C** exchange | 値札 | **3** price tag | 値下げ価格 | **10** sale price |
| 試着する | **D** try on | レシート | **4** receipt | 値段 | **11** price |
| ～の代金を払う | **E** pay for | 割引 | **5** discount | 売上税 | **12** sales tax |
| ～についての情報を得る | **F** get some information about | サイズ | **6** size | 合計金額 | **13** total price |
| | | 素材 | **7** material | | |

A. May I help you?
B. Yes, please. I want to ___[A–F]___ this item.
A. Certainly. I'll be glad to help you.

A. { What's the ___[5–7, 9–13]___?
What are the ___[8]___? }
B. ________.
A. Are you sure?
B. Yes. Look at the ___[1–4]___!

Which stores in your area have sales? How often?

Tell about something you bought on sale.

# VIDEO AND AUDIO EQUIPMENT

## ビデオ・オーディオ機器

テレビ **1** TV/television
プラズマTV **2** plasma TV
液晶TV **3** LCD TV
プロジェクションTV **4** projection TV
ポータブルTV **5** portable TV
リモコン **6** remote (control)
DVD **7** DVD
DVDプレーヤー **8** DVD player
ビデオテープ **9** video/videocassette/videotape
ビデオデッキ **10** VCR/videocassette recorder
ビデオカメラ **11** camcorder/video camera
バッテリーパック **12** battery pack
バッテリーチャージャー／充電器 **13** battery charger
ラジオ **14** radio
ラジオ付き時計 **15** clock radio
短波ラジオ **16** shortwave radio
テープレコーダー **17** tape recorder/cassette recorder
マイク **18** microphone

ステレオ **19** stereo system/sound system
レコード **20** record
レコードプレーヤー **21** turntable
CD(コンパクトディスク) **22** CD/compact disc
CDプレーヤー **23** CD player
チューナー **24** tuner
カセットテープ **25** (audio)tape/(audio)cassette
テープデッキ／カセットデッキ **26** tape deck/cassette deck
スピーカー **27** speakers
ミニコンポ **28** portable stereo system/boombox
ポータブルCDプレーヤー **29** portable/personal CD player
ポータブルカセットプレーヤー **30** portable/personal cassette player
ヘッドホン **31** headphones
ポータブルデジタルオーディオプレーヤー **32** portable/personal digital audio player
テレビゲーム機 **33** video game system
ゲームソフト **34** video game
携帯用ゲーム機 **35** hand-held video game

A. May I help you?
B. Yes, please. I'm looking for a **TV**.

* *With 27 & 31, use:* I'm looking for ______.

A. I like your new ______.
Where did you get it/them?
B. At ......*(name of store)*......

A. Which company makes the best ______?
B. In my opinion, the best ______ is/are made by ..............

What video and audio equipment do you have or want?

In your opinion, which brands of video and audio equipment are the best?

# 電話・カメラ

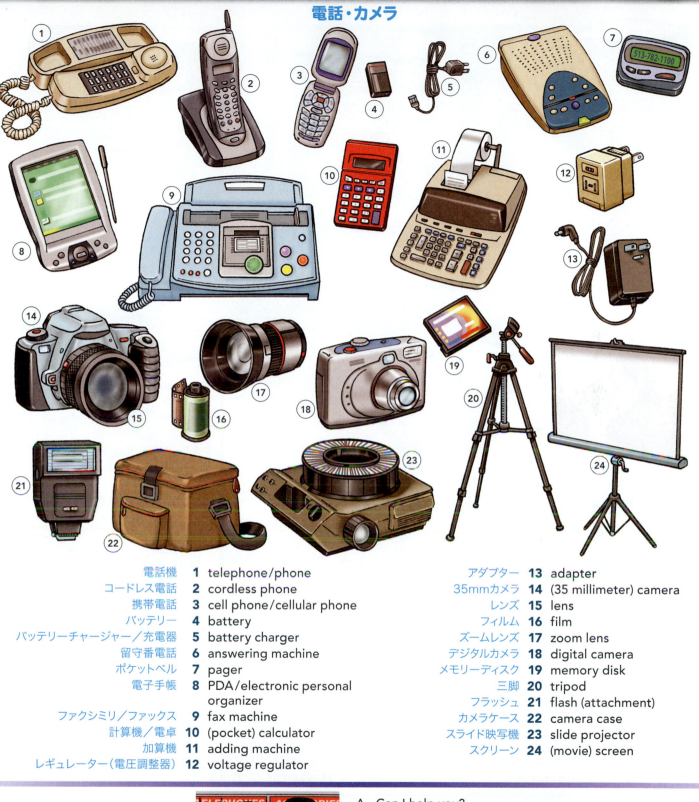

| | | |
|---|---|---|
| 電話機 | **1** | telephone/phone |
| コードレス電話 | **2** | cordless phone |
| 携帯電話 | **3** | cell phone/cellular phone |
| バッテリー | **4** | battery |
| バッテリーチャージャー／充電器 | **5** | battery charger |
| 留守番電話 | **6** | answering machine |
| ポケットベル | **7** | pager |
| 電子手帳 | **8** | PDA/electronic personal organizer |
| ファクシミリ／ファックス | **9** | fax machine |
| 計算機／電卓 | **10** | (pocket) calculator |
| 加算機 | **11** | adding machine |
| レギュレーター（電圧調整器） | **12** | voltage regulator |
| アダプター | **13** | adapter |
| 35mmカメラ | **14** | (35 millimeter) camera |
| レンズ | **15** | lens |
| フィルム | **16** | film |
| ズームレンズ | **17** | zoom lens |
| デジタルカメラ | **18** | digital camera |
| メモリーディスク | **19** | memory disk |
| 三脚 | **20** | tripod |
| フラッシュ | **21** | flash (attachment) |
| カメラケース | **22** | camera case |
| スライド映写機 | **23** | slide projector |
| スクリーン | **24** | (movie) screen |

A. Can I help you?
B. Yes. I want to buy a **telephone**.*

* *With 16, use:* I want to buy ____.

A. Excuse me. Do you sell ______s?*
B. Yes. We have a large selection of ______s.

* *With 16, use the singular.*

A. Which ______ is the best?
B. This one here. It's made by ......*(company)*......

What kind of telephone do you use?

Do you have a camera? What kind is it? What do you take pictures of?

Does anyone you know have an answering machine? When you call, what message do you hear?

# COMPUTERS

# コンピュータ

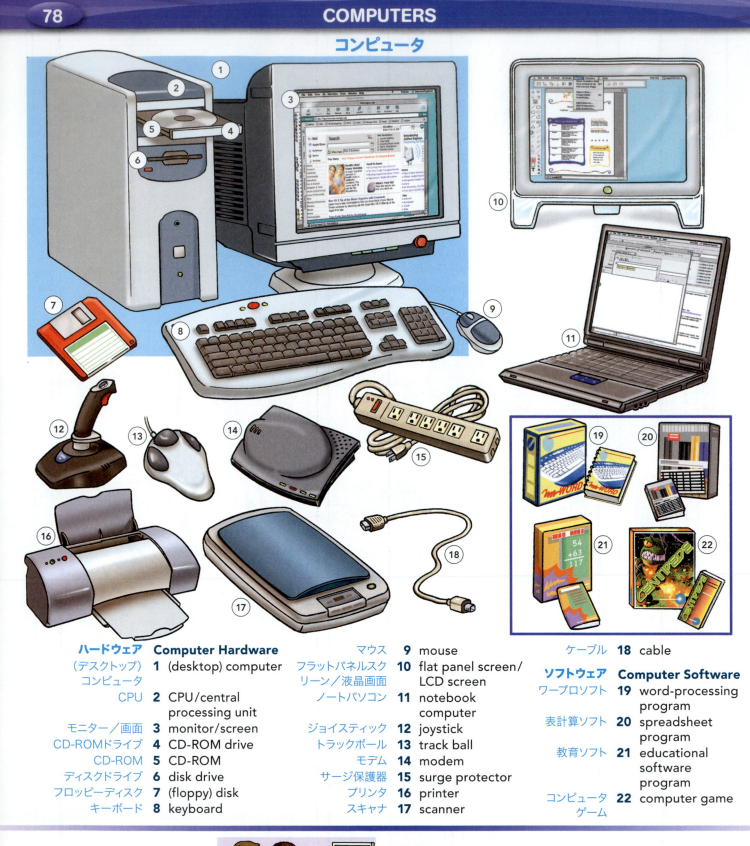

## ハードウェア Computer Hardware

(デスクトップ)コンピュータ **1** (desktop) computer
CPU **2** CPU/central processing unit
モニター/画面 **3** monitor/screen
CD-ROMドライブ **4** CD-ROM drive
CD-ROM **5** CD-ROM
ディスクドライブ **6** disk drive
フロッピーディスク **7** (floppy) disk
キーボード **8** keyboard
マウス **9** mouse
フラットパネルスクリーン/液晶画面 **10** flat panel screen/LCD screen
ノートパソコン **11** notebook computer
ジョイスティック **12** joystick
トラックボール **13** track ball
モデム **14** modem
サージ保護器 **15** surge protector
プリンタ **16** printer
スキャナ **17** scanner
ケーブル **18** cable

## ソフトウェア Computer Software

ワープロソフト **19** word-processing program
表計算ソフト **20** spreadsheet program
教育ソフト **21** educational software program
コンピュータゲーム **22** computer game

A. Can you recommend a good **computer**?
B. Yes. This **computer** here is excellent.

A. Is that a new ________?
B. Yes.
A. Where did you get it?
B. At .....*(name of store)*.....

A. May I help you?
B. Yes, please. Do you sell ________s?
A. Yes. We carry a complete line of ________s.

Do you use a computer? When?

In your opinion, how have computers changed the world?

# おもちゃ屋

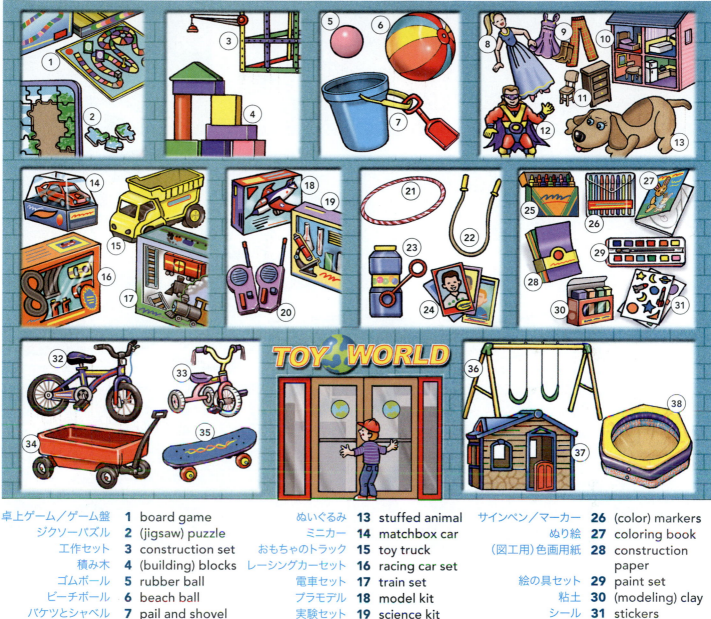

| | | |
|---|---|---|
| 卓上ゲーム／ゲーム盤 | **1** | board game |
| ジクソーパズル | **2** | (jigsaw) puzzle |
| 工作セット | **3** | construction set |
| 積み木 | **4** | (building) blocks |
| ゴムボール | **5** | rubber ball |
| ビーチボール | **6** | beach ball |
| バケツとシャベル | **7** | pail and shovel |
| 人形 | **8** | doll |
| 着せ替え人形の洋服 | **9** | doll clothing |
| ドールハウス（ミニチュアの家） | **10** | doll house |
| ドールハウスの家具 | **11** | doll house furniture |
| アクションフィギュア | **12** | action figure |
| ぬいぐるみ | **13** | stuffed animal |
| ミニカー | **14** | matchbox car |
| おもちゃのトラック | **15** | toy truck |
| レーシングカーセット | **16** | racing car set |
| 電車セット | **17** | train set |
| プラモデル | **18** | model kit |
| 実験セット | **19** | science kit |
| トランシーバー | **20** | walkie-talkie (set) |
| フラフープ | **21** | hula hoop |
| なわとび | **22** | jump rope |
| シャボン玉 | **23** | bubble soap |
| トレーディングカード（野球カードなど） | **24** | trading cards |
| クレヨン | **25** | crayons |
| サインペン／マーカー | **26** | (color) markers |
| ぬり絵 | **27** | coloring book |
| （図工用）色画用紙 | **28** | construction paper |
| 絵の具セット | **29** | paint set |
| 粘土 | **30** | (modeling) clay |
| シール | **31** | stickers |
| 自転車 | **32** | bicycle |
| 三輪車 | **33** | tricycle |
| ワゴン | **34** | wagon |
| スケートボード | **35** | skateboard |
| ブランコ | **36** | swing set |
| 屋外用プレイハウス | **37** | play house |
| ビニールプール | **38** | kiddie pool/ inflatable pool |

A. Excuse me. I'm looking for (a/an) _______(s) for my *grandson*.*
B. Look in the next aisle.
A. Thank you.

* *grandson/granddaughter/. . .*

A. I don't know what to get my ............-year-old son/daughter for his/her birthday.
B. What about (a) ________?
A. Good idea! Thanks.

A. Mom/Dad? Can we buy this/these ________?
B. No, *Johnny*. Not today.

What toys are most popular in your country?

What were your favorite toys when you were a child?

# THE BANK
## 銀行

預金する **A** make a deposit
預金を引き出す **B** make a withdrawal
小切手を換金する **C** cash a check
トラベラーズチェック（旅行者用小切手）を購入する **D** get traveler's checks
口座を開く **E** open an account
ローンを申し込む **F** apply for a loan
両替する **G** exchange currency

預金伝票 **1** deposit slip
払戻伝票 **2** withdrawal slip
小切手 **3** check
トラベラーズチェック（旅行者用小切手） **4** traveler's check
預金通帳 **5** bankbook/passbook
キャッシュカード **6** ATM card
クレジットカード **7** credit card
金庫 **8** (bank) vault
貸金庫 **9** safe deposit box
金銭出納係 **10** teller
警備員 **11** security guard
ATM／自動預払機 **12** ATM (machine)/cash machine
行員 **13** bank officer

[A–G]
A. Where are you going?
B. I'm going to the bank. I have to ______.

[5–7]
A. What are you looking for?
B. My ______. I can't find it anywhere!

[8–13]
A. How many ______s does the State Street Bank have?
B. ..............

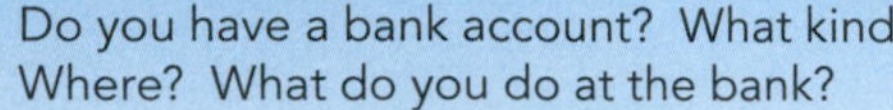

Do you have a bank account? What kind? Where? What do you do at the bank?

Do you ever use traveler's checks? When?

Do you have a credit card? What kind? When do you use it?

# 金融

## 支払いの形態 Forms of Payment

現金 1 cash
小切手 2 check
小切手番号 a check number
口座番号 b account number
クレジットカード 3 credit card
クレジットカード番号 a credit card number
為替 4 money order
トラベラーズチェック（旅行者用小切手） 5 traveler's check

## 一般的な支払い関係 Household Bills

家賃 6 rent
住宅ローン返済金 7 mortgage payment
電気料金請求書 8 electric bill
電話料金請求書 9 telephone bill
ガス料金請求書 10 gas bill
燃料費請求書 11 oil bill/heating bill
水道料金請求書 12 water bill
ケーブルテレビ請求書 13 cable TV bill
自動車ローン支払い 14 car payment
クレジッドカード利用代金請求書 15 credit card bill

## 家計 Family Finances

口座の残高計算をする 16 balance the checkbook
小切手を切る 17 write a check
オンラインバンキングする 18 bank online
小切手帳 19 checkbook
小切手記録薄 20 check register
月々の利用明細書 21 monthly statement

## ATMの利用 Using an ATM Machine

バンクカードを入れる 22 insert the ATM card
暗証番号を入力する 23 enter your PIN number/personal identification number
取引の種類を選ぶ 24 select a transaction
預金する 25 make a deposit
現金をおろす 26 withdraw/get cash
振替をする 27 transfer funds
カードを取り出す 28 remove your card
利用明細書をとる 29 take your transaction slip/receipt

A. Can I pay by [1, 2] / with a [3–5] ?
B. Yes. We accept [1] / [2–5] s.

A. What are you doing?
B. I'm paying the [6–15] .
I'm [16–18] ing.
I'm looking for the [19–21] .

A. What should I do?
B. [22–29] .

What household bills do you receive?
How much do you pay for the different bills?

Who takes care of the finances in your household? What does that person do?

Do you use ATM machines?
If you do, how do you use them?

# 郵便局

手紙 **1** letter
はがき **2** postcard
航空郵便／航空書簡 **3** air letter/aerogramme
小包 **4** package/parcel
第一種（封書） **5** first class
優先扱い郵便 **6** priority mail
速達 **7** express mail/overnight mail
小包郵便 **8** parcel post
配達証明郵便 **9** certified mail
切手 **10** stamp
切手シート **11** sheet of stamps
ロール切手 **12** roll of stamps
切手帳 **13** book of stamps
郵便為替 **14** money order
転居届 **15** change-of-address form
選抜徴兵登録用紙 **16** selective service registration form
パスポート申請用紙 **17** passport application form
封筒 **18** envelope
差出人住所氏名 **19** return address
送り先住所 **20** mailing address
郵便番号 **21** zip code
消印 **22** postmark
切手／郵便料金 **23** stamp/postage
投函口 **24** mail slot
郵便局員 **25** postal worker/postal clerk
はかり **26** scale
切手自動販売機 **27** stamp machine
郵便配達人 **28** letter carrier/mail carrier
郵便車 **29** mail truck
郵便ポスト **30** mailbox

[1–4]
A. Where are you going?
B. To the post office. I have to mail a/an ________.

[10–17]
A. Next!
B. I'd like a ________, please.
A. Here you are.

[5–9]
A. How do you want to send it?
B. ________, please.

[19–21, 23]
A. Do you want me to mail this letter?
B. Yes, thanks.
A. Oops! You forgot the ________!

How often do you go to the post office? What do you do there?

Tell about the postal system in your country.

# 図書館

- オンライン目録 **1** online catalog
- カード目録 **2** card catalog
- 著者名 **3** author
- 書名 **4** title
- 貸出カード **5** library card
- コピー機 **6** copier/ photocopier/ copy machine
- 書棚 **7** shelves
- 児童書コーナー **8** children's section
- 児童書 **9** children's books
- 定期刊行物コーナー **10** periodical section
- 定期刊行物／専門雑誌 **11** journals
- 雑誌 **12** magazines
- 新聞 **13** newspapers
- 視聴覚コーナー **14** media section
- 朗読テープ **15** books on tape
- 録音テープ **16** audiotapes
- CD **17** CDs
- ビデオ **18** videotapes
- (コンピュータ) ソフト **19** (computer) software
- DVD **20** DVDs
- 外国語コーナー **21** foreign language section
- 外国語図書 **22** foreign language books
- 参考図書室 **23** reference section
- マイクロフィルム **24** microfilm
- マイクロリーダー **25** microfilm reader
- 辞書 **26** dictionary
- 百科事典 **27** encyclopedia
- 地図帳 **28** atlas
- レファレンスデスク **29** reference desk
- (参考)図書案内員 **30** (reference) librarian
- 貸出カウンター **31** checkout desk
- 図書館事務員 **32** library clerk

[1, 2, 6–32]
A. Excuse me. Where's/Where are the ________?
B. Over there, at/near/next to the ________.

[8–23, 26–28]
A. Excuse me. Where can I find a/an ___[26–28]___ /___[9, 11–13, 15–20, 22]___?
B. Look in the ___[8, 10, 14, 21, 23]___ over there.

A. I'm having trouble finding a book.
B. Do you know the ___[3–4]___?
A. Yes. ..............

A. Excuse me. I'd like to check out this ___[26–28]___/these ___[11–13]___.
B. I'm sorry. It/They must remain in the library.

Do you go to a library? Where?
What does this library have?

Tell about how you use the library.

# COMMUNITY INSTITUTIONS

## コミュニティ組織

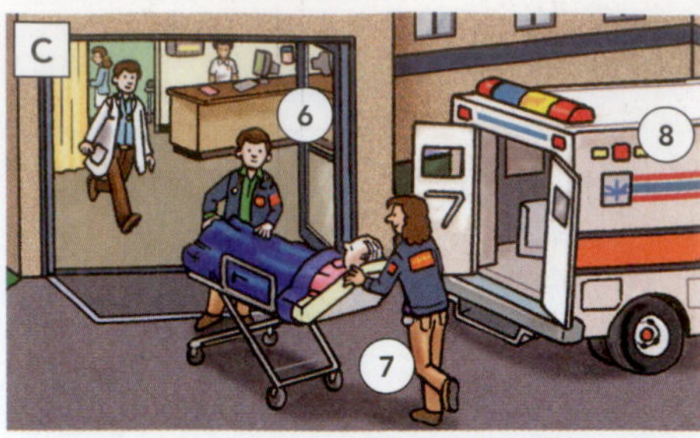

| | | |
|---|---|---|
| 警察署 | **A** | police station |
| 消防署 | **B** | fire station |
| 病院 | **C** | hospital |
| 市庁舎／市役所 | **D** | town hall/city hall |
| レクリエーションセンター | **E** | recreation center |
| ゴミ集積場 | **F** | dump |
| 託児所 | **G** | child-care center |
| 高齢者福祉センター | **H** | senior center |
| 教会 | **I** | church |
| シナゴーグ | **J** | synagogue |
| モスク | **K** | mosque |
| 寺院 | **L** | temple |
| 緊急応答オペレーター | **1** | emergency operator |
| 警官 | **2** | police officer |
| パトカー | **3** | police car |
| 消防車 | **4** | fire engine |
| 消防士 | **5** | firefighter |
| 救急室 | **6** | emergency room |
| 緊急医療士／救急隊員 | **7** | EMT/paramedic |
| 救急車 | **8** | ambulance |
| 市長／市政管理官 | **9** | mayor/city manager |
| 会議室 | **10** | meeting room |
| 体育館 | **11** | gym |
| アクティビティディレクター | **12** | activities director |
| ゲーム室 | **13** | game room |
| プール | **14** | swimming pool |
| 清掃課員 | **15** | sanitation worker |
| リサイクルセンター | **16** | recycling center |
| 保育士 | **17** | child-care worker |
| 育児室 | **18** | nursery |
| プレイルーム | **19** | playroom |
| 老人介護士 | **20** | eldercare worker/ senior care worker |

[A–L]
A. Where are you going?
B. I'm going to the ______.

[1, 2, 5, 7, 12, 15, 17, 20]
A. What do you do?
B. I'm a/an ______.

[3, 4, 8]
A. Do you hear a siren?
B. Yes. There's a/an ______ coming up behind us.

What community institutions are in your city or town? Where are they located?

Which community institutions do you use? When?

# 犯罪・緊急事態

| | | |
|---|---|---|
| 交通事故 | 1 | car accident |
| 火事 | 2 | fire |
| 爆発 | 3 | explosion |
| 強盗 | 4 | robbery |
| 泥棒 | 5 | burglary |
| 引ったくり | 6 | mugging |
| 誘拐 | 7 | kidnapping |
| 迷子 | 8 | lost child |
| カージャック | 9 | car jacking |
| 銀行強盗 | 10 | bank robbery |
| 暴行 | 11 | assault |
| 殺人 | 12 | murder |
| 停電 | 13 | blackout/ power outage |
| ガス漏れ | 14 | gas leak |
| 水道管破裂 | 15 | water main break |
| 電線の切断 | 16 | downed power line |
| 薬品の流出 | 17 | chemical spill |
| 脱線 | 18 | train derailment |
| 破壊行為 | 19 | vandalism |
| ギャングによる暴力行為 | 20 | gang violence |
| 飲酒運転 | 21 | drunk driving |
| 麻薬取引 | 22 | drug dealing |

[1–13]
A. I want to report a/an ________.
B. What's your location?
A. .............

[14–18]
A. Why is this street closed?
B. It's closed because of a ________.

[19–22]
A. I'm very concerned about the amount of ________ in our community.
B. I agree. ________ is a very serious problem.

Is there much crime in your community? Tell about it.

Have you ever experienced a crime or emergency? What happened?

## からだ

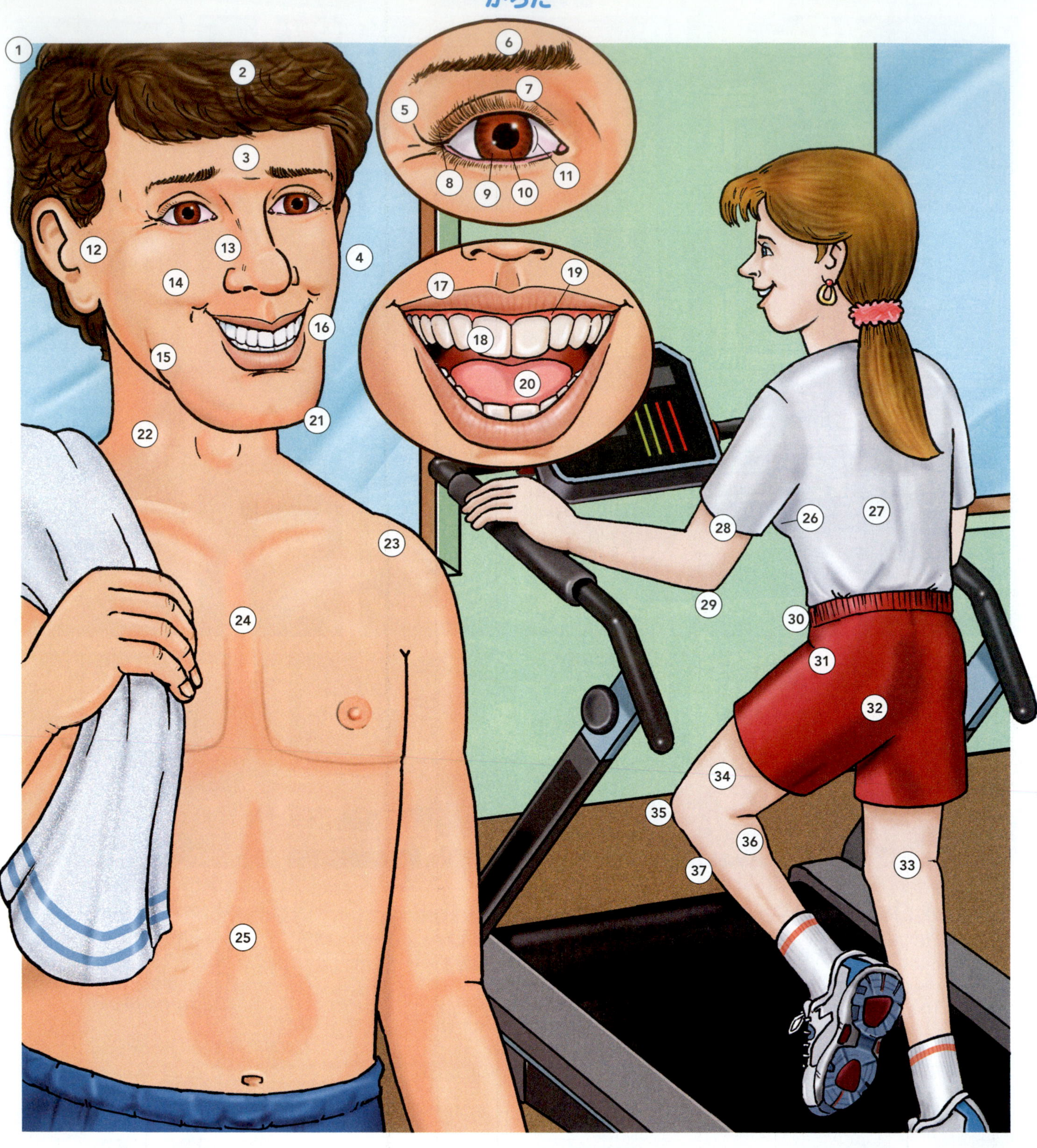

| | | |
|---|---|---|
| 頭 | **1** | head |
| 髪 | **2** | hair |
| 額 | **3** | forehead |
| 顔 | **4** | face |
| 目 | **5** | eye |
| まゆ | **6** | eyebrow |
| まぶた | **7** | eyelid |
| まつげ | **8** | eyelashes |
| こう彩 | **9** | iris |
| どう孔（ひとみ） | **10** | pupil |
| 角膜 | **11** | cornea |
| 耳 | **12** | ear |
| 鼻 | **13** | nose |
| ほお | **14** | cheek |
| あご | **15** | jaw |
| 口 | **16** | mouth |
| 唇 | **17** | lip |
| 歯 | **18** | tooth–teeth |
| 歯茎 | **19** | gums |
| 舌 | **20** | tongue |
| あご | **21** | chin |
| 首 | **22** | neck |
| 肩 | **23** | shoulder |
| 胸 | **24** | chest |
| 腹 | **25** | abdomen |
| 胸 | **26** | breast |
| 背中 | **27** | back |
| 腕 | **28** | arm |
| ひじ | **29** | elbow |
| ウエスト（胴のくびれ） | **30** | waist |
| 腰 | **31** | hip |
| しり（でん部） | **32** | buttocks |
| 脚 | **33** | leg |
| 太もも | **34** | thigh |
| ひざ | **35** | knee |
| ふくらはぎ | **36** | calf |
| むこうずね | **37** | shin |

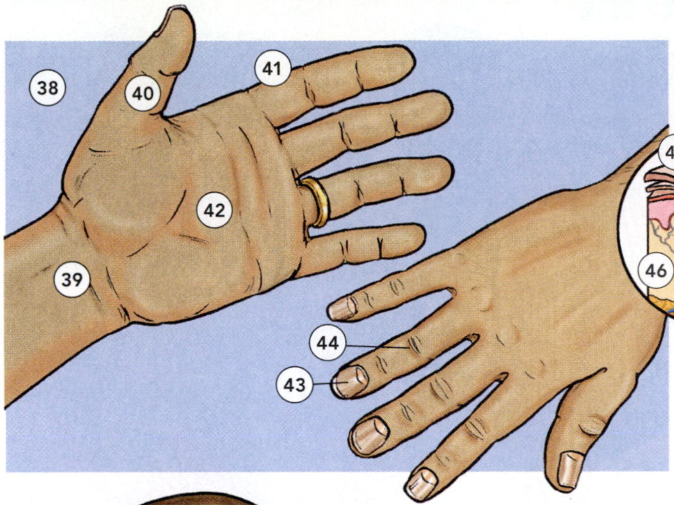

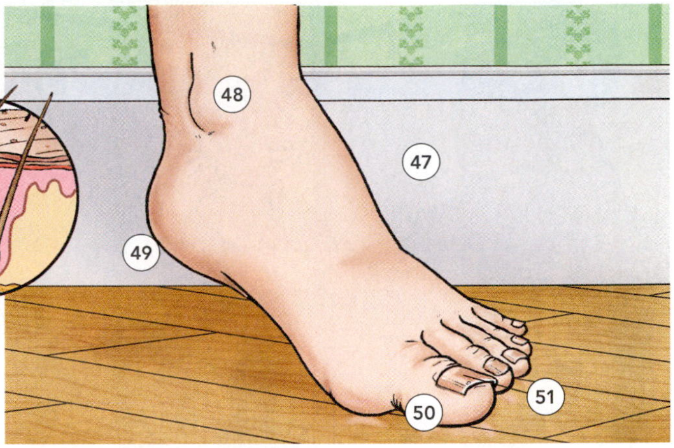

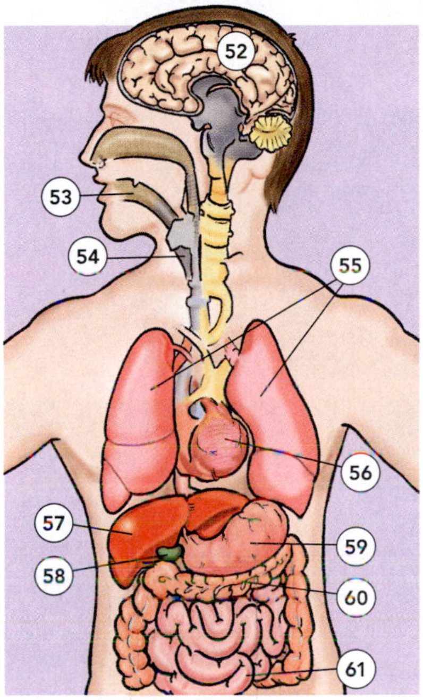

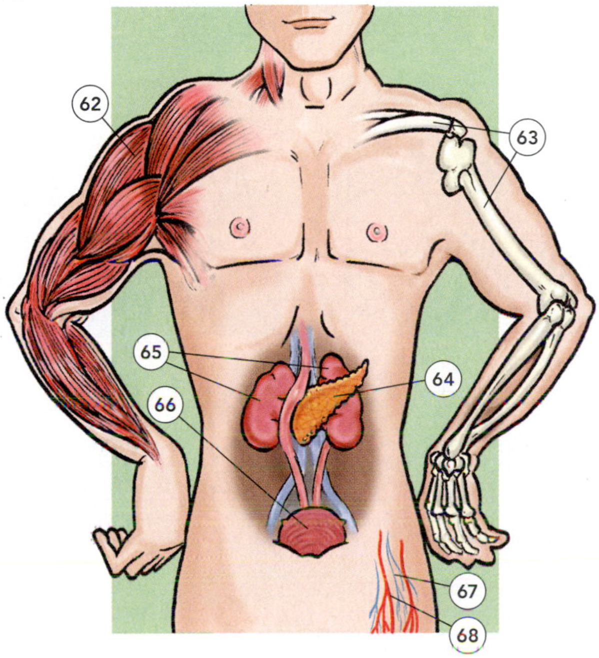

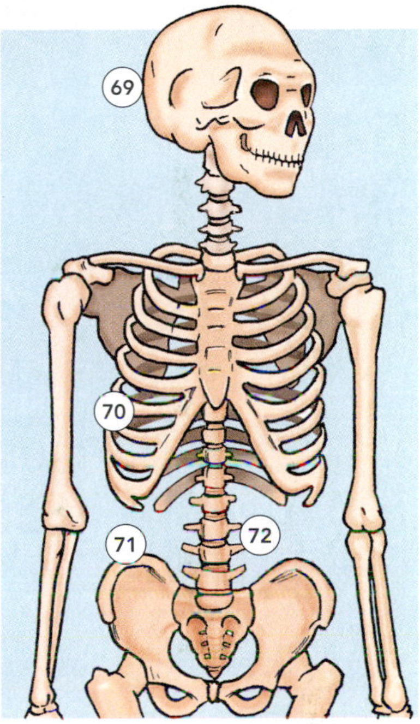

| | | |
|---|---|---|
| 手 | **38** | hand |
| 手首 | **39** | wrist |
| 親指 | **40** | thumb |
| 指 | **41** | finger |
| 手のひら | **42** | palm |
| 手のつめ | **43** | fingernail |
| 指関節 | **44** | knuckle |
| 皮膚 | **45** | skin |
| 神経 | **46** | nerve |
| 足 | **47** | foot |
| くるぶし | **48** | ankle |
| かかと | **49** | heel |
| つま先 | **50** | toe |
| 足のつめ | **51** | toenail |
| 脳 | **52** | brain |
| のど | **53** | throat |
| 食道 | **54** | esophagus |
| 肺 | **55** | lungs |
| 心臓 | **56** | heart |
| 肝臓 | **57** | liver |
| 胆のう | **58** | gallbladder |
| 胃 | **59** | stomach |
| 大腸 | **60** | large intestine |
| 小腸 | **61** | small intestine |
| 筋肉 | **62** | muscles |
| 骨 | **63** | bones |
| すい臓 | **64** | pancreas |
| 腎臓 | **65** | kidneys |
| ぼうこう | **66** | bladder |
| 静脈 | **67** | veins |
| 動脈 | **68** | arteries |
| 頭蓋骨 | **69** | skull |
| 胸郭 | **70** | ribcage |
| 骨盤 | **71** | pelvis |
| 脊柱／脊髄 | **72** | spinal column/ spinal cord |

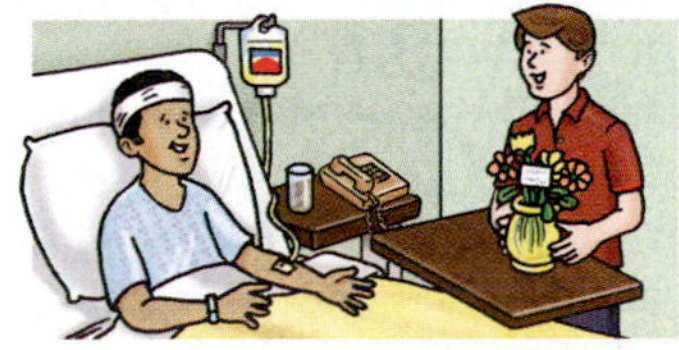

A. My doctor checked my **head** and said everything is okay.
B. I'm glad to hear that.

[1, 3–7, 12–29, 31–51]
A. Ooh!
B. What's the matter?
{ My ________ hurts!
{ My ________s hurt!

[52–72]
A. My doctor wants me to have some tests.
B. Why?
A. She's concerned about my ________.

Describe yourself as completely as you can.

Which parts of the body are most important at school? at work? when you play your favorite sport?

# AILMENTS, SYMPTOMS, AND INJURIES

## 病気・症状・傷害

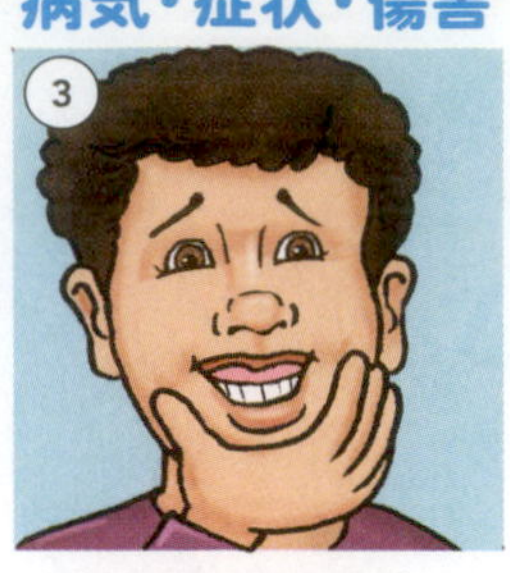
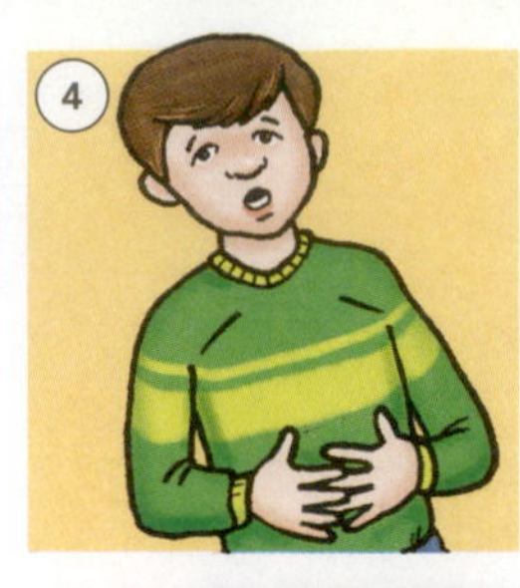
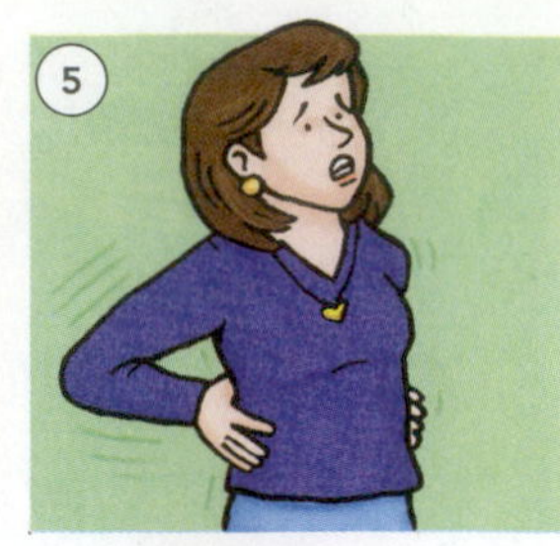

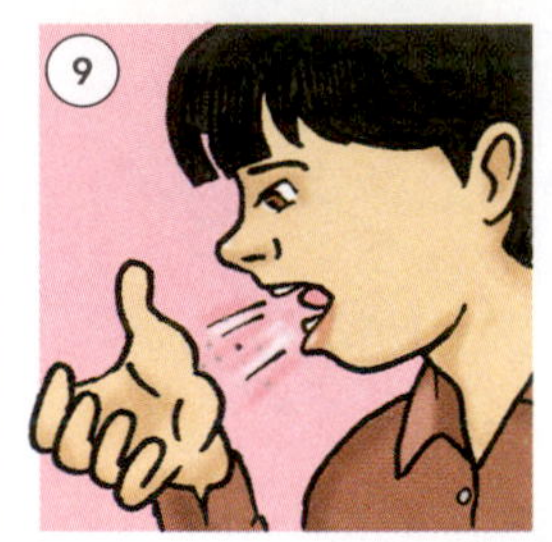
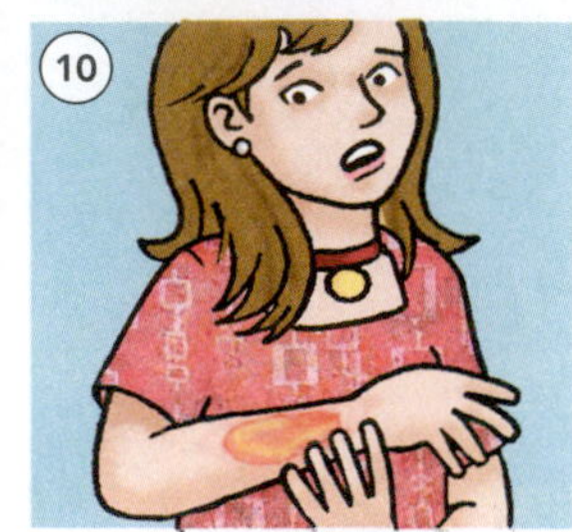
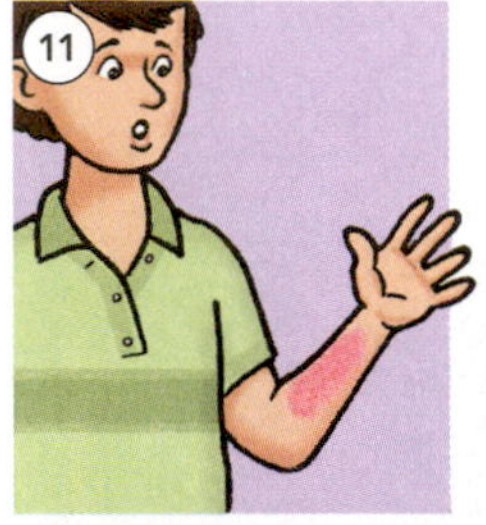

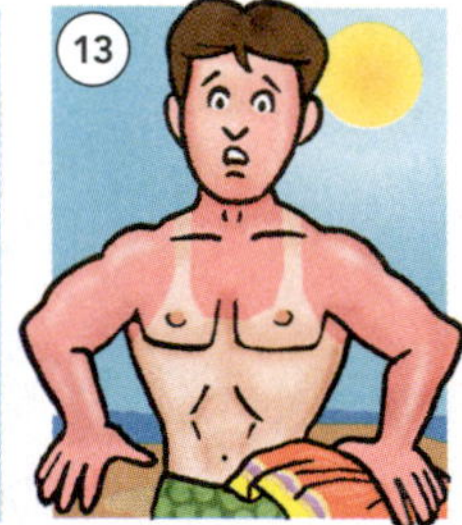

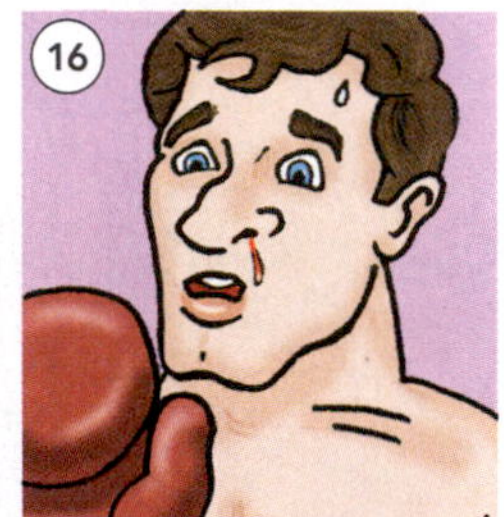
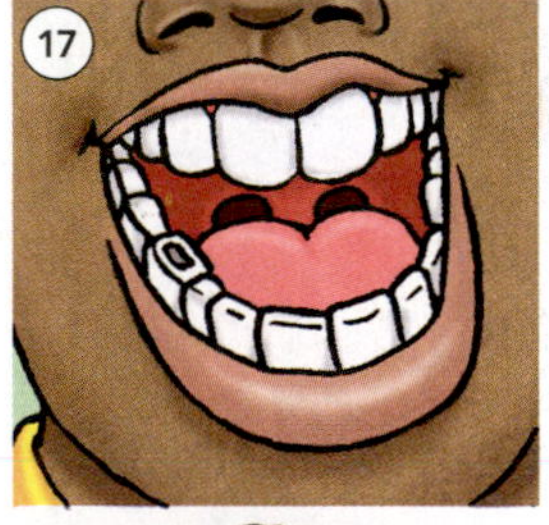
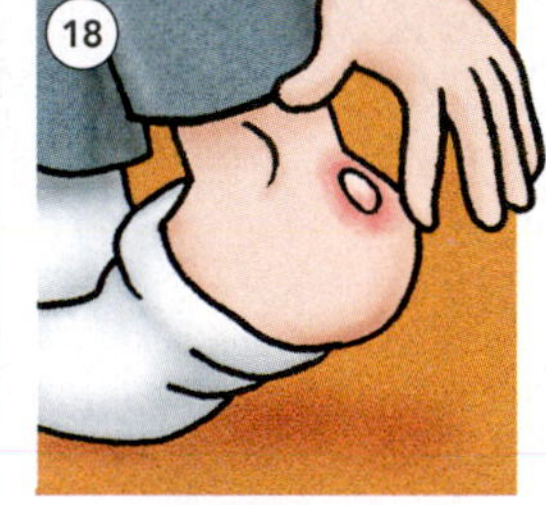
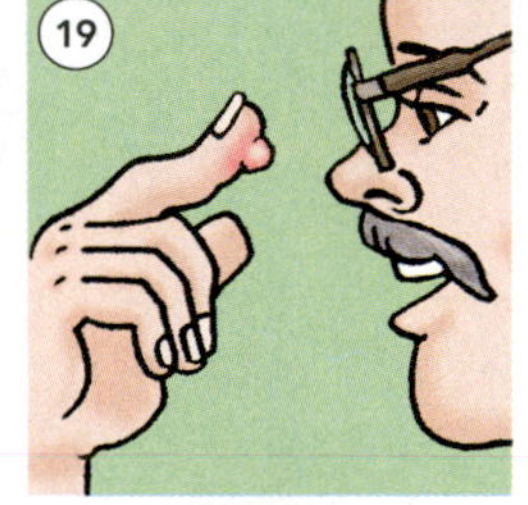

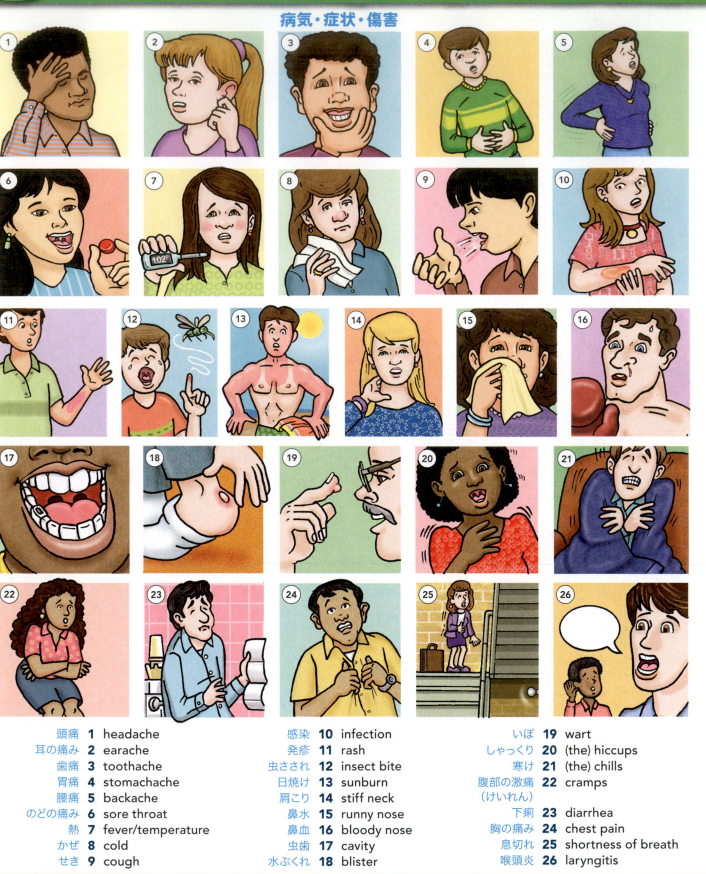

頭痛 **1** headache
耳の痛み **2** earache
歯痛 **3** toothache
胃痛 **4** stomachache
腰痛 **5** backache
のどの痛み **6** sore throat
熱 **7** fever/temperature
かぜ **8** cold
せき **9** cough
感染 **10** infection
発疹 **11** rash
虫さされ **12** insect bite
日焼け **13** sunburn
肩こり **14** stiff neck
鼻水 **15** runny nose
鼻血 **16** bloody nose
虫歯 **17** cavity
水ぶくれ **18** blister
いぼ **19** wart
しゃっくり **20** (the) hiccups
寒け **21** (the) chills
腹部の激痛（けいれん） **22** cramps
下痢 **23** diarrhea
胸の痛み **24** chest pain
息切れ **25** shortness of breath
喉頭炎 **26** laryngitis

A. What's the matter?
B. I have a/an ___[1–19]___.

A. What's the matter?
B. I have ___[20–26]___.

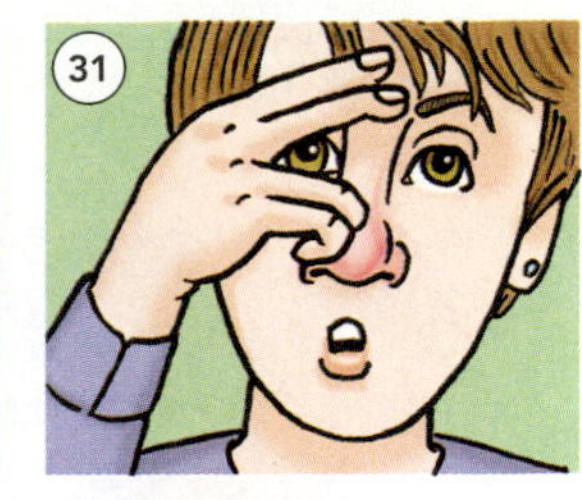

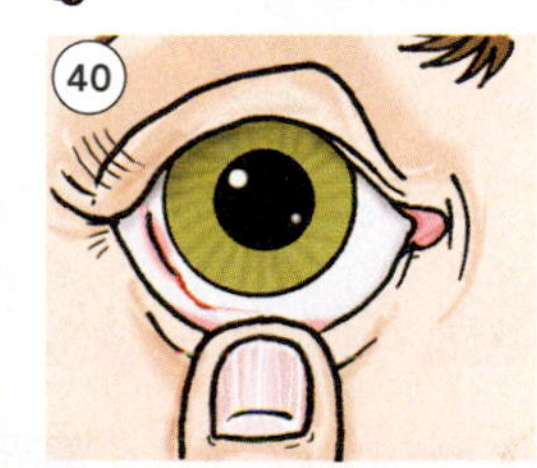

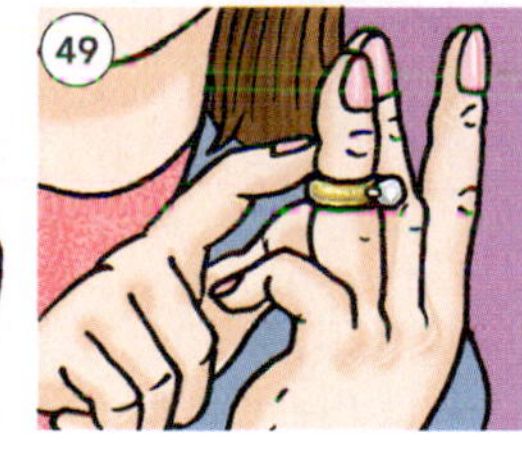

| | | |
|---|---|---|
| 気が遠くなる | **27** | faint |
| めまいがする | **28** | dizzy |
| 吐き気がする | **29** | nauseous |
| むくみがある | **30** | bloated |
| 詰まった | **31** | congested |
| 疲労した | **32** | exhausted |
| せきをする | **33** | cough |
| くしゃみをする | **34** | sneeze |
| ゼーゼー息をする | **35** | wheeze |
| げっぷをする | **36** | burp |
| 嘔吐する | **37** | vomit/throw up |
| 出血する | **38** | bleed |
| ひねる | **39** | twist |
| かき傷をつける | **40** | scratch |
| すりむく | **41** | scrape |
| あざができる | **42** | bruise |
| やけどする | **43** | burn |
| 痛める | **44** | hurt–hurt |
| 切り傷をつける | **45** | cut–cut |
| ねんざする | **46** | sprain |
| 脱臼する | **47** | dislocate |
| 骨折する | **48** | break–broke |
| むくんだ | **49** | swollen |
| かゆい | **50** | itchy |

A. What's the problem?

B. I feel [27–30] .
I'm [31–32] .
I've been [33–38] ing a lot.

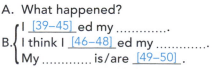

A. What happened?

B. I [39–45] ed my .............
I think I [46–48] ed my .............
My ............. is/are [49–50] .

A. How do you feel?
B. Not so good. / Not very well. / Terrible!
A. What's the matter?
B. ............., ............., and .............
A. I'm sorry to hear that.

Tell about the last time you didn't feel well. What was the matter?

Tell about a time you hurt yourself. What happened? How? What did you do about it?

What do you do when you have a cold? a stomachache? an insect bite? the hiccups?

## 応急手当

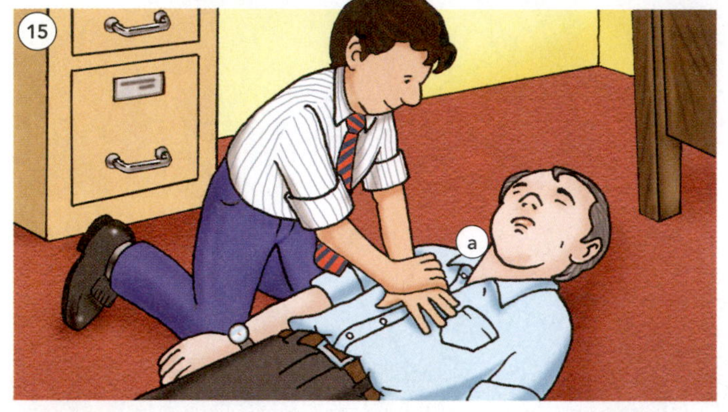

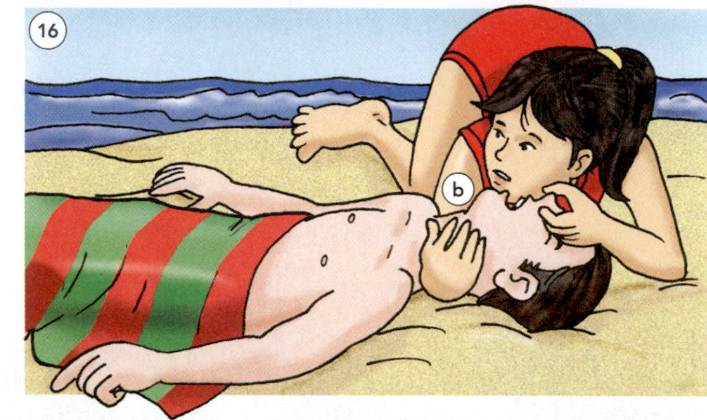

| | | |
|---|---|---|
| 応急手当の手引き | 1 | first-aid manual |
| 救急箱 | 2 | first-aid kit |
| 絆創膏／バンドエイド（商標名） | 3 | (adhesive) bandage/ Band-Aid™ |
| 消毒綿 | 4 | antiseptic cleansing wipe |
| 滅菌ガーゼ | 5 | sterile (dressing) pad |
| オキシドール | 6 | hydrogen peroxide |
| 抗生物質の軟膏 | 7 | antibiotic ointment |
| ガーゼ | 8 | gauze |
| サージカルテープ | 9 | adhesive tape |
| とげ抜き | 10 | tweezers |
| 抗ヒスタミンクリーム | 11 | antihistamine cream |
| 伸縮性包帯／Ace（商標名）包帯 | 12 | elastic bandage/ Ace™ bandage |
| アスピリン | 13 | aspirin |
| 非アスピリン系鎮痛剤 | 14 | non-aspirin pain reliever |
| 心肺機能蘇生法 | 15 | CPR (cardiopulmonary resuscitation) |
| 脈がない | a | has no pulse |
| 人工呼吸 | 16 | rescue breathing |
| 呼吸していない | b | isn't breathing |
| ハイムリッヒ法 | 17 | the Heimlich maneuver |
| 窒息している | c | is choking |
| 副木 | 18 | splint |
| 指の骨を折る | d | broke a finger |
| 止血帯 | 19 | tourniquet |
| 出血している | e | is bleeding |

A. Do we have any [3–5, 12] s/ [6–11, 13, 14] ?
B. Yes. Look in the first-aid kit.

A. Help! My friend [a–e] !
B. I can help!
{I know how to do [15–17] .
{I can make a [18, 19] .

Do you have a first-aid kit? If you do, what's in it? If you don't, where can you buy one?

Tell about a time when you gave or received first aid.

Where can a person learn first aid in your community?

# 救急・病気

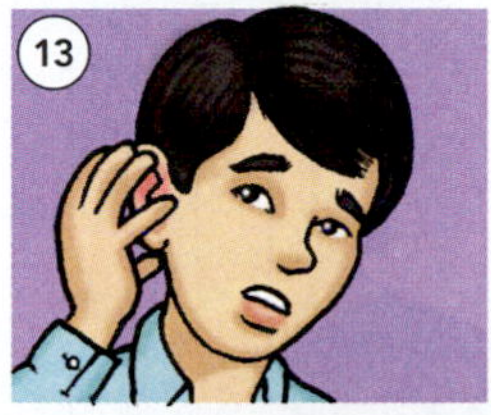

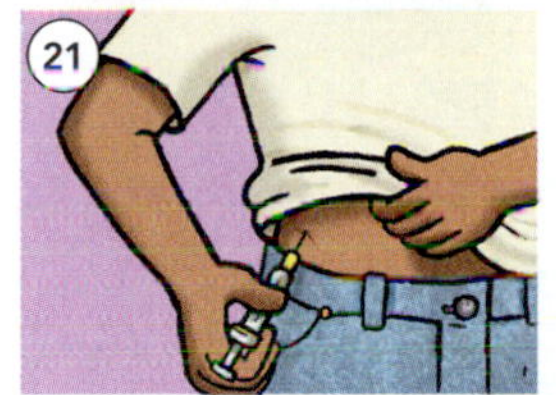

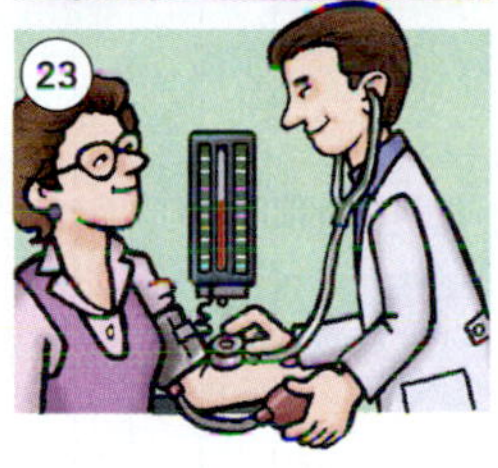
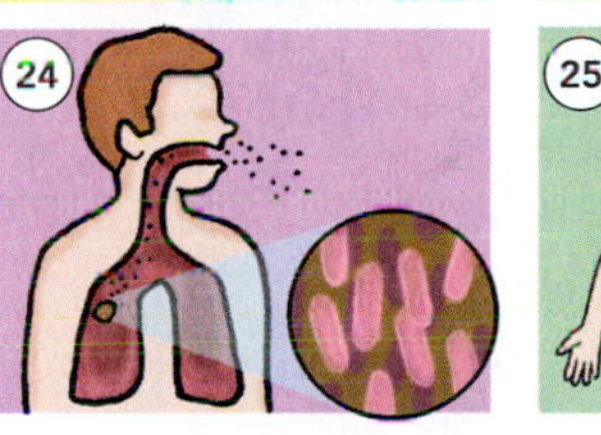
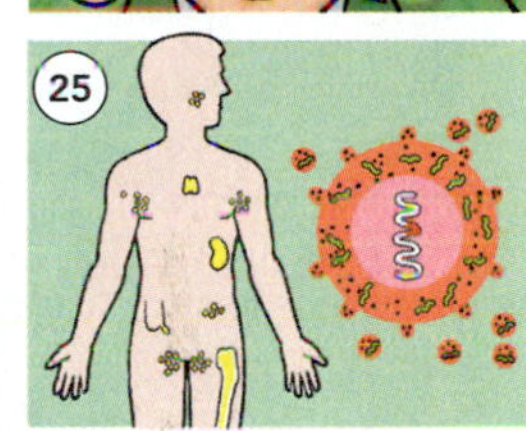

痛める／けがをする **1** hurt/injured
ショック状態にある **2** in shock
意識不明になっている **3** unconscious
熱射病 **4** heatstroke
しもやけ／凍傷 **5** frostbite
心臓発作 **6** heart attack
アレルギー反応 **7** allergic reaction
毒物を誤飲する **8** swallow poison
薬の適量を超過する **9** overdose on drugs
落ちる **10** fall–fell
電気ショックを受ける **11** get–got an electric shock
インフルエンザ **12** the flu/influenza
耳感染 **13** an ear infection

咽頭炎 **14** strep throat
はしか **15** measles
おたふく風邪 **16** mumps
水ぼうそう **17** chicken pox
喘息 **18** asthma
ガン **19** cancer
うつ **20** depression
糖尿病 **21** diabetes
心臓病 **22** heart disease
高血圧 **23** high blood pressure/hypertension
結核 **24** TB/tuberculosis
エイズ **25** AIDS*

* Acquired Immune Deficiency Syndrome

A. What happened?
B. My ............ { is [1–3]. / has [4–5]. / is having a/an [6–7]. / [8–11]ed. }
A. What's your location?
B. ....(address)....

A. My ............ is sick.
B. What's the matter?
A. He/She has [12–25].
B. I'm sorry to hear that.

Tell about a medical emergency that happened to you or someone you know.

Which illnesses in this lesson are you familiar with?

# THE MEDICAL EXAM

## 診察

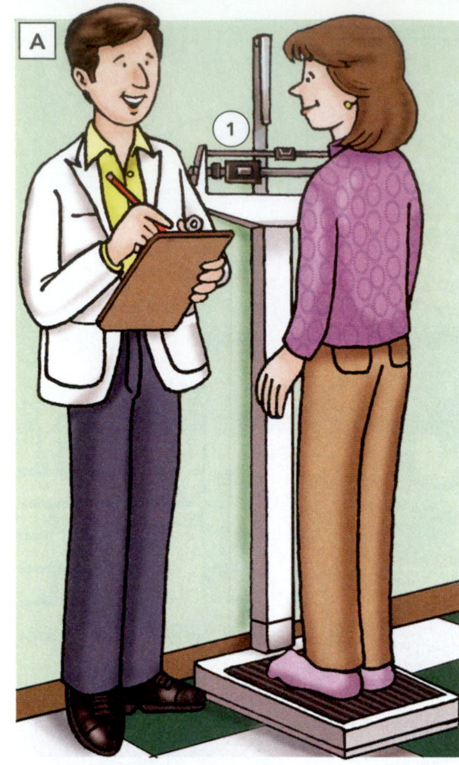

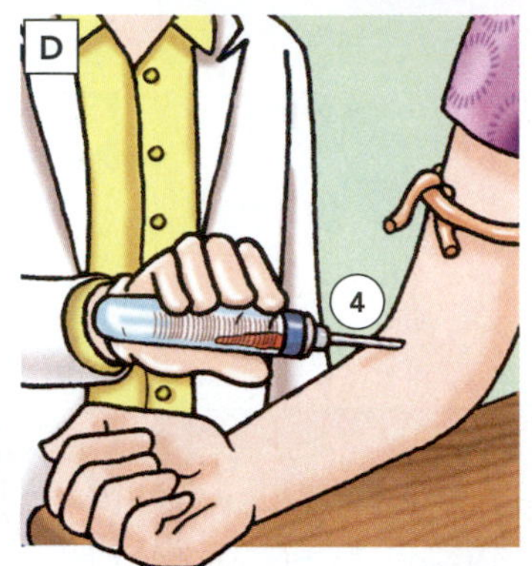


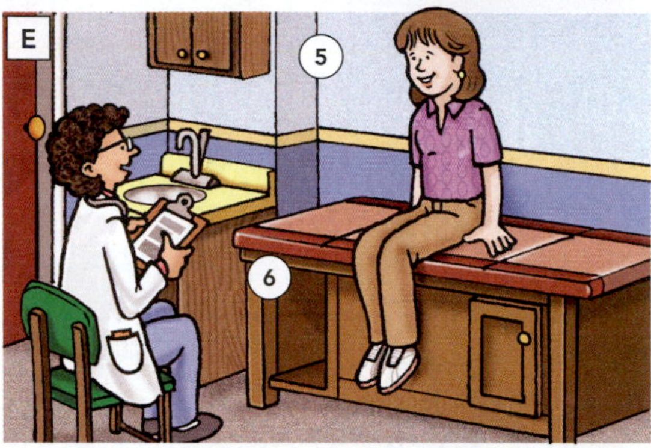

身長・体重を測る **A** measure *your* height and weight
体温を測る **B** take *your* temperature
血圧を測る **C** check *your* blood pressure
採血する **D** draw some blood
自分の健康状態について質問する **E** ask *you* some questions about *your* health
目、耳、鼻、喉を検査する **F** examine *your* eyes, ears, nose, and throat
心音を聞く **G** listen to *your* heart
胸部レントゲンを撮る **H** take a chest X-ray

体重計 **1** scale
体温計 **2** thermometer
血圧計 **3** blood pressure gauge
注射針／注射器 **4** needle/syringe
診察室 **5** examination room
診察台 **6** examination table
視力検査表 **7** eye chart
聴診器 **8** stethoscope
レントゲン写真機 **9** X-ray machine

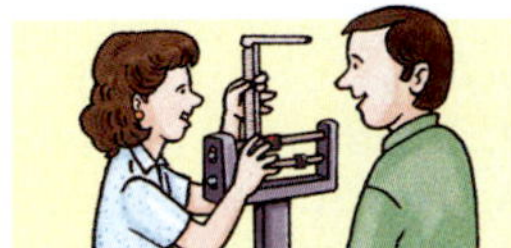

[A–H]
A. Now I'm going to **measure your height and weight.**
B. All right.

[A–H]
A. What did the doctor/nurse do during the examination?
B. She/He **measured my height and weight.**

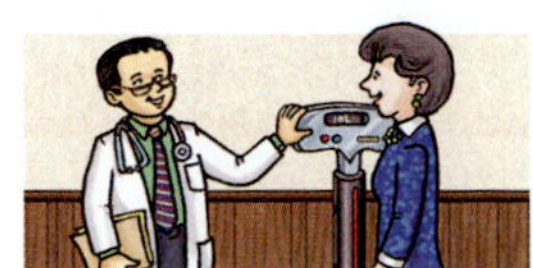

[1–3, 5–9]
A. So, how do you like our new **scale?**
B. It's very nice, doctor.

How often do you have a medical exam? What does the doctor/nurse do?

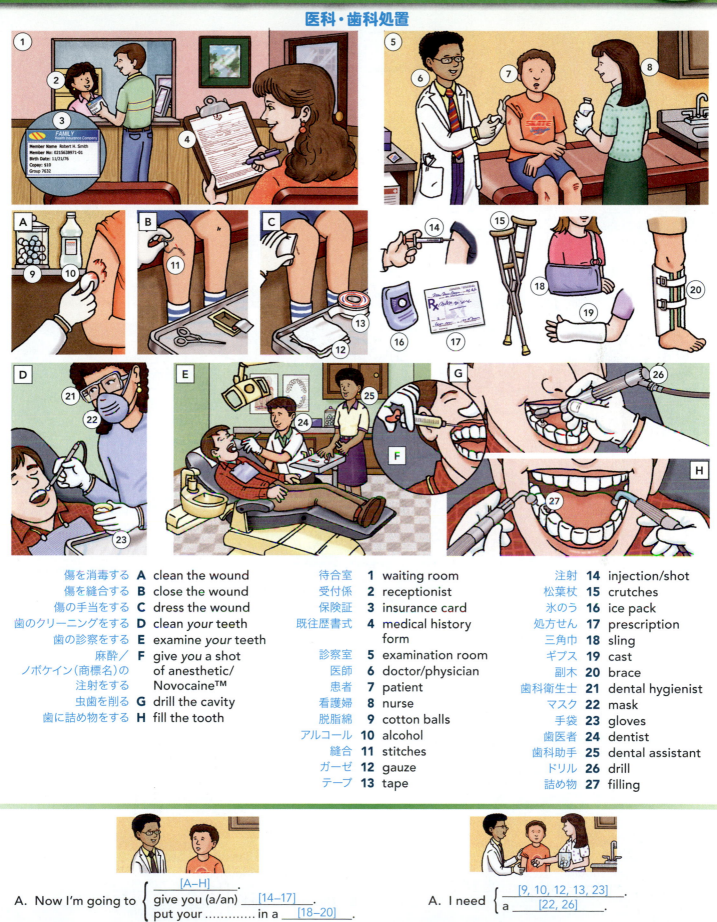

## 医科・歯科処置

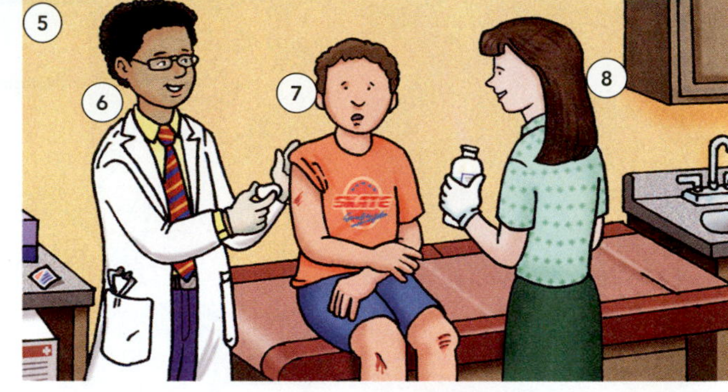


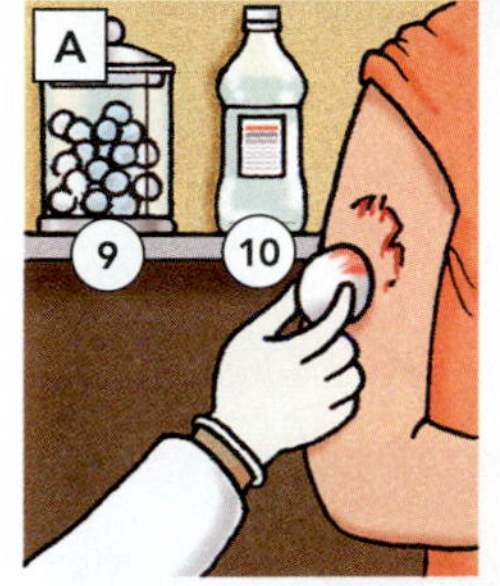


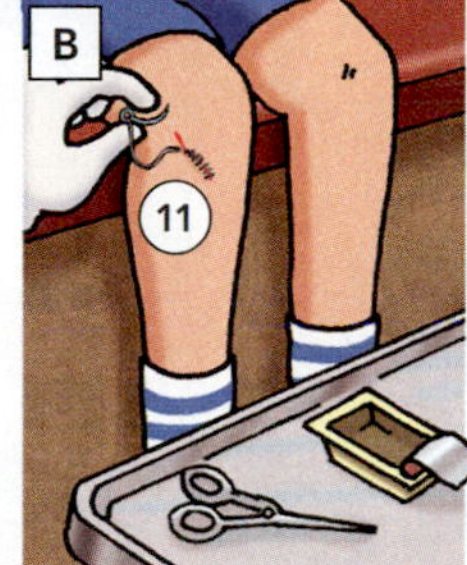


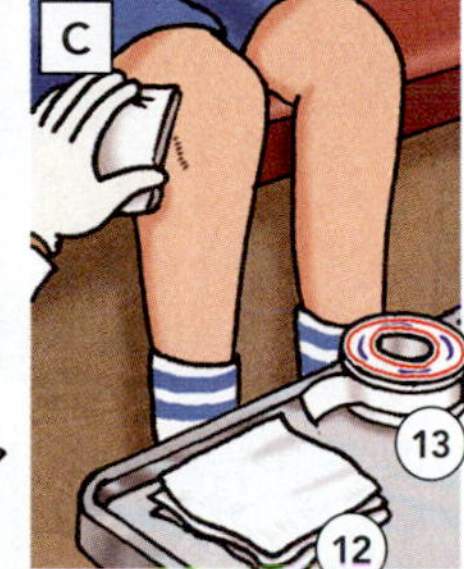


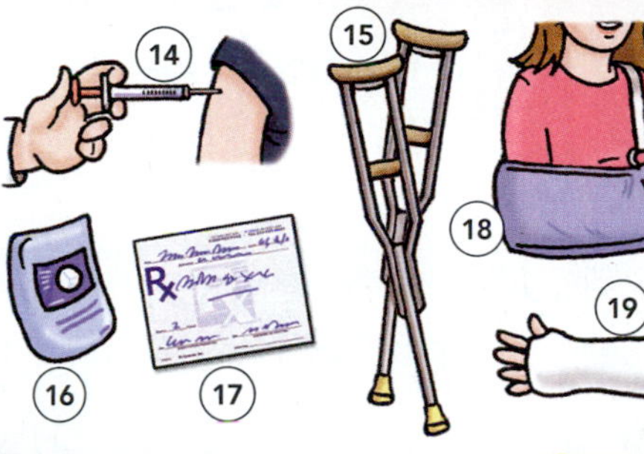

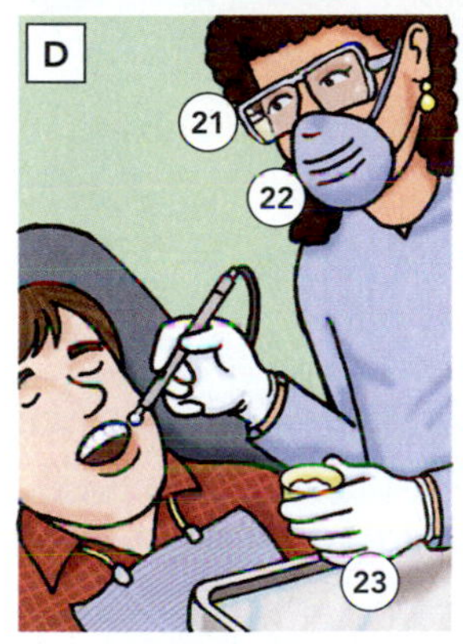


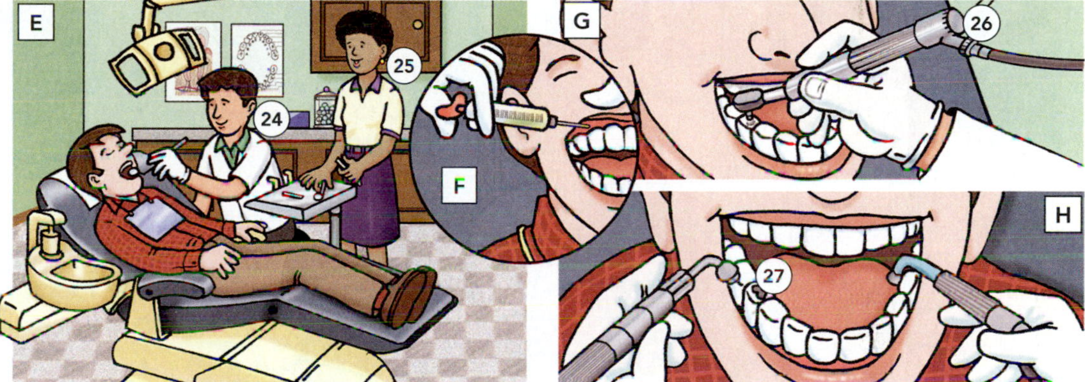


- 傷を消毒する **A** clean the wound
- 傷を縫合する **B** close the wound
- 傷の手当をする **C** dress the wound
- 歯のクリーニングをする **D** clean *your* teeth
- 歯の診察をする **E** examine *your* teeth
- 麻酔／ノボケイン(商標名)の注射をする **F** give *you* a shot of anesthetic/ Novocaine™
- 虫歯を削る **G** drill the cavity
- 歯に詰め物をする **H** fill the tooth

- 待合室 **1** waiting room
- 受付係 **2** receptionist
- 保険証 **3** insurance card
- 既往歴書式 **4** medical history form
- 診察室 **5** examination room
- 医師 **6** doctor/physician
- 患者 **7** patient
- 看護婦 **8** nurse
- 脱脂綿 **9** cotton balls
- アルコール **10** alcohol
- 縫合 **11** stitches
- ガーゼ **12** gauze
- テープ **13** tape

- 注射 **14** injection/shot
- 松葉杖 **15** crutches
- 氷のう **16** ice pack
- 処方せん **17** prescription
- 三角巾 **18** sling
- ギプス **19** cast
- 副木 **20** brace
- 歯科衛生士 **21** dental hygienist
- マスク **22** mask
- 手袋 **23** gloves
- 歯医者 **24** dentist
- 歯科助手 **25** dental assistant
- ドリル **26** drill
- 詰め物 **27** filling

A. Now I'm going to { ____[A–H]____. / give you (a/an) ____[14–17]____. / put your ............ in a ____[18–20]____.

B. Okay.

A. I need { ____[9, 10, 12, 13, 23]____. / a ____[22, 26]____.

B. Here you are.

Tell about a personal experience you had with a medical or dental procedure.

# MEDICAL ADVICE

## 医療アドバイス

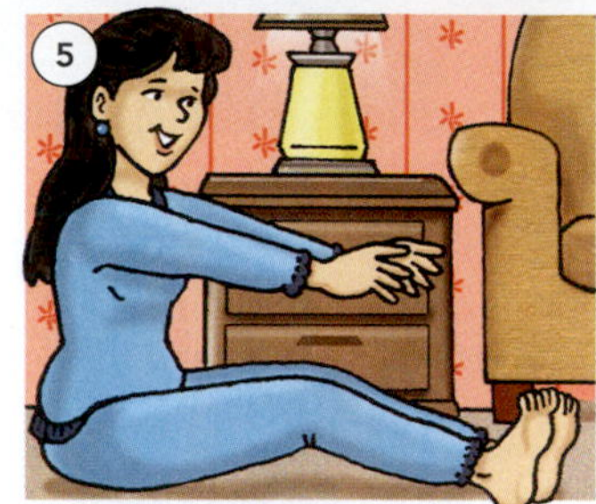

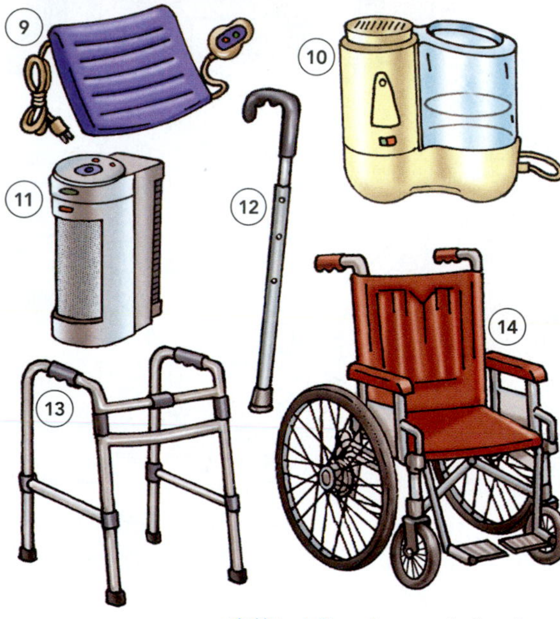
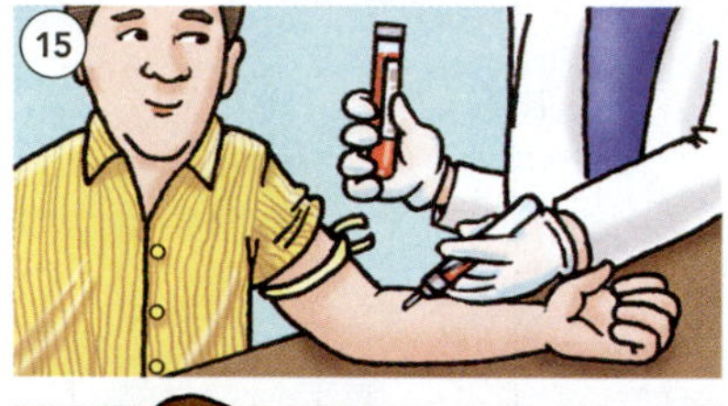
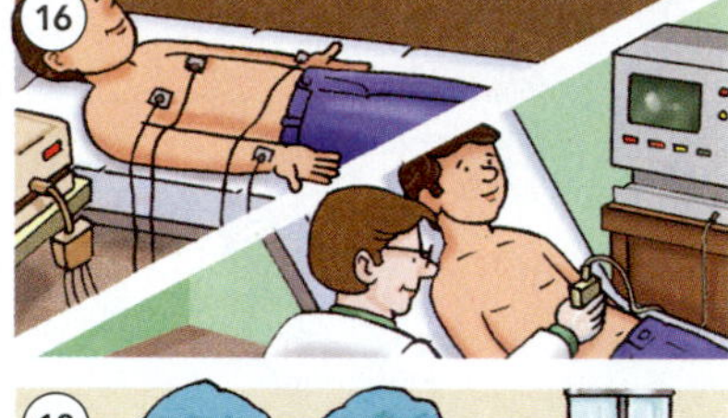
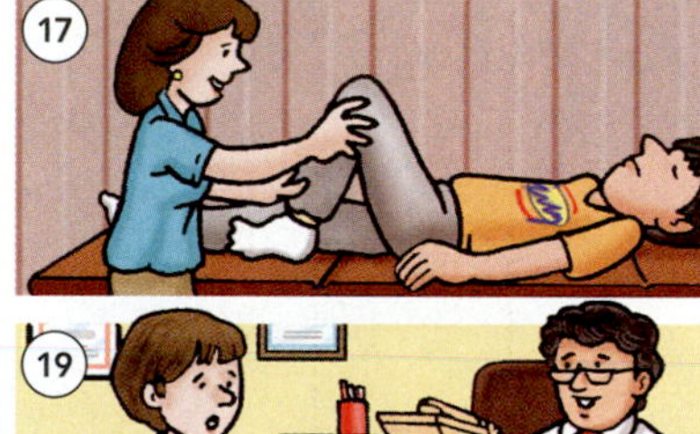
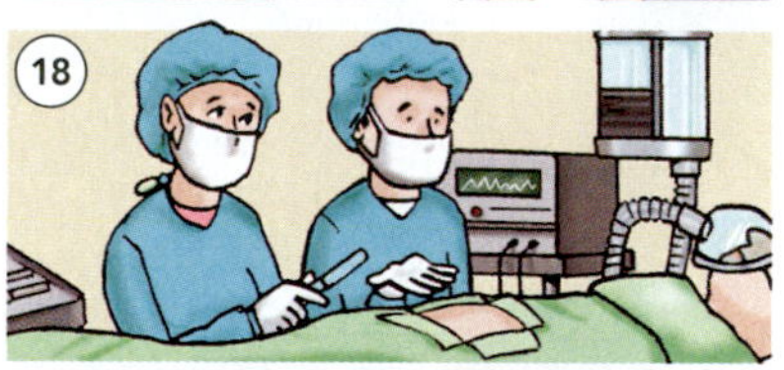

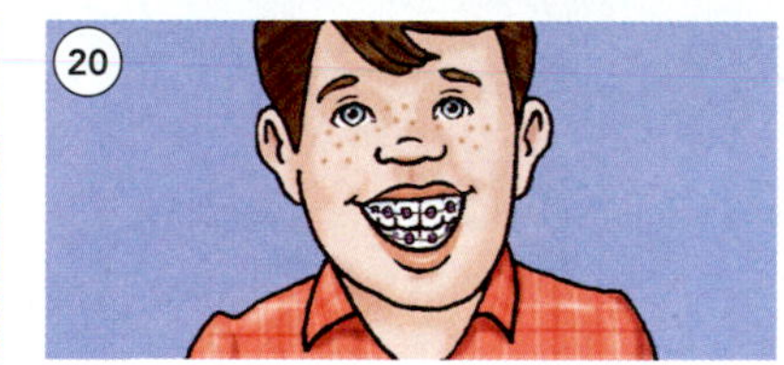

安静にする **1** rest in bed
流動食をとる **2** drink fluids
うがいをする **3** gargle
食餌療法を行う **4** go on a diet
からだを動かす **5** exercise
ビタミン剤を飲む **6** take vitamins
専門医にみてもらう **7** see a specialist
鍼治療を受ける **8** get acupuncture
ヒーティングパッド(加温器) **9** heating pad
保湿器 **10** humidifier

空気清浄機 **11** air purifier
杖 **12** cane
歩行補助器 **13** walker
車いす **14** wheelchair
血液検査 **15** blood work/blood tests
検査 **16** tests
理学療法 **17** physical therapy
手術 **18** surgery
カウンセリング **19** counseling
歯列矯正器 **20** braces

A. I think { you should __[1–8]__. / you should use a/an __[9–14]__. / you need __[15–20]__.
B. I see.

A. What did the doctor say?
B. The doctor thinks { I should __[1–8]__. / I should use a/an __[9–14]__. / I need __[15–20]__.

Tell about medical advice a doctor gave you. What did the doctor say? Did you follow the advice?

# 薬

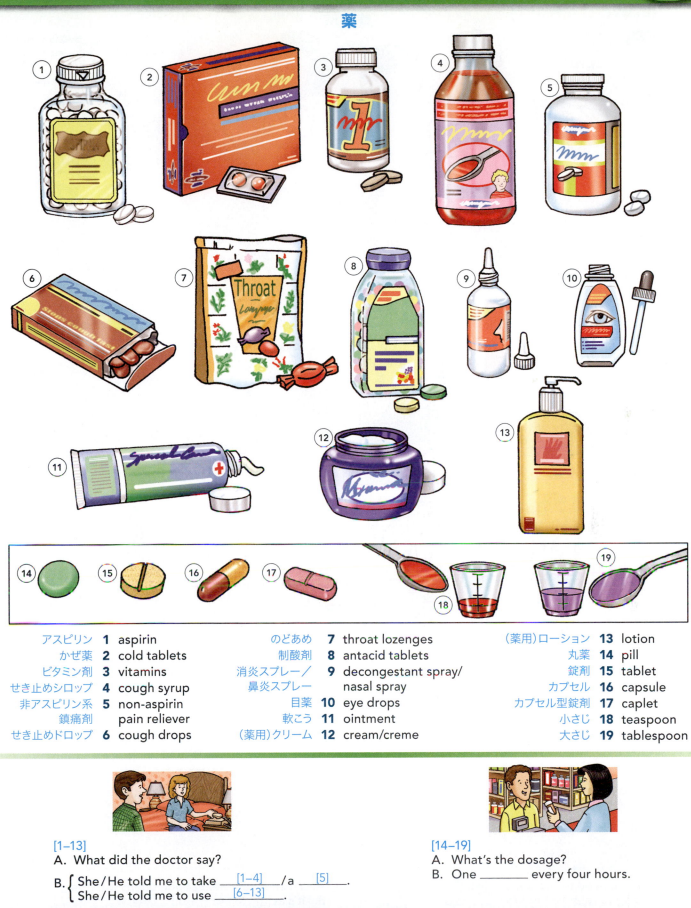

| | | |
|---|---|---|
| アスピリン **1** aspirin | のどあめ **7** throat lozenges | (薬用)ローション **13** lotion |
| かぜ薬 **2** cold tablets | 制酸剤 **8** antacid tablets | 丸薬 **14** pill |
| ビタミン剤 **3** vitamins | 消炎スプレー／鼻炎スプレー **9** decongestant spray/ nasal spray | 錠剤 **15** tablet |
| せき止めシロップ **4** cough syrup | 目薬 **10** eye drops | カプセル **16** capsule |
| 非アスピリン系鎮痛剤 **5** non-aspirin pain reliever | 軟こう **11** ointment | カプセル型錠剤 **17** caplet |
| せき止めドロップ **6** cough drops | (薬用)クリーム **12** cream/creme | 小さじ **18** teaspoon |
| | | 大さじ **19** tablespoon |

[1–13]
A. What did the doctor say?
B. She/He told me to take __[1–4]__/a __[5]__.
She/He told me to use __[6–13]__.

[14–19]
A. What's the dosage?
B. One ________ every four hours.

What medicines in this lesson do you have at home? What other medicines do you have?

What do you take or use for a fever? a headache? a stomachache? a sore throat? a cold? a cough?

Tell about any medicines in your country that are different from the ones in this lesson.

# MEDICAL SPECIALISTS

## 専門医

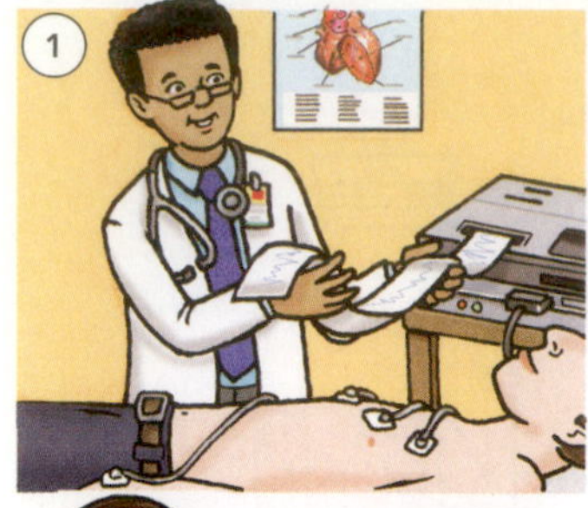
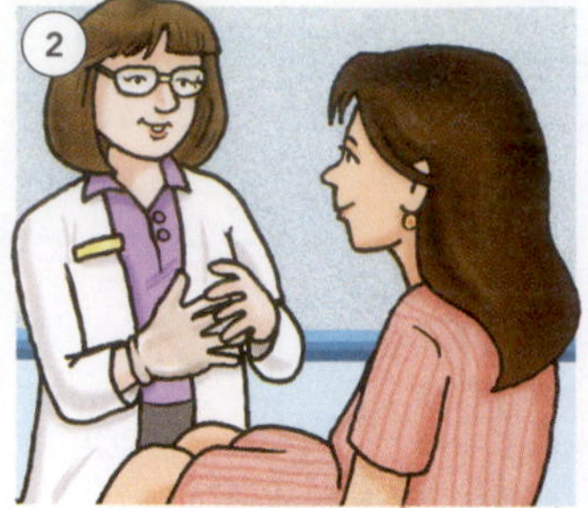
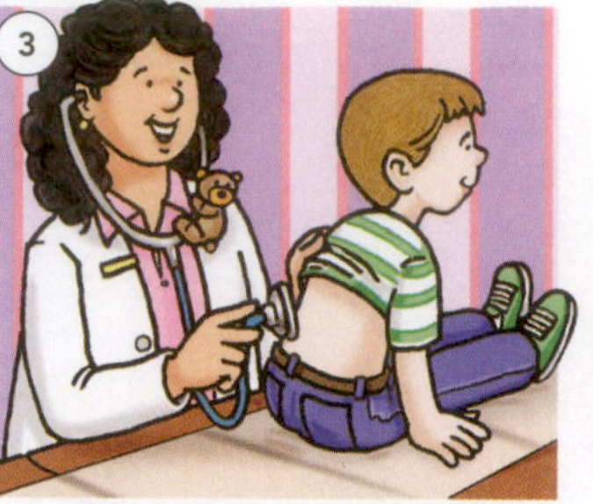

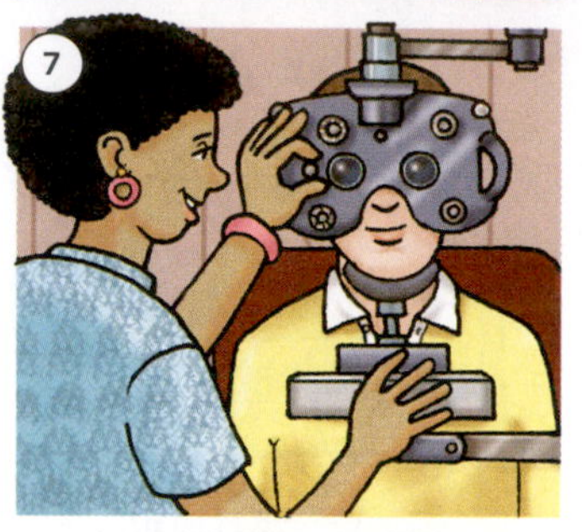

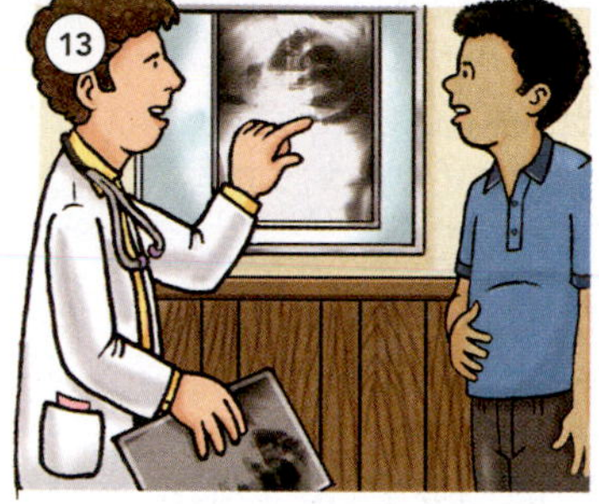
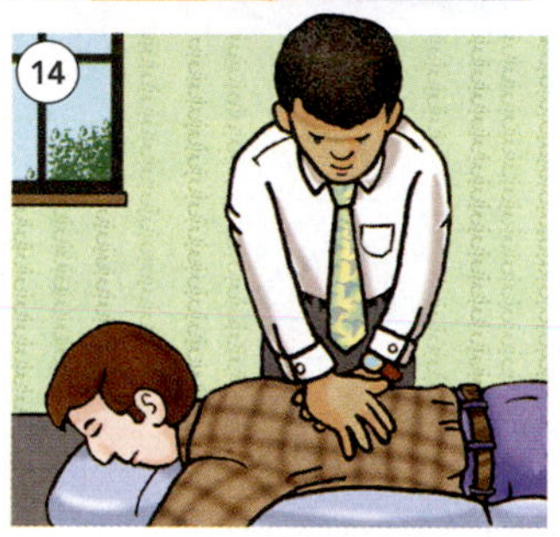
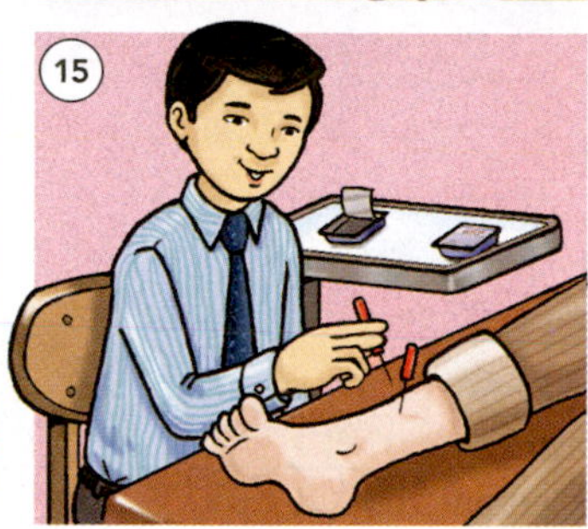

心臓病専門医 **1** cardiologist
婦人科医 **2** gynecologist
小児科医 **3** pediatrician
老年病専門医 **4** gerontologist
アレルギー専門医 **5** allergist
整形外科医 **6** orthopedist
眼科医 **7** ophthalmologist
耳鼻咽喉科医 **8** ear, nose, and throat (ENT) specialist
聴覚科医 **9** audiologist
理学療法士 **10** physical therapist
カウンセラー／セラピスト／療法士 **11** counselor/therapist
精神科医 **12** psychiatrist
胃腸病専門医 **13** gastroenterologist
カイロプラクター／脊柱指圧療法師 **14** chiropractor
鍼医 **15** acupuncturist
歯列矯正医 **16** orthodontist

A. I think you need to see a specialist.
 I'm going to refer you to a/an _______.
B. A/An _______?
A. Yes.

A. When is your next appointment with the _______?
B. It's at ......(time)...... on ......(date)........

Do you or members of your family see any of these medical specialists? Which ones?

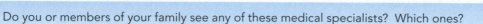

# 病院

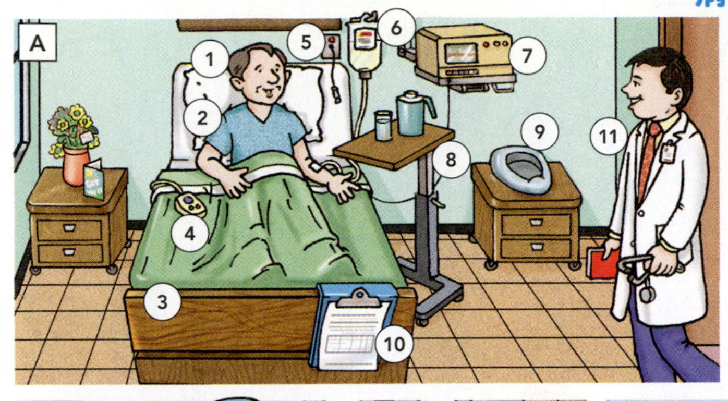

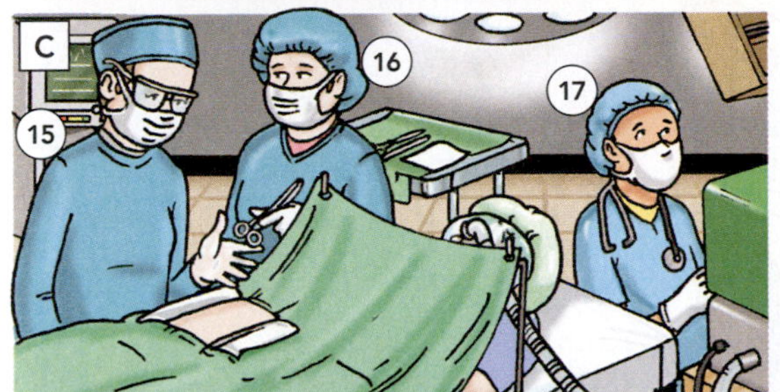

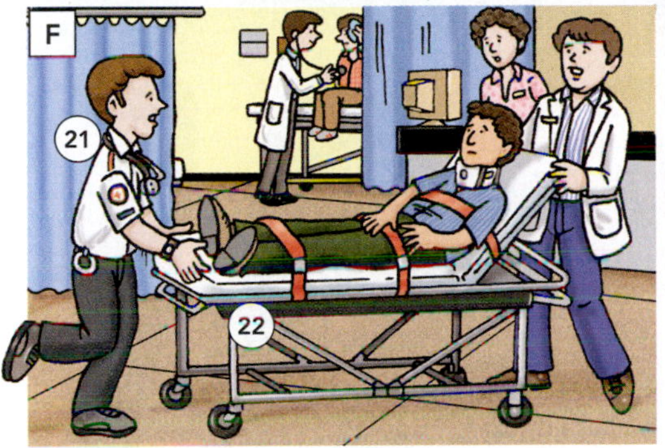


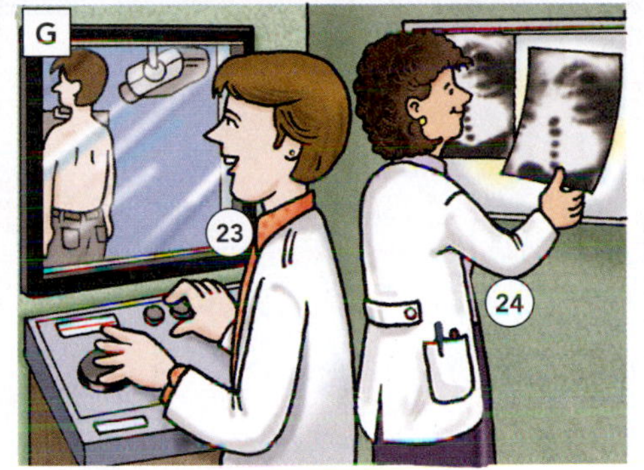

**病室 A patient's room**
- 患者 1 patient
- 患者用ガウン 2 hospital gown
- 治療用ベッド 3 hospital bed
- ベッド調節器 4 bed control
- 呼び出しボタン 5 call button
- 点滴 6 I.V.
- 心拍出量モニター 7 vital signs monitor
- (寝室用の)テーブル 8 bed table
- (病人用)便器 9 bed pan
- カルテ 10 medical chart
- 医師 11 doctor/physician

**ナースステーション B nurse's station**
- 看護師 12 nurse
- 栄養士 13 dietitian
- 付き添い 14 orderly

**手術室 C operating room**
- 外科医 15 surgeon
- 手術室看護士 16 surgical nurse
- 麻酔科医 17 anesthesiologist

**待合室 D waiting room**
- ボランティア 18 volunteer

**出産室 E birthing room/delivery room**
- 産科医 19 obstetrician
- 助産婦 20 midwife/nurse-midwife

**救急室 F emergency room/ER**
- 緊急医療士 21 emergency medical technician/EMT
- 車輪付き担架 22 gurney

**放射線科 G radiology department**
- レントゲン技師 23 X-ray technician
- 放射線技師 24 radiologist

**検査室 H laboratory/lab**
- 検査技師 25 lab technician

A. This is your [2–10].
B. I see.

A. Do you work here?
B. Yes. I'm a/an [11–21, 23–25].

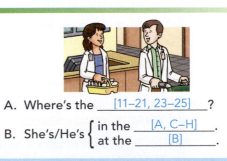

A. Where's the [11–21, 23–25]?
B. She's/He's { in the [A, C–H]. / at the [B]. }

Tell about an experience you or a family member had in the hospital.

# 保健衛生

A 
1 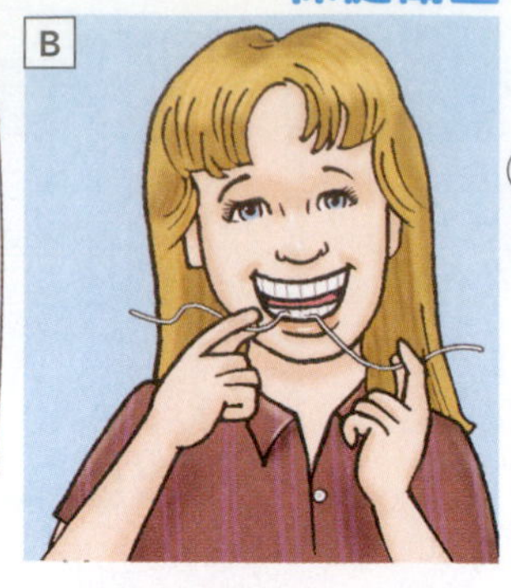
2
B 
3
C 
4 
D 
5 
E 
6 7 
F 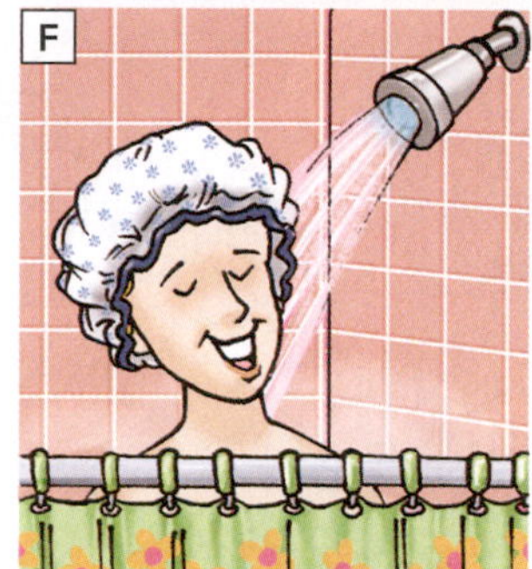
8 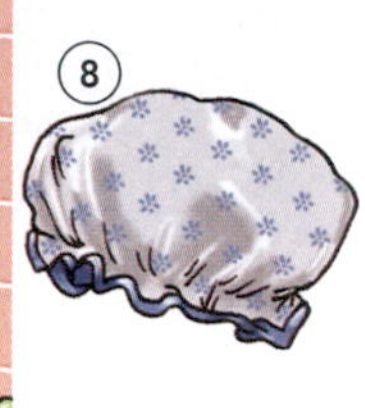
G 
9 10 
H 
11 
I 
12 
J 
13 
K 
14 15 16 
17 18 19 

| | | |
|---|---|---|
| **歯を磨く** | **A** | **brush *my* teeth** |
| 歯ブラシ | **1** | toothbrush |
| 歯みがき粉 | **2** | toothpaste |
| **デンタルフロスする** | **B** | **floss *my* teeth** |
| デンタルフロス | **3** | dental floss |
| **うがいする** | **C** | **gargle** |
| うがい薬 | **4** | mouthwash |
| **歯を白くする** | **D** | **whiten *my* teeth** |
| 歯の美白剤 | **5** | teeth whitener |
| **風呂に入る** | **E** | **bathe/take a bath** |
| 石けん | **6** | soap |
| バブルバス／泡風呂 | **7** | bubble bath |
| **シャワーを浴びる** | **F** | **take a shower** |
| シャワーキャップ | **8** | shower cap |
| **髪の毛を洗う／シャンプーする** | **G** | **wash *my* hair** |
| シャンプー | **9** | shampoo |
| コンディショナー／リンス | **10** | conditioner/ rinse |
| **髪の毛を乾かす** | **H** | **dry *my* hair** |
| ドライヤー | **11** | hair dryer/ blow dryer |
| **髪の毛をくしでとかす** | **I** | **comb *my* hair** |
| くし | **12** | comb |
| **髪の毛をブラシでとかす** | **J** | **brush *my* hair** |
| ブラシ | **13** | (hair) brush |
| **髪をスタイリングする** | **K** | **style *my* hair** |
| ヘアアイロン | **14** | hot comb/ curling iron |
| ヘアスプレー | **15** | hairspray |
| ヘアジェル | **16** | hair gel |
| ボビーピン | **17** | bobby pin |
| 髪止め飾りピン | **18** | barrette |
| クリップ | **19** | hairclip |

**ひげを剃る　L　shave**

- ひげ剃り用クリーム　20　shaving cream
- カミソリ　21　razor
- カミソリの刃　22　razor blade
- 電気カミソリ　23　electric shaver
- 止血棒剤(ひげそり傷の止血用)　24　styptic pencil
- アフターシェイブ(ローション)　25　aftershave (lotion)

**爪の手入れをする　M　do *my* nails**

- つめやすり　26　nail file
- (マニキュア用の)つめやすり　27　emery board
- つめ切り　28　nail clipper
- (マニキュア用の)つめブラシ　29　nail brush
- はさみ　30　scissors
- マニキュア液　31　nail polish
- 除光液　32　nail polish remover

**～をつける　N　put on . . .**

- デオドラント　33　deodorant
- ハンドローション　34　hand lotion
- ボディローション　35　body lotion
- パウダー(粉おしろい)　36　powder
- 香水／ボディコロン　37　cologne/perfume
- 日焼け止め　38　sunscreen

**化粧する　O　put on makeup**

- ほお紅　39　blush/rouge
- ファンデーション　40　foundation/base
- モイスチャライザー　41　moisturizer
- フェースパウダー　42　face powder
- アイライナー　43　eyeliner
- アイシャドウ　44　eye shadow
- マスカラ　45　mascara
- アイブロウペンシル　46　eyebrow pencil
- 口紅／リップスティック　47　lipstick

**靴を磨く　P　polish *my* shoes**

- 靴みがき　48　shoe polish
- 靴ひも　49　shoelaces

[A–M, N (33–38), O, P]
A. What are you doing?
B. I'm ________ing.

[1, 8, 11–14, 17–19, 21–24, 26–30, 46, 49]
A. Excuse me. Where can I find ________(s)?
B. They're in the next aisle.

[2–7, 9, 10, 15, 16, 20, 25, 31–45, 47, 48]
A. Excuse me. Where can I find ________?
B. It's in the next aisle.

Which of these personal care products do you use?

You're going on a trip. Make a list of the personal care products you need to take with you.

# 育児

| | | |
|---|---|---|
| 赤ちゃんに食事をさせる | A | **feed** |
| ベビーフード | 1 | baby food |
| よだれかけ | 2 | bib |
| 哺乳ビン | 3 | bottle |
| 乳首 | 4 | nipple |
| 乳児用人口乳（栄養食） | 5 | formula |
| （液体）ビタミン剤 | 6 | (liquid) vitamins |
| 赤ちゃんのおむつを取り替える | B | **change the baby's diaper** |
| 紙おむつ | 7 | disposable diaper |
| 布おむつ | 8 | cloth diaper |
| おむつ止めピン | 9 | diaper pin |
| おしり拭き | 10 | (baby) wipes |
| ベビーパウダー | 11 | baby powder |
| トレーニングパンツ | 12 | training pants |
| 軟こう | 13 | ointment |
| お風呂に入れる | C | **bathe** |
| ベビーシャンプー | 14 | baby shampoo |
| 綿棒 | 15 | cotton swab |
| ベビーローション | 16 | baby lotion |
| 抱く | D | **hold** |
| おしゃぶり | 17 | pacifier |
| 歯がため | 18 | teething ring |
| 授乳する | E | **nurse** |
| 着せる | F | **dress** |
| 揺れる | G | **rock** |
| 託児所 | 19 | child-care center |
| 保育士 | 20 | child-care worker |
| ロッキングチェア | 21 | rocking chair |
| ～に読む | H | **read to** |
| 収納ボックス | 22 | cubby |
| ～と遊ぶ | I | **play with** |
| おもちゃ | 23 | toys |

A. What are you doing?
B. { I'm __[A, C–I]__ing the baby.
I'm __[B]__ing.

A. Do we need anything from the store?
B. Yes. We need some more { __[2–4, 7–9, 15, 17, 18]__s
__[1, 5, 6, 10–14, 16]__.

In your opinion, which are better: cloth diapers or disposable diapers? Why?

Tell about baby products in your country.

# 学校の種類

保育園 **1** preschool/nursery school
小学校 **2** elementary school
中学校 **3** middle school/ junior high school
高等学校 **4** high school
成人学校 **5** adult school
職業専門学校 **6** vocational school/trade school
コミュニティカレッジ **7** community college
単科大学 **8** college
総合大学 **9** university
大学院 **10** graduate school
ロースクール **11** law school
医科大学 **12** medical school

A. Are you a student?
B. Yes. I'm in ___[1–4, 8, 10–12]___.

A. Are you a student?
B. Yes. I go to a/an ___[5–7, 9]___.

A. Is this apartment building near a/an ________?
B. Yes. ......*(name of school)*...... is nearby.

A. Tell me about your previous education.
B. I went to ......*(name of school)*.......
A. Did you like it there?
B. Yes. It was an excellent ________.

What types of schools are there in your community? What are their names, and where are they located?

What types of schools have you gone to?

Where? When? What did you study?

# THE SCHOOL

## 学校

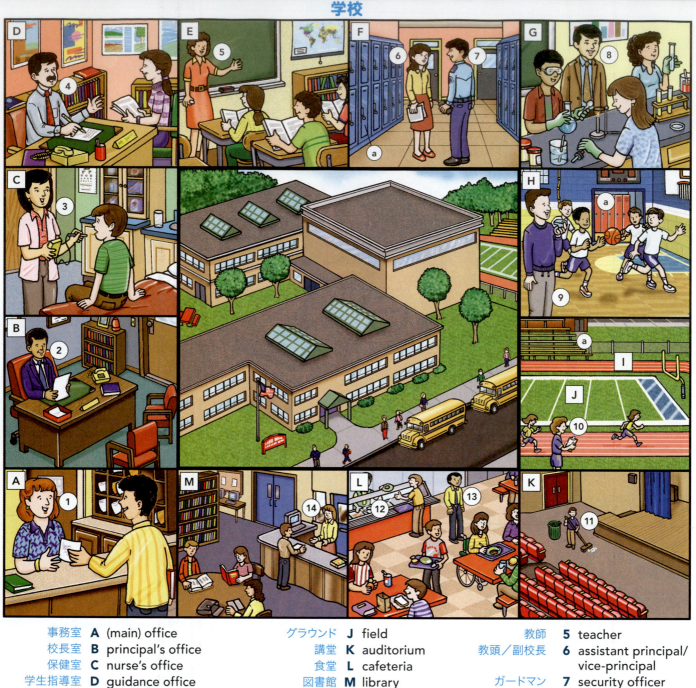

事務室 **A** (main) office
校長室 **B** principal's office
保健室 **C** nurse's office
学生指導室 **D** guidance office
教室 **E** classroom
廊下 **F** hallway
ロッカー **a** locker
理科実験室 **G** science lab
体育館 **H** gym/gymnasium
更衣室 **a** locker room
競技用トラック **I** track
(屋外)観覧席 **a** bleachers

グラウンド **J** field
講堂 **K** auditorium
食堂 **L** cafeteria
図書館 **M** library

事務員／学校職員 **1** clerk/(school) secretary
校長 **2** principal
保健婦／養護の先生 **3** (school) nurse
学生指導員 **4** (guidance) counselor

教師 **5** teacher
教頭／副校長 **6** assistant principal/vice-principal
ガードマン **7** security officer
理科の先生 **8** science teacher
体育の先生 **9** P.E. teacher
コーチ **10** coach
用務員 **11** custodian
食堂従業員 **12** cafeteria worker
学食監視員 **13** lunchroom monitor
学校図書館の司書 **14** (school) librarian

A. Where are you going?
B. I'm going to the [A–D, G–M].
A. Do you have a hall pass?
B. Yes. Here it is.

A. Where's the [1–14]?
B. He's/She's in the [A–M].

Describe the school where you study English.
Tell about the rooms, offices, and people.

Tell about differences between the school in this lesson and schools in your country.

# 学校の教科

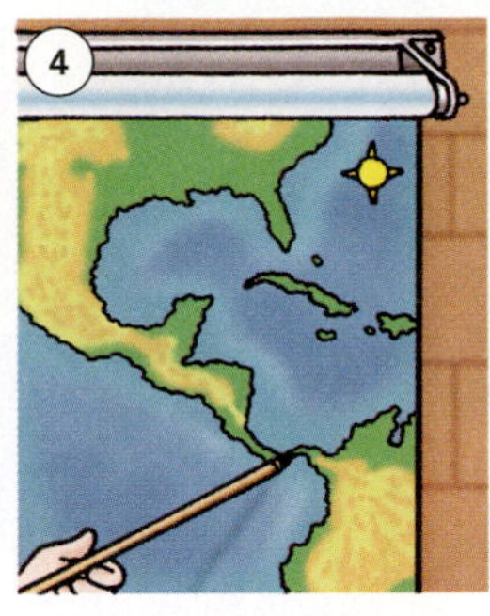

| | | |
|---|---|---|
| 数学 | **1** | math/mathematics |
| 英語 | **2** | English |
| 歴史 | **3** | history |
| 地理 | **4** | geography |
| 政治 | **5** | government |
| 科学／理科 | **6** | science |
| 生物 | **7** | biology |
| 化学 | **8** | chemistry |
| 物理 | **9** | physics |
| 保健 | **10** | health |
| コンピュータ科学 | **11** | computer science |
| スペイン語 | **12** | Spanish |
| フランス語 | **13** | French |
| 家庭科 | **14** | home economics |
| 技術／工芸 | **15** | industrial arts/shop |
| ビジネス教育 | **16** | business education |
| 体育 | **17** | physical education/P.E. |
| 自動車運転教習 | **18** | driver's education/driver's ed |
| 美術 | **19** | art |
| 音楽 | **20** | music |

A. What do you have next period?
B. **Math**. How about you?
A. **English**.
B. There's the bell. I've got to go.

What is/was your favorite subject? Why?

In your opinion, what's the most interesting subject? the most difficult subject? Why do you think so?

# 課外活動

| | | |
|---|---|---|
| バンド／楽隊 | 1 | band |
| オーケストラ | 2 | orchestra |
| 合唱団 | 3 | choir/chorus |
| 演劇 | 4 | drama |
| (アメリカン)フットボール | 5 | football |
| チアリーダー | 6 | cheerleading/pep squad |
| 生徒会 | 7 | student government |
| 地域サービス | 8 | community service |
| 校内新聞 | 9 | school newspaper |
| 卒業記念アルバム | 10 | yearbook |
| 文芸誌 | 11 | literary magazine |
| A.V. クルー | 12 | A.V. crew |
| 討論クラブ | 13 | debate club |
| コンピュータクラブ | 14 | computer club |
| 国際クラブ | 15 | international club |
| チェスクラブ | 16 | chess club |

A. Are you going home right after school?

B. { No. I have ___[1–6]___ practice.
No. I have a ___[7–16]___ meeting.

What extracurricular activities do/did you participate in?

Which extracurricular activities in this lesson are there in schools in your country? What other activities are there?

# 数学

## Arithmetic 算数

2+1=3 8-3=5 4x2=8 10÷2=5

| たし算 addition | ひき算 subtraction | かけ算 multiplication | わり算 division |
|---|---|---|---|
| 2 **plus** 1 **equals*** 3. | 8 **minus** 3 **equals*** 5. | 4 **times** 2 **equals*** 8. | 10 **divided by** 2 **equals*** 5. |

**You can also say:* **is**

A. How much is *two plus one?*
B. *Two plus one* equals/is *three.*

Make conversations for the arithmetic problems above and others.

## Fractions 分数

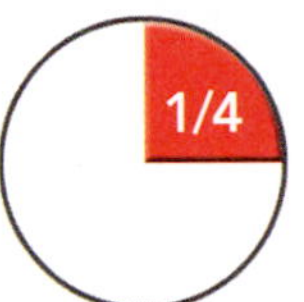

one quarter/ one fourth

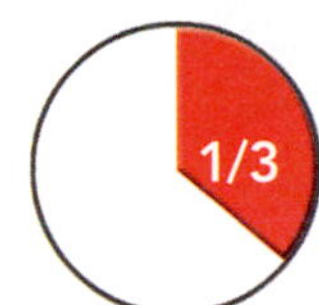

one third

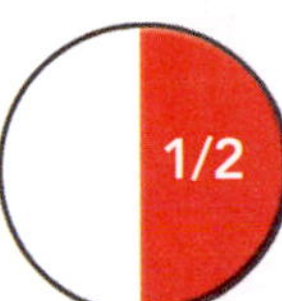

one half/ half

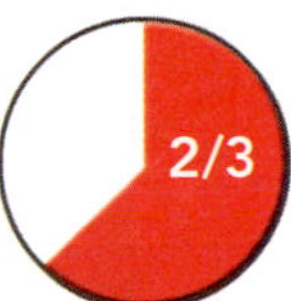

two thirds

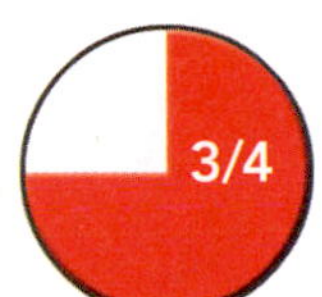

three quarters/ three fourths

A. Is this on sale?
B. Yes. It's ________ off the regular price.

A. Is the gas tank almost empty?
B. It's about ________ full.

## Percents パーセント

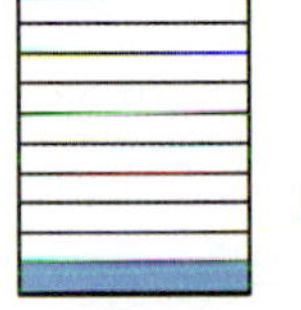
10% ten percent

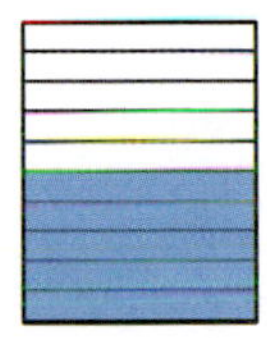
50% fifty percent

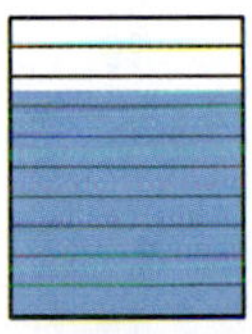
75% seventy-five percent

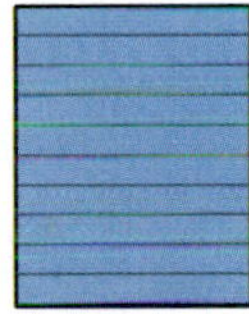
100% one-hundred percent

A. How did you do on the test?
B. I got ________ percent of the answers right.

A. What's the weather forecast?
B. There's a ________ percent chance of rain.

## Types of Math 数学の種類

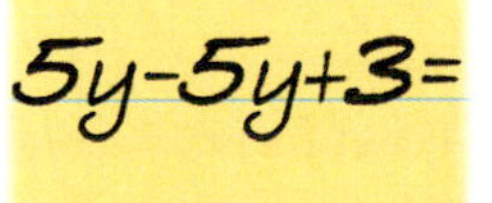

algebra
代数

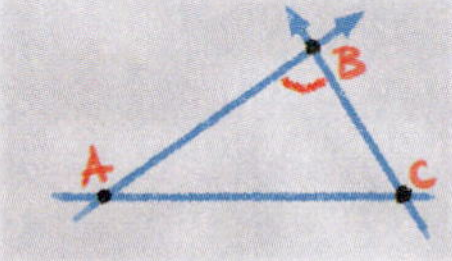

geometry
幾何

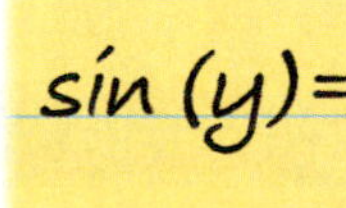

trigonometry
三角法

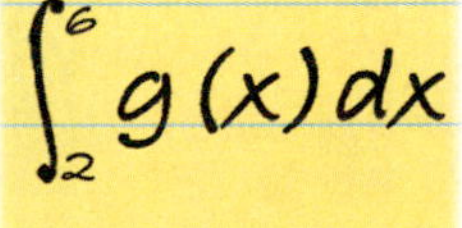

calculus
微分・積分(計算法)

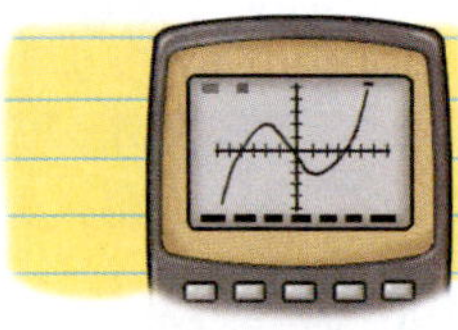
statistics
統計

A. What math course are you taking this year?
B. I'm taking ________.

Are you good at math?

What math courses do/did you take in school?

Tell about something you bought on sale. How much off the regular price was it?

Research and discuss: What percentage of people in your country live in cities? live on farms? work in factories? vote in general elections?

# 寸法・幾何図形

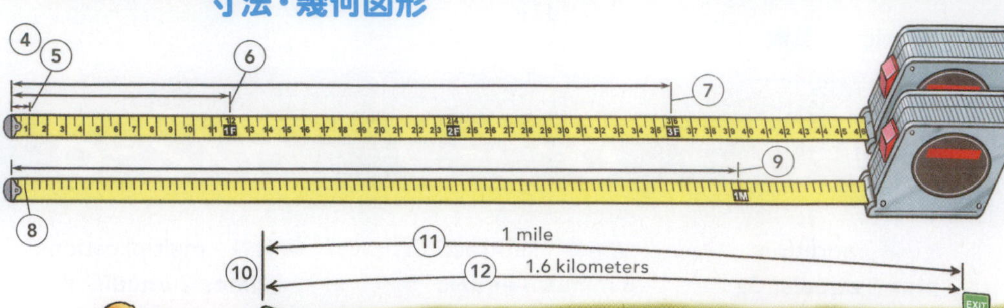


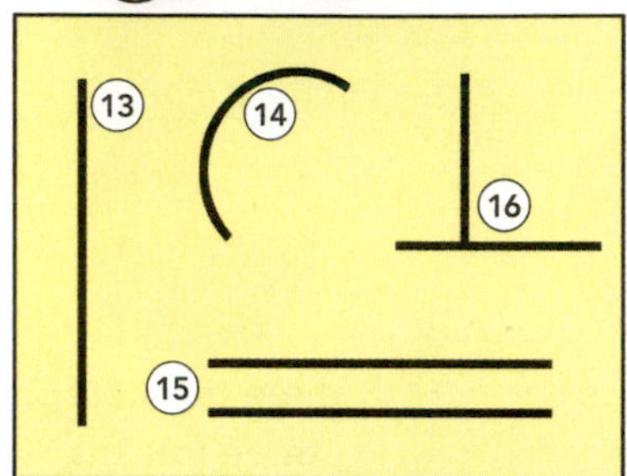


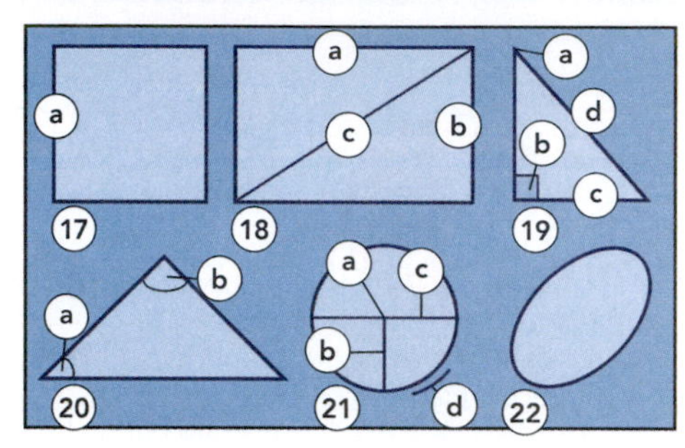


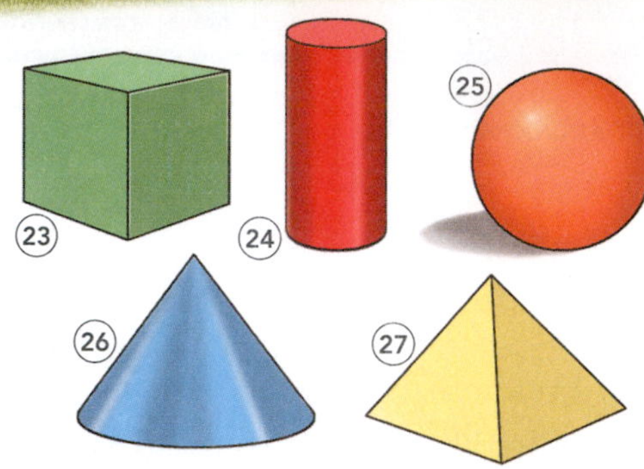

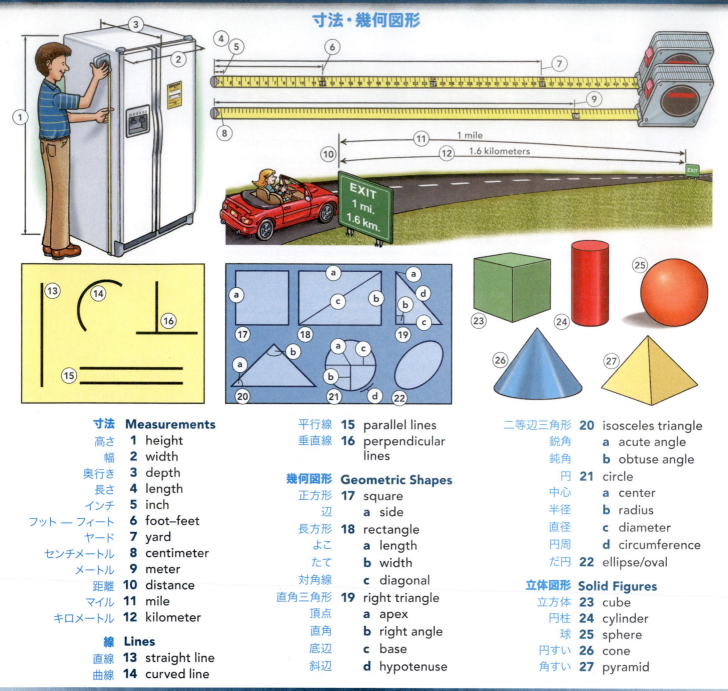

**寸法 Measurements**

- 高さ **1** height
- 幅 **2** width
- 奥行き **3** depth
- 長さ **4** length
- インチ **5** inch
- フット — フィート **6** foot–feet
- ヤード **7** yard
- センチメートル **8** centimeter
- メートル **9** meter
- 距離 **10** distance
- マイル **11** mile
- キロメートル **12** kilometer

**線 Lines**

- 直線 **13** straight line
- 曲線 **14** curved line
- 平行線 **15** parallel lines
- 垂直線 **16** perpendicular lines

**幾何図形 Geometric Shapes**

- 正方形 **17** square
  - 辺 **a** side
- 長方形 **18** rectangle
  - よこ **a** length
  - たて **b** width
  - 対角線 **c** diagonal
- 直角三角形 **19** right triangle
  - 頂点 **a** apex
  - 直角 **b** right angle
  - 底辺 **c** base
  - 斜辺 **d** hypotenuse
- 二等辺三角形 **20** isosceles triangle
  - 鋭角 **a** acute angle
  - 鈍角 **b** obtuse angle
- 円 **21** circle
  - 中心 **a** center
  - 半径 **b** radius
  - 直径 **c** diameter
  - 円周 **d** circumference
- だ円 **22** ellipse/oval

**立体図形 Solid Figures**

- 立方体 **23** cube
- 円柱 **24** cylinder
- 球 **25** sphere
- 円すい **26** cone
- 角すい **27** pyramid

[1–9]
A. What's the ______[1–4]______?
B. .................. ______[5–9]______(s).

[11–12]
A. What's the distance?
B. .................. ________(s).

| | | |
|---|---|---|
| 1 inch (1″) | = | 2.54 centimeters (cm) |
| 1 foot (1′) | = | 0.305 meters (m) |
| 1 yard (1 yd.) | = | 0.914 meters (m) |
| 1 mile (mi.) | = | 1.6 kilometers (km) |

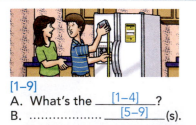

[17–22]
A. Who can tell me what shape this is?
B. I can. It's a/an ________.

[23–27]
A. Who knows what figure this is?
B. I do. It's a/an ________.

[13–27]
A. This painting is magnificent!
B. Hmm. I don't think so. It just looks like a lot of ________s and ________s to me!

# 英語・英作文

## Types of Sentences & Parts of Speech　センテンスの種類・品詞

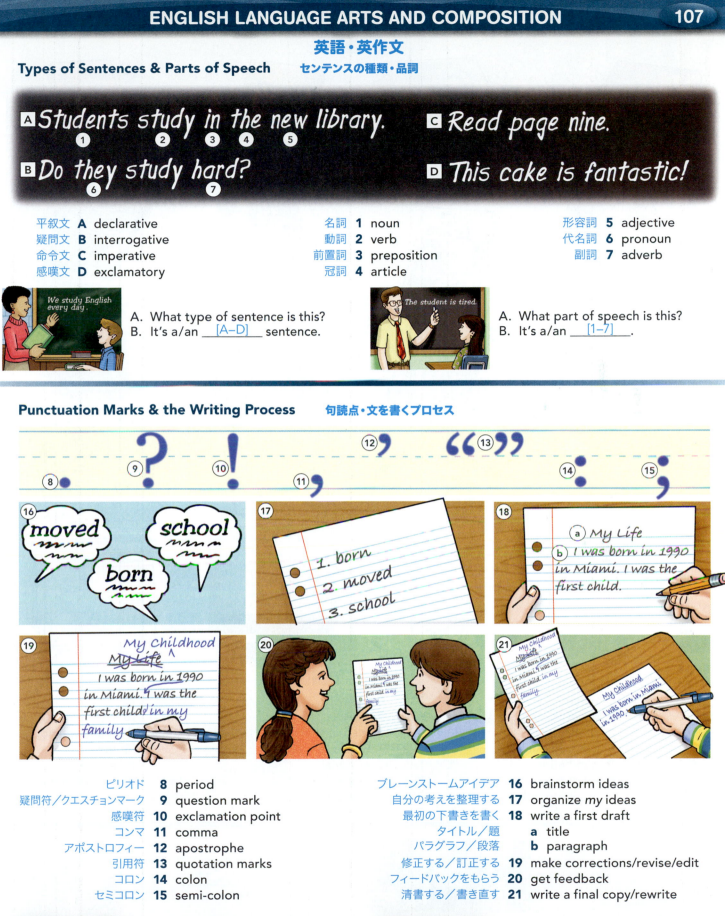

**A** Students(1) study(2) in(3) the(4) new(5) library.

**B** Do they(6) study hard(7)?

**C** Read page nine.

**D** This cake is fantastic!

平叙文 **A** declarative
疑問文 **B** interrogative
命令文 **C** imperative
感嘆文 **D** exclamatory

名詞 **1** noun
動詞 **2** verb
前置詞 **3** preposition
冠詞 **4** article

形容詞 **5** adjective
代名詞 **6** pronoun
副詞 **7** adverb

We study English every day.


A. What type of sentence is this?
B. It's a/an __[A–D]__ sentence.

The student is tired.


A. What part of speech is this?
B. It's a/an __[1–7]__.

## Punctuation Marks & the Writing Process　句読点・文を書くプロセス

moved
school
born
1. born
2. moved
3. school
a My Life
b I was born in 1990 in Miami. I was the first child.
My Childhood
My Life
I was born in 1990 in Miami. I was the first child in my family
My Childhood
I was born in Miami in 1990.


ピリオド **8** period
疑問符／クエスチョンマーク **9** question mark
感嘆符 **10** exclamation point
コンマ **11** comma
アポストロフィー **12** apostrophe
引用符 **13** quotation marks
コロン **14** colon
セミコロン **15** semi-colon

ブレーンストームアイデア **16** brainstorm ideas
自分の考えを整理する **17** organize *my* ideas
最初の下書きを書く **18** write a first draft
タイトル／題 **a** title
パラグラフ／段落 **b** paragraph
修正する／訂正する **19** make corrections/revise/edit
フィードバックをもらう **20** get feedback
清書する／書き直す **21** write a final copy/rewrite

A. Did you find any mistakes?
B. Yes. You forgot to put a/an __[8–15]__ in this sentence.

A. Are you working on your composition?
B. Yes. I'm __[16–21]__ing.

# 文学・書き物

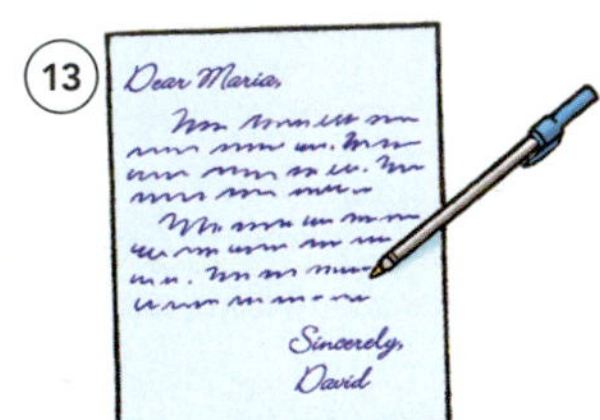

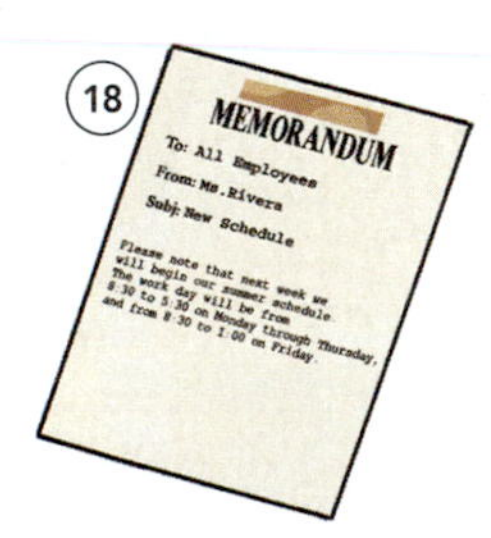

| | | |
|---|---|---|
| フィクション **1** fiction | エッセイ **8** essay | 短い手紙 **15** note |
| 小説 **2** novel | レポート **9** report | 招待状 **16** invitation |
| 短編小説 **3** short story | 雑誌の記事 **10** magazine article | 礼状 **17** thank-you note |
| 詩 **4** poetry/poems | 新聞の記事 **11** newspaper article | メモ **18** memo |
| ノンフィクション **5** non-fiction | 社説／論説 **12** editorial | メール／eメール **19** e-mail |
| 伝記 **6** biography | 手紙 **13** letter | インスタントメッセージ **20** instant message |
| 自伝 **7** autobiography | はがき **14** postcard | |

A. What are you doing?

B. I'm writing { ___[1, 4, 5]___. / a/an ___[2, 3, 6–20]___.

What kind of literature do you like to read? What are some of your favorite books? Who is your favorite author?

Do you like to read newspapers and magazines? Which ones do you read?

Do you sometimes send or receive letters, postcards, notes, e-mail, or instant messages? Tell about the people you communicate with, and how.

# 地理

森／森林 **1** forest/woods
丘 **2** hill
山脈 **3** mountain range
山頂 **4** mountain peak
谷 **5** valley
湖 **6** lake
平地／平原 **7** plains
牧草地 **8** meadow

小川 **9** stream/brook
池 **10** pond
台地 **11** plateau
峡谷 **12** canyon
砂丘 **13** dune/sand dune
砂漠 **14** desert
ジャングル **15** jungle
海岸 **16** seashore/shore

入り江 **17** bay
海 **18** ocean
島 **19** island
半島 **20** peninsula
熱帯雨林 **21** rainforest
川 **22** river
滝 **23** waterfall

A. {Isn't this a beautiful ________?!
{Aren't these beautiful ________s?!
B. Yes. It's/They're magnificent!

Tell about the geography of your country.
Describe the different geographic features.

Have you seen some of the geographic features in this lesson? Which ones? Where?

# 科学

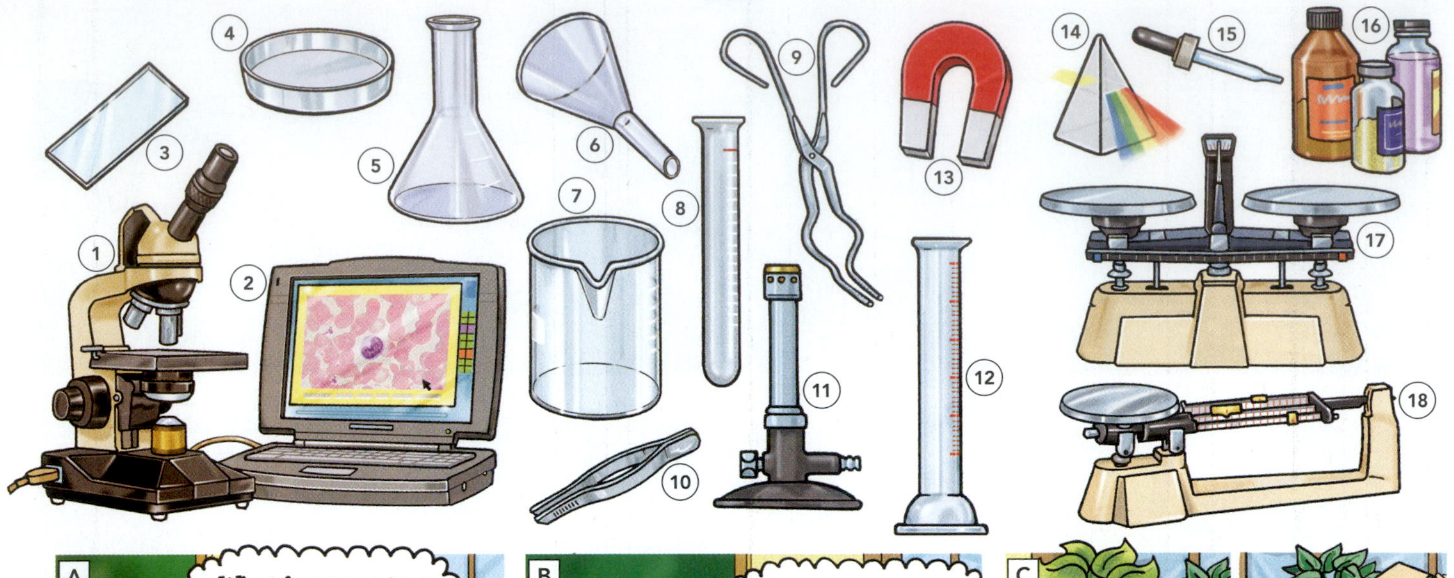

## 科学実験器具 Science Equipment

| | | |
|---|---|---|
| 顕微鏡 | 1 | microscope |
| コンピュータ | 2 | computer |
| スライド | 3 | slide |
| シャーレ | 4 | Petri dish |
| フラスコ | 5 | flask |
| じょうご | 6 | funnel |
| ビーカー | 7 | beaker |
| 試験管 | 8 | test tube |
| 鉗子 | 9 | forceps |
| ピンセット | 10 | crucible tongs |
| ブンゼン式バーナー | 11 | Bunsen burner |
| 目盛り付きシリンダー | 12 | graduated cylinder |
| マグネット／磁石 | 13 | magnet |
| プリズム | 14 | prism |
| スポイト | 15 | dropper |
| 薬品 | 16 | chemicals |
| 天秤 | 17 | balance |
| はかり | 18 | scale |

## 科学的方法 The Scientific Method

| | | |
|---|---|---|
| 問題提起する | A | state the problem |
| 仮説を立てる | B | form a hypothesis |
| 手順を考える | C | plan a procedure |
| 手順を実行する | D | do a procedure |
| 観察する／観察を記録する | E | make/record observations |
| 結論を導き出す | F | draw conclusions |

A. What do we need to do this procedure?
B. We need a/an/the [1–18].

A. How is your experiment coming along?
B. I'm getting ready to [A–F].

Do you have experience with the scientific equipment in this lesson? Tell about it.

What science courses do/did you take in school?

Think of an idea for a science experiment.
What question about science do you want to answer? State the problem.
What do you think will happen in the experiment? Form a hypothesis.
How can you test your hypothesis? Plan a procedure.

# 宇宙

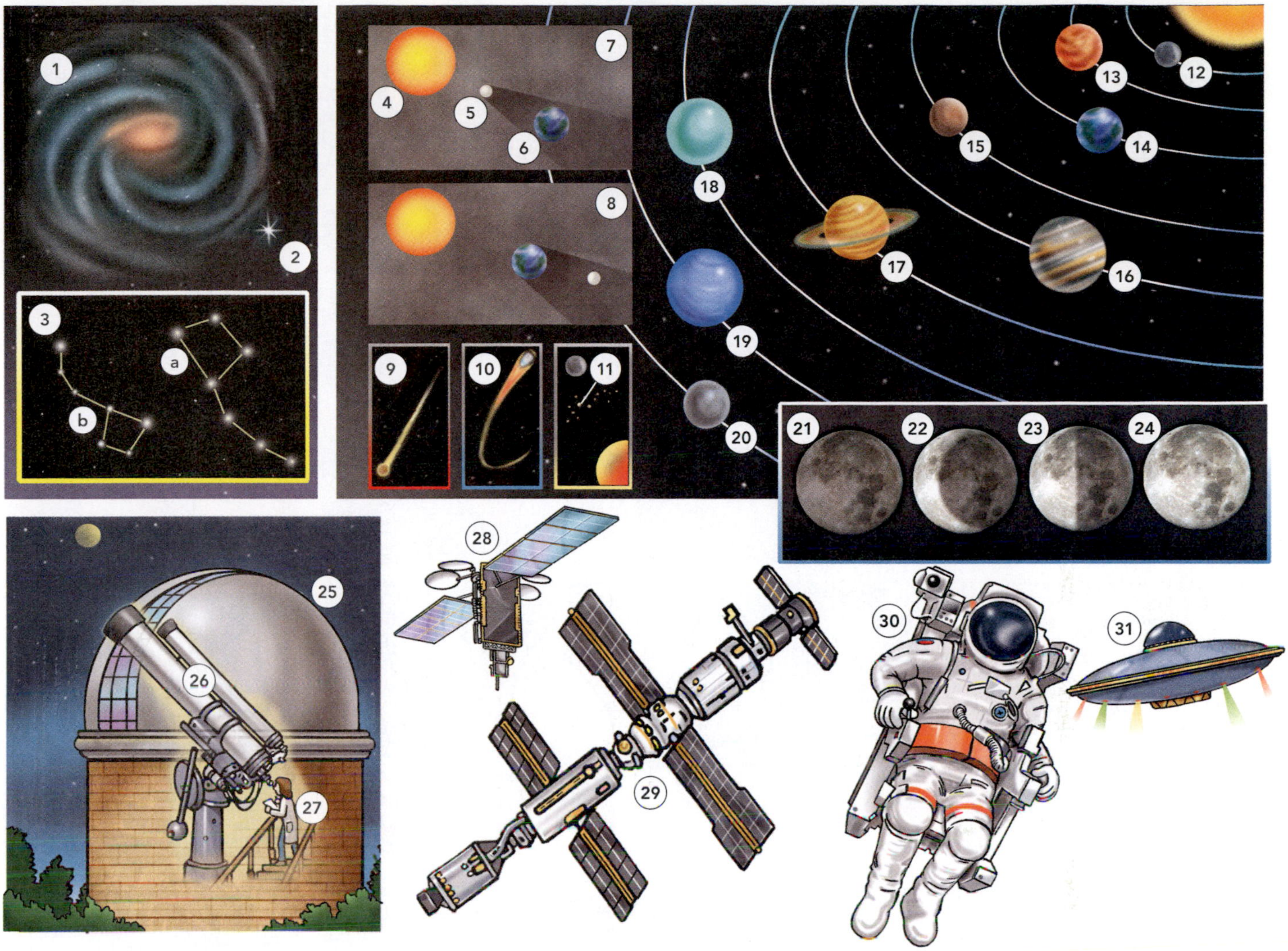

## 宇宙 The Universe

星雲 1 galaxy
星 2 star
星座 3 constellation
北斗七星 a The Big Dipper
小熊座の小びしゃく b The Little Dipper

## 太陽系 The Solar System

太陽 4 sun
月 5 moon
惑星 6 planet
日食 7 solar eclipse
月食 8 lunar eclipse
流れ星 9 meteor
彗星 10 comet
小惑星 11 asteroid
水星 12 Mercury
金星 13 Venus
地球 14 Earth
火星 15 Mars
木星 16 Jupiter
土星 17 Saturn
天王星 18 Uranus
海王星 19 Neptune
冥王星 20 Pluto
新月 21 new moon
三日月 22 crescent moon
半月 23 quarter moon
満月 24 full moon

## 天文学 Astronomy

天文台／観測所 25 observatory
天体望遠鏡 26 telescope
天文学者 27 astronomer

## 宇宙探検 Space Exploration

人工衛星 28 satellite
宇宙ステーション 29 space station
宇宙飛行士 30 astronaut
UFO／未確認飛行物体 31 U.F.O./ Unidentified Flying Object/ flying saucer

[1–24]
A. Is that (a/an/the) ________?
B. I'm not sure. I think it might be (a/an/the) ________.

[28–30]
A. Is the ________ ready for tomorrow's launch?
B. Yes. "All systems are go!"

Pretend you are an astronaut traveling in space. What do you see?

Draw and name a constellation you are familiar with.

Do you think space exploration is important? Why?

Have you ever seen a U.F.O.? Do you believe there is life in outer space? Why?

# 職業 1

| | | |
|---|---|---|
| 会計士 | 1 | accountant |
| 男優／俳優 | 2 | actor |
| 女優 | 3 | actress |
| 建築家 | 4 | architect |
| 画家 | 5 | artist |
| 組立工 | 6 | assembler |
| ベビーシッター | 7 | babysitter |
| パン屋 | 8 | baker |
| 床屋 | 9 | barber |
| 石工 | 10 | bricklayer/mason |
| ビジネスマン | 11 | businessman |
| ビジネスウーマン | 12 | businesswoman |
| 肉屋 | 13 | butcher |
| 大工 | 14 | carpenter |
| レジ係 | 15 | cashier |
| シェフ／コック | 16 | chef/cook |
| 保育士 | 17 | child day-care worker |
| コンピュータソフトウェアエンジニア | 18 | computer software engineer |
| 建設作業員 | 19 | construction worker |
| 用務員 | 20 | custodian/janitor |
| カスタマーサービス係 | 21 | customer service representative |
| データ入力作業員 | 22 | data entry clerk |

配達員 **23** delivery person
港湾作業者 **24** dockworker
エンジニア **25** engineer
工員 **26** factory worker
農夫 **27** farmer
消防士 **28** firefighter
漁師 **29** fisher

外食サービス従事者 **30** food-service worker
作業長 **31** foreman
庭師／造園家 **32** gardener/landscaper
仕立て屋 **33** garment worker
美容師 **34** hairdresser

介護士 **35** health-care aide/attendant
家庭介護人 **36** home health aide/home attendant
主婦（主夫） **37** homemaker
家政婦 **38** housekeeper

A. What do you do?
B. I'm an **accountant**. How about you?
A. I'm a **carpenter**.

[At a job interview]

A. Are you an experienced ________?
B. Yes. I'm a very experienced ________.

A. How long have you been a/an ________?
B. I've been a/an ________ for ............ months/years.

Which of these occupations do you think are the most interesting? the most difficult? Why?

# 職業 2

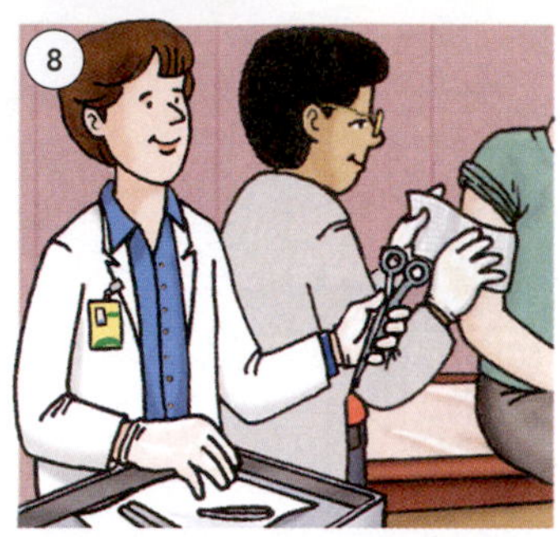

記者 **1** journalist/reporter
弁護士 **2** lawyer
機械オペレーター **3** machine operator
郵便配達人 **4** mail carrier/letter carrier
マネージャー **5** manager
マニキュア師 **6** manicurist
機械整備工 **7** mechanic
医療助手 **8** medical assistant/physician assistant
送達吏／配達人 **9** messenger/courier
引越屋 **10** mover
音楽家 **11** musician
ペンキ屋 **12** painter
薬剤師 **13** pharmacist
写真家 **14** photographer
パイロット **15** pilot
警官 **16** police officer
郵便局員 **17** postal worker
受付係 **18** receptionist
修繕屋 **19** repairperson
販売員 **20** salesperson

清掃職員 **21** sanitation worker/trash collector
秘書 **22** secretary
警備員 **23** security guard
軍人 **24** serviceman
軍人 **25** servicewoman
倉庫係 **26** stock clerk
小売店経営者 **27** store owner/shopkeeper
監督者 **28** supervisor
仕立て屋 **29** tailor
教師／インストラクター **30** teacher/instructor
電話勧誘員 **31** telemarketer
翻訳者／通訳 **32** translator/interpreter
旅行代理業者 **33** travel agent
トラック運転手 **34** truck driver
獣医 **35** veterinarian/vet
ウエイター／給仕 **36** waiter/server
ウエイトレス／給仕 **37** waitress/server
溶接工 **38** welder

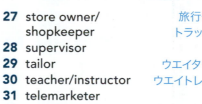

A. What's your occupation?
B. I'm a **journalist**.
A. A **journalist**?
B. Yes. That's right.

A. Are you still a ________?
B. No. I'm a ________.
A. Oh. That's interesting.

A. What kind of job would you like in the future?
B. I'd like to be a ________.

Do you work? What's your occupation?

What are the occupations of people in your family?

# 職業技能

演技する **1** act
(部品を)組み立てる **2** assemble *components*
(患者の)めんどうをみる **3** assist *patients*
焼く **4** bake
(ものを)組み立てる／建造する **5** build *things*/construct *things*
掃除する **6** clean
料理する **7** cook
(ピザを)配達する **8** deliver *pizzas*
(建物を)設計する **9** design *buildings*
絵を描く **10** draw
(トラックを)運転する **11** drive *a truck*
ファイルする **12** file
(飛行機を)操縦する **13** fly *an airplane*
(野菜を)育てる **14** grow *vegetables*
(ビルを)警備する **15** guard *buildings*
(レストランを)経営する **16** manage *a restaurant*
(芝を)刈る **17** mow *lawns*
(装置を)操作する **18** operate *equipment*
ペンキを塗る **19** paint
(ピアノを)弾く **20** play the *piano*

(食事を)準備する **21** prepare *food*
(ものを)修繕する **22** repair *things*/fix *things*
(車を)販売する **23** sell *cars*
(食事を)給仕する **24** serve *food*
縫う **25** sew
歌う **26** sing
(スペイン語を)話す **27** speak *Spanish*
(人々を)監督する **28** supervise *people*

(老人の)世話をする **29** take care of *elderly people*
在庫確認をする **30** take inventory
教える **31** teach
訳す **32** translate
タイプを打つ **33** type
(レジ機を)使う **34** use *a cash register*
(食器を)洗う **35** wash *dishes*
文章を書く **36** write

A. Can you **act**?
B. Yes, I can.

A. Do you know how to ________?
B. Yes. I've been ________ing for years.

A. Tell me about your skills.
B. I can ________, and I can ________.

Tell about your job skills.
What can you do?

# 仕事探し

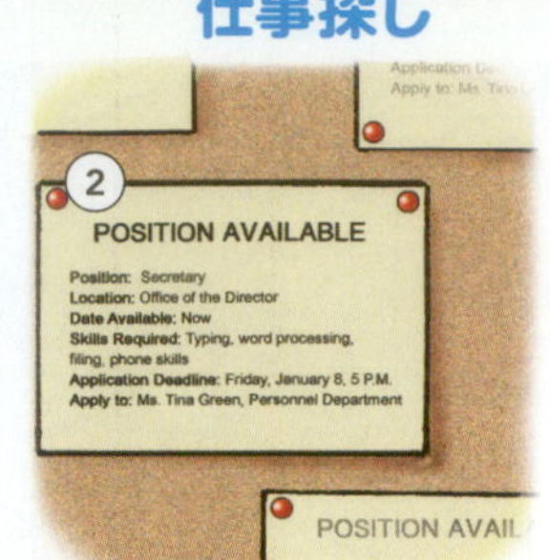

2
POSITION AVAILABLE
Position: Secretary
Location: Office of the Director
Date Available: Now
Skills Required: Typing, word processing, filing, phone skills
Application Deadline: Friday, January 8, 5 P.M.
Apply to: Ms. Tina Green, Personnel Department
POSITION AVAIL


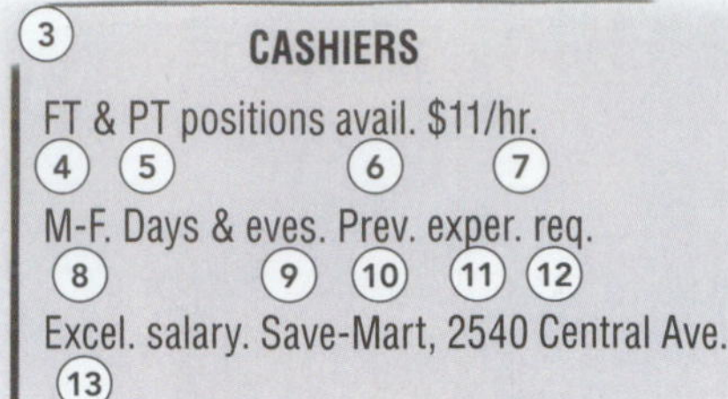

3
CASHIERS
FT & PT positions avail. $11/hr.
4 5 6 7
M-F. Days & eves. Prev. exper. req.
8 9 10 11 12
Excel. salary. Save-Mart, 2540 Central Ave.
13

| | **Types of Job Ads** |
|---|---|
| **求人広告の種類** | |
| 人材募集の看板 | **1** help wanted sign |
| 求人案内 | **2** job notice/ job announcement |
| 求人広告 | **3** classified ad/want ad |

| **求人広告の略語** | **Job Ad Abbreviations** |
|---|---|
| フルタイム | **4** full-time |
| パートタイム | **5** part-time |
| 募集 | **6** available |
| 時間 | **7** hour |
| 月曜から金曜まで | **8** Monday through Friday |
| 夕方 | **9** evenings |
| 過去の | **10** previous |
| 経験 | **11** experience |
| 要 | **12** required |
| 高 | **13** excellent |

| **仕事探し** | **Job Search** |
|---|---|
| 広告に応える | **A** respond to an ad |
| 情報を要求する | **B** request information |
| 面接を希望する | **C** request an interview |
| 履歴書を用意する | **D** prepare a resume |
| 適切な身なりをする | **E** dress appropriately |
| 申込書に記入する | **F** fill out an application (form) |
| 面接に臨む | **G** go to an interview |
| 自分の技能と資格について話す | **H** talk about your skills and qualifications |
| 自分の経験について話す | **I** talk about your experience |
| 給与について質問する | **J** ask about the salary |
| 福利厚生について質問する | **K** ask about the benefits |
| 礼状を書く | **L** write a thank-you note |
| 採用される | **M** get hired |

A. How did you find your job?
B. I found it through a ___[1–3]___.

A. How was your job interview?
B. It went very well.
A. Did you ___[D–F, H–M]___?
B. Yes, I did.

Tell about a job you are familiar with. What are the skills and qualifications required for the job? What are the hours? What is the salary?

Tell about how people you know found their jobs.

Tell about your own experience with a job search or a job interview.

# 職場

| | | |
|---|---|---|
| 受付 | **A** | reception area |
| 会議室 | **B** | conference room |
| 郵便仕分け室 | **C** | mailroom |
| 仕事場 | **D** | work area |
| オフィス（事務室） | **E** | office |
| 事務用品置き場／備品置き場 | **F** | supply room |
| 倉庫 | **G** | storage room |
| 休憩室 | **H** | employee lounge |
| コート掛け | **1** | coat rack |
| クローゼット | **2** | coat closet |
| 受付係 | **3** | receptionist |
| 会議用テーブル | **4** | conference table |
| プレゼンテーション用ボード | **5** | presentation board |
| 郵便ばかり | **6** | postal scale |
| 郵便料金メーター | **7** | postage meter |
| 事務アシスタント | **8** | office assistant |
| 郵便箱 | **9** | mailbox |
| 小部屋 | **10** | cubicle |
| 回転いす | **11** | swivel chair |
| タイプライター | **12** | typewriter |
| 加算機 | **13** | adding machine |
| コピー機 | **14** | copier/photocopier |
| シュレッダー（書類裁断機） | **15** | paper shredder |
| 紙裁断機 | **16** | paper cutter |
| 書類整理係 | **17** | file clerk |
| 書類キャビネット | **18** | file cabinet |
| 秘書 | **19** | secretary |
| コンピュータワークステーション | **20** | computer workstation |
| 社長／雇用主 | **21** | employer/boss |
| 事務アシスタント | **22** | administrative assistant |
| オフィスマネージャー | **23** | office manager |
| 事務用品入れ | **24** | supply cabinet |
| 保管品戸棚 | **25** | storage cabinet |
| 自動販売機 | **26** | vending machine |
| 冷水機 | **27** | water cooler |
| コーヒーメーカー | **28** | coffee machine |
| メッセージボード | **29** | message board |
| メッセージを受ける | **a** | take a message |
| プレゼンテーションをする | **b** | give a presentation |
| 郵便物を仕分けする | **c** | sort the mail |
| コピーを取る | **d** | make copies |
| ファイルする | **e** | file |
| 手紙をタイプする | **f** | type a letter |

[A–H]
A. Where's .....(name).....?
B. He's/She's in the ______.

[1–29]
A. What do you think of the new ______?
B. He's/She's/It's very nice.

[a–f]
A. What's .....(name)..... doing?
B. He's/She's ______ing.

Describe a workplace you are familiar with. Tell about the rooms, the areas, and the employees.

# OFFICE SUPPLIES AND EQUIPMENT

## オフィスの事務用品・備品

| | | |
|---|---|---|
| 机 | 1 | desk |
| ホッチキス | 2 | stapler |
| レタートレー | 3 | letter tray/ stacking tray |
| 回転式カードファイル | 4 | rotary card file |
| デスクマット | 5 | desk pad |
| スケジュールノート | 6 | appointment book |
| クリップボード | 7 | clipboard |
| メモ用紙 | 8 | note pad/ memo pad |
| 電動鉛筆削り | 9 | electric pencil sharpener |
| 卓上カレンダー | 10 | desk calendar |
| (商標名)ポスト・イット／付箋紙 | 11 | Post-It note pad |
| システム手帳 | 12 | organizer/ personal planner |
| 輪ゴム | 13 | rubber band |
| クリップ | 14 | paper clip |
| ホッチキス針 | 15 | staple |
| 画びょう | 16 | thumbtack |
| 画びょう／ピン | 17 | pushpin |
| リーガルパッド (8.5x14インチの用紙) | 18 | legal pad |
| ファイルフォルダー | 19 | file folder |
| 索引カード | 20 | index card |
| 封筒 | 21 | envelope |
| レターヘッド／レターヘッド付き便せん | 22 | stationery/ letterhead (paper) |
| 郵便封筒 | 23 | mailer |
| 宛名(用)ラベル | 24 | mailing label |
| タイプライター用カートリッジ | 25 | typewriter cartridge |
| インクカートリッジ | 26 | ink cartridge |
| ゴム印 | 27 | rubber stamp |
| スタンプ台 | 28 | ink pad |
| スティックのり | 29 | glue stick |
| 接着剤 | 30 | glue |
| ゴムのり | 31 | rubber cement |
| 修正液 | 32 | correction fluid |
| セロテープ | 33 | cellophane tape/ clear tape |
| 梱包テープ／ガムテープ | 34 | packing tape/ sealing tape |

A. My desk is a mess!
I can't find my [2–12]!
B. Here it is next to your [2–12].

A. Could you get some more [13–21, 23–29] s/ [22, 30–34] from the supply room?
B. Some more [13–21, 23–29] s/ [22, 30–34]? Sure. I'd be happy to.

Which supplies and equipment do you use?
What do you use them for?

Which supplies in this lesson do you have at home? at school?

| | | |
|---|---|---|
| タイムレコーダー | **1** | time clock |
| タイムカード | **2** | time cards |
| 更衣室 | **3** | locker room |
| 組みたてライン | **4** | (assembly) line |
| 工員 | **5** | (factory) worker |
| 作業場 | **6** | work station |
| ライン監督官 | **7** | line supervisor |
| 品質管理監督 | **8** | quality control supervisor |
| 機械 | **9** | machine |
| ベルトコンベア | **10** | conveyor belt |
| 倉庫 | **11** | warehouse |
| 荷造り係 | **12** | packer |
| フォークリフト | **13** | forklift |
| 荷物用エレベーター | **14** | freight elevator |
| 組合掲示 | **15** | union notice |
| 投書箱 | **16** | suggestion box |
| 出荷部 | **17** | shipping department |
| 出荷係 | **18** | shipping clerk |
| 台車 | **19** | hand truck/dolly |
| 荷積み台 | **20** | loading dock |
| 給与課(部) | **21** | payroll office |
| 人事課(部) | **22** | personnel office |

A. Excuse me. I'm a new employee. Where's/Where are the ______?
B. Next to/Near/In/On the ______.

A. Have you seen *Tony*?
B. Yes. *He's* in/on/at/next to/near the ______.

Are there any factories where you live? What kind? What are the working conditions there?

What products do factories in your country produce?

# THE CONSTRUCTION SITE

## 建設現場

| | | |
|---|---|---|
| 大ハンマー | **1** | sledgehammer |
| つるはし | **2** | pickax |
| スコップ | **3** | shovel |
| 手押し車 | **4** | wheelbarrow |
| 削岩機／削岩ドリル | **5** | jackhammer/ pneumatic drill |
| 青写真 | **6** | blueprints |
| はしご | **7** | ladder |
| 巻き尺 | **8** | tape measure |
| 工具ベルト | **9** | toolbelt |
| こて | **10** | trowel |
| セメントミキサー | **11** | cement mixer |
| セメント | **a** | cement |
| 足場 | **12** | scaffolding |
| ダンプカー | **13** | dump truck |
| シャベルローダー | **14** | front-end loader |
| クレーン車 | **15** | crane |
| 高所作業用クレーン | **16** | cherry picker |
| ブルドーザー | **17** | bulldozer |
| ショベルカー | **18** | backhoe |
| コンクリートミキサー車 | **19** | concrete mixer truck |
| コンクリート | **a** | concrete |
| ピックアップトラック | **20** | pickup truck |
| トレーラー | **21** | trailer |
| 石壁 | **22** | drywall |
| 木材 | **23** | wood/lumber |
| ベニヤ板 | **24** | plywood |
| 断縁材 | **25** | insulation |
| 針金 | **26** | wire |
| れんが | **27** | brick |
| こけら板 | **28** | shingle |
| 導管 | **29** | pipe |
| 梁 | **30** | girder/beam |

A. Could you get me that/those [1–10]?
B. Sure.

A. Watch out for that [11–21]!
B. Oh! Thanks for the warning!

A. Do we have enough [22–26]/[27–30]s?
B. I think so.

What building materials is your home made of? When was it built?

Describe a construction site near your home or school. Tell about the construction equipment and the materials.

# JOB SAFETY

## 作業安全

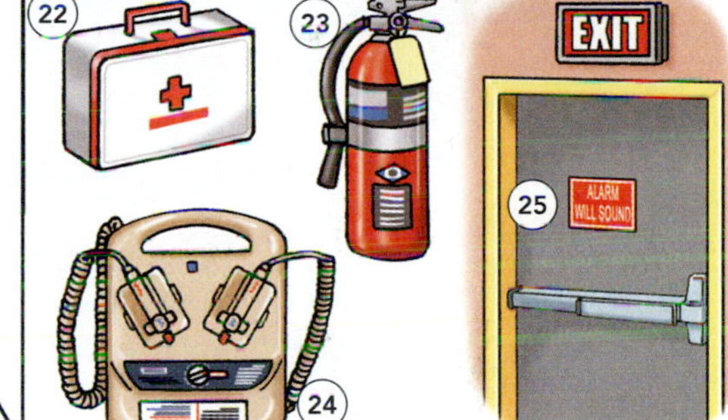

| | | |
|---|---|---|
| ヘルメット | **1** | hard hat/helmet |
| 耳栓 | **2** | earplugs |
| ゴーグル | **3** | goggles |
| 安全ベスト | **4** | safety vest |
| 安全靴 | **5** | safety boots |
| トウガード | **6** | toe guard |
| バックサポートベルト | **7** | back support |
| 安全イヤーマフ | **8** | safety earmuffs |
| ヘアネット | **9** | hairnet |
| マスク | **10** | mask |
| ラテックスの手袋 | **11** | latex gloves |
| 防毒マスク | **12** | respirator |
| 保護めがね | **13** | safety glasses |
| 可燃性の | **14** | flammable |
| 毒性の | **15** | poisonous |
| 腐食性の | **16** | corrosive |
| 放射性の | **17** | radioactive |
| 危険な | **18** | dangerous |
| 有害な | **19** | hazardous |
| 生物学的危険物質 | **20** | biohazard |
| 感電の危険 | **21** | electrical hazard |
| 救急箱 | **22** | first-aid kit |
| 消火器 | **23** | fire extinguisher |
| 除細動器 | **24** | defibrillator |
| 非常口 | **25** | emergency exit |

A. Don't forget to wear your [1–13]!
B. Thanks for reminding me.

A. Be careful! That material is [14–17]! / That machine is [18]! / That work area is [19]! / That's a [20]! / That's an [21]!
B. Thanks for the warning.

A. Where's the [22–25]?
B. It's over there.

Have you ever used any of the safety equipment in this lesson? What have you used? When? Where?

Where do you see people using safety equipment in your community?

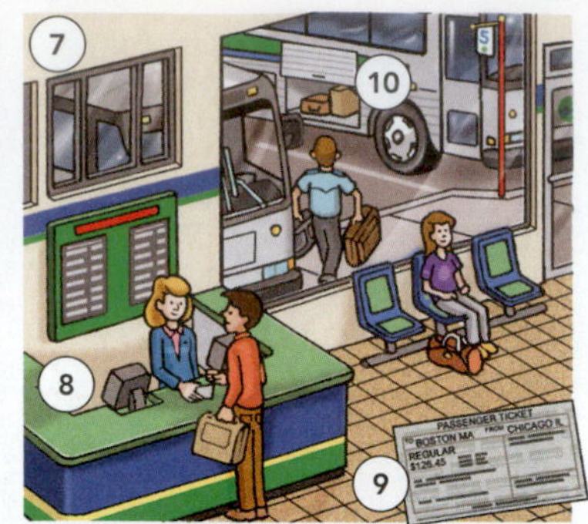

**バス A bus**
- バス停 1 bus stop
- バスの通り道 2 bus route
- 乗客 3 passenger/rider
- 運賃 4 (bus) fare
- 乗り換え切符 5 transfer
- バス運転手 6 bus driver
- バス発着所 7 bus station
- 乗車券売場 8 ticket counter
- 乗車券 9 ticket
- 荷物室 10 baggage compartment/ luggage compartment

**列車 B train**
- 駅 11 train station
- 切符売り場 12 ticket window
- （列車）発着案内板 13 arrival and departure board
- 鉄道案内所 14 information booth
- 時刻表 15 schedule/timetable
- プラットホーム 16 platform
- 線路 17 track
- 車掌 18 conductor

**地下鉄 C subway**
- 地下鉄駅 19 subway station
- トークン（地下鉄の切符に当たるコイン） 20 (subway) token
- 回転式改札口 21 turnstile
- フェアカード（乗車カード） 22 fare card
- フェアカード販売機 23 fare card machine

**タクシー D taxi**
- タクシー乗り場 24 taxi stand
- タクシー 25 taxi/cab/taxicab
- 料金メーター 26 meter
- タクシー運転手 27 cab driver/ taxi driver

**フェリー E ferry**

[A–E]
A. How are you going to get there?
B. { I'm going to take the [A–C, E] .
  { I'm going to take a [D] .

[1, 7, 8, 10–19, 21, 23–25]
A. Excuse me. Where's the ______?
B. Over there.

How do you get to different places in your community? Describe public transportation where you live.

In your country, can you travel far by train or by bus? Where can you go? How much do tickets cost? Describe the buses and trains.

## 車両の種類

| | | |
|---|---|---|
| セダン（普通乗用車） | **1** | sedan |
| ハッチバック | **2** | hatchback |
| コンバーチブル | **3** | convertible |
| スポーツカー | **4** | sports car |
| ハイブリッド | **5** | hybrid |
| ライトバン | **6** | station wagon |
| SUV | **7** | S.U.V. (sport utility vehicle) |
| ジープ | **8** | jeep |
| ワゴン車 | **9** | van |
| ミニワゴン車 | **10** | minivan |
| 小型トラック | **11** | pickup truck |
| リムジン | **12** | limousine |
| レッカー車 | **13** | tow truck |
| キャンピングカー | **14** | R.V. (recreational vehicle)/camper |
| 引っ越しトラック | **15** | moving van |
| トラック | **16** | truck |
| トレーラートラック／セミトレーラー | **17** | tractor trailer/semi |
| 自転車 | **18** | bicycle/bike |
| スクーター | **19** | motor scooter |
| 原動機付き自転車 | **20** | moped |
| オートバイ | **21** | motorcycle |

A. What kind of vehicle are you looking for?
B. I'm looking for a **sedan**.

A. Do you drive a/an ________?
B. No. I drive a/an ________.

A. I just saw an accident between a/an ________ and a/an ________!
B. Was anybody hurt?
A. No. Fortunately, nobody was hurt.

What are the most common types of vehicles in your country?

What's your favorite type of vehicle? Why? In your opinion, which company makes the best one?

- バンパー **1** bumper
- ヘッドライト **2** headlight
- 方向指示灯／ウインカー **3** turn signal
- 駐車灯 **4** parking light
- フェンダー **5** fender
- タイヤ **6** tire
- ホイールキャップ **7** hubcap
- ボンネット **8** hood
- フロントガラス **9** windshield
- ワイパー **10** windshield wipers
- サイドミラー **11** side mirror
- ルーフラック **12** roof rack
- サンルーフ **13** sunroof
- アンテナ **14** antenna
- 後部ガラス **15** rear window
- （後部ガラス用）デフロスター **16** rear defroster
- トランク **17** trunk
- テールランプ **18** taillight
- ブレーキランプ **19** brake light
- バックライト **20** backup light
- ナンバープレート **21** license plate
- 排気管 **22** tailpipe/exhaust pipe
- マフラー **23** muffler
- トランスミッション（変速機） **24** transmission
- ガソリンタンク **25** gas tank
- ジャッキ **26** jack
- スペアタイヤ **27** spare tire
- ラグレンチ **28** lug wrench
- 照明筒 **29** flare
- （バッテリー充電用）ブースターケーブル **30** jumper cables
- 点火プラグ **31** spark plugs
- エアーフィルター **32** air filter
- エンジン **33** engine
- 燃料噴射システム **34** fuel injection system
- ラジエーター **35** radiator
- ラジエーターホース **36** radiator hose
- ファンベルト **37** fan belt
- 発電機 **38** alternator
- オイルレベルゲージ **39** dipstick
- バッテリー **40** battery
- 空気ポンプ **41** air pump
- ガソリンポンプ **42** gas pump
- ノズル **43** nozzle
- ガソリンタンクキャップ **44** gas cap
- ガソリン **45** gas
- オイル **46** oil
- 冷却液 **47** coolant
- 空気 **48** air

エアバッグ **49** air bag
日よけ **50** visor
バックミラー **51** rearview mirror
ダッシュボード／計器パネル **52** dashboard/instrument panel
水温計 **53** temperature gauge
ガソリンメーター **54** gas gauge/fuel gauge
スピードメーター **55** speedometer
オドメーター（走行距離計） **56** odometer
警告灯 **57** warning lights
ウインカーレバー **58** turn signal
ハンドル **59** steering wheel
クラクション **60** horn

イグニッション（点火スイッチ） **61** ignition
通気孔 **62** vent
ナビゲーションシステム **63** navigation system
ラジオ **64** radio
CDプレーヤー **65** CD player
ヒーター **66** heater
エアコン **67** air conditioning
デフロスター **68** defroster
電源 **69** power outlet
グローブボックス **70** glove compartment
サイドブレーキ **71** emergency brake
ブレーキペダル **72** brake (pedal)
アクセルペダル **73** accelerator/gas pedal

自動変速機（オートマチックトランスミッション） **74** automatic transmission
シフトレバー **75** gearshift
手動変速機（マニュアルトランスミッション） **76** manual transmission
シフトレバー **77** stickshift
クラッチペダル **78** clutch
ドアロック **79** door lock
ドア取っ手 **80** door handle
肩ベルト **81** shoulder harness
ひじ掛け **82** armrest
ヘッドレスト **83** headrest
座席（シート） **84** seat
シートベルト **85** seat belt

[2, 3, 9–16, 24, 35–39, 49–85]
A. What's the matter with your car?
B. The ________(s) is/are broken.

[45–48]
A. Can I help you?
B. {Yes. My car needs [45–47].
Yes. My tires need [48].

[1, 2, 4–15, 17–23, 25]
A. I was just in a car accident!
B. Oh, no! Were you hurt?
A. No. But my ________(s) was/were damaged.

In your opinion, what are the most important features to look for when you buy a car?

Do you own a car? What kind? Tell about any repairs your car has needed.

## 幹線道路（高速道路）・街路

| | | |
|---|---|---|
| トンネル | 1 | tunnel |
| 橋 | 2 | bridge |
| 料金所 | 3 | tollbooth |
| 案内標識 | 4 | route sign |
| 幹線道路／高速道路 | 5 | highway |
| 道路 | 6 | road |
| 中央分離壁 | 7 | divider/barrier |
| 高架路 | 8 | overpass |
| ガード下路 | 9 | underpass |
| 高速道路入口 | 10 | entrance ramp/ on ramp |
| 州間道路（高速道路） | 11 | interstate (highway) |
| 中央分離帯 | 12 | median |
| 追越車線 | 13 | left lane |
| 走行車線 | 14 | middle lane/ center lane |
| 減速車線 | 15 | right lane |
| 路側帯 | 16 | shoulder |
| 車両通行帯境界線 | 17 | broken line |
| 車両通行帯最外側線 | 18 | solid line |
| 速度制限標識 | 19 | speed limit sign |
| （高速道路）出口 | 20 | exit (ramp) |
| 出口案内標識 | 21 | exit sign |
| 街路 | 22 | street |
| 一方通行道路 | 23 | one-way street |
| 車道中央線 | 24 | double yellow line |
| 横断歩道 | 25 | crosswalk |
| 交差点 | 26 | intersection |
| 交通信号／信号機 | 27 | traffic light/ traffic signal |
| 曲がり角 | 28 | corner |
| 区画 | 29 | block |

[1–28]
A. Where's the accident?
B. It's on / in / at / near the _______.

Describe a highway you travel on.

Describe an intersection near where you live.

In your area, on which highways and streets do most accidents occur? Why are these places dangerous?

# 場所・方向を表す前置詞

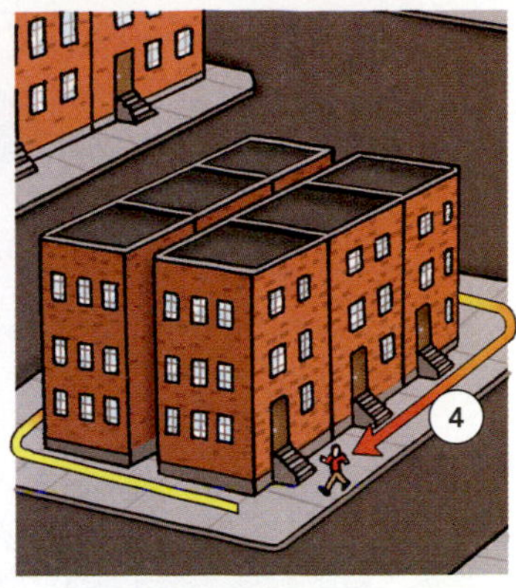

〜の上に **1** over
〜の下に **2** under
〜を通って **3** through
〜の周り **4** around

上に向かう **5** up
下に向かう **6** down
〜を横切る **7** across
〜を過ぎて **8** past

〜の上に **9** on
〜から離れる **10** off
〜の中に入る **11** into
〜から外にでる **12** out of
〜の上に乗る **13** onto

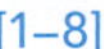

[1–8]
A. Go **over** *the bridge.*
B. **Over** *the bridge*?
A. Yes.

[9–13]
A. I can't talk right now. I'm getting **on** *a train.*
B. You're getting **on** *a train*?
A. Yes. I'll call you later.

What places do you go past on your way to school?

Tell how to get to different places from your home or your school.

# TRAFFIC SIGNS AND DIRECTIONS
道路標識・方向

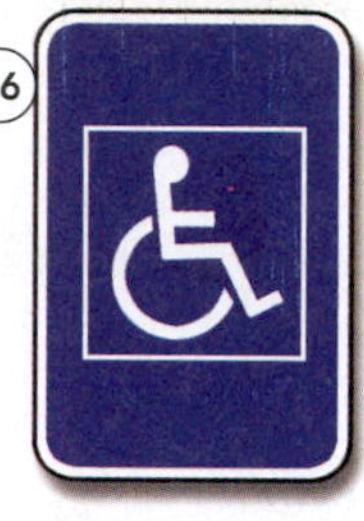


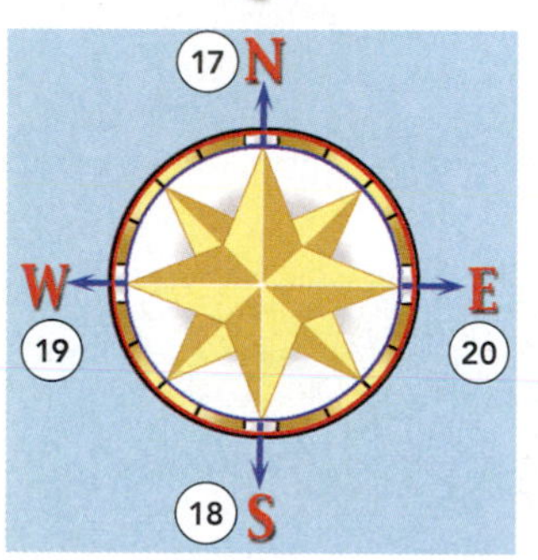


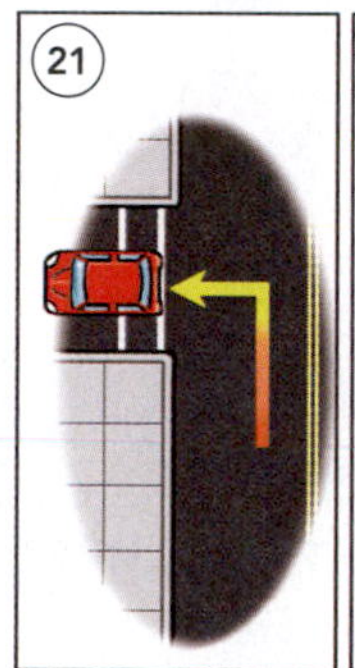


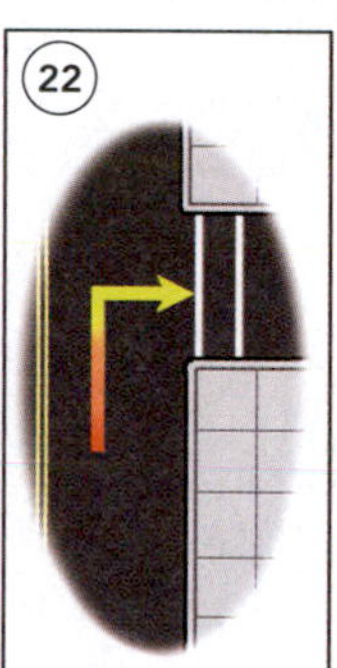


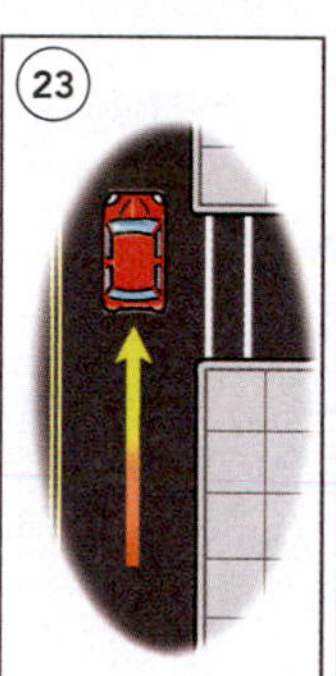


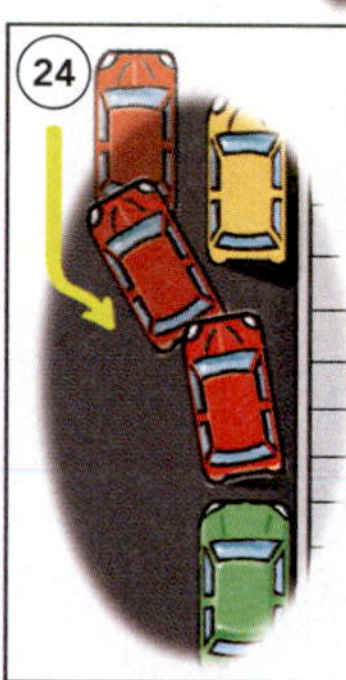


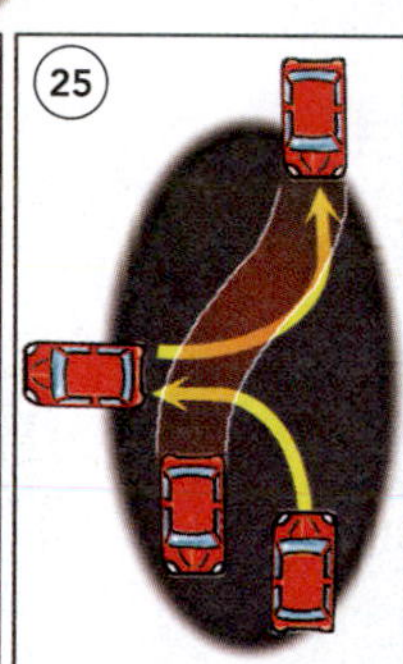

**交通標識 Traffic Signs**

止まれ **1** stop
左折禁止 **2** no left turn
右折禁止 **3** no right turn
Uターン禁止 **4** no U-turn
右折のみ可 **5** right turn only
進入禁止 **6** do not enter
一方通行 **7** one way
この先行き止まり **8** dead end/no outlet
横断歩道 **9** pedestrian crossing
踏切注意 **10** railroad crossing
学童横断路 **11** school crossing
この先合流あり **12** merging traffic
徐行 **13** yield
迂回路 **14** detour
スリップ注意 **15** slippery when wet
障害者用駐車スペース **16** handicapped parking only

**磁石の方角 Compass Directions**

北 **17** north
南 **18** south
西 **19** west
東 **20** east

**路上試験の指示 Road Test Instructions**

左折せよ。 **21** Turn left.
右折せよ。 **22** Turn right.
直進せよ。 **23** Go straight.
縦列駐車せよ。 **24** Parallel park.
スリーポイントターンせよ。／方向転換せよ。 **25** Make a 3-point turn.
手信号を使用せよ。 **26** Use hand signals.

[1–16]
A. Careful! That sign says "**stop**"!
B. Oh. Thanks.

[17–20]
A. Which way should I go?
B. Go **north**.

[21–26]
A. Turn **right**.
B. Turn **right**?
A. Yes.

Which of these traffic signs are in your neighborhood? What other traffic signs do you usually see?

Describe any differences between traffic signs in different countries you know.

# 空港

**搭乗手続き A Check-In**

- 航空券 1 ticket
- 発券カウンター 2 ticket counter
- 航空券取扱人 3 ticket agent
- スーツケース 4 suitcase
- 発着便案内表示 5 arrival and departure monitor

**手荷物検査 B Security**

- 手荷物検査所 6 security checkpoint
- 金属探知機 7 metal detector
- 航空保安官 8 security officer
- X線探知機 9 X-ray machine
- 機内持ち込み手荷物 10 carry-on bag

**搭乗口 C The Gate**

- 搭乗カウンター 11 check-in counter
- 搭乗券 12 boarding pass
- 搭乗口(ゲート) 13 gate
- 搭乗エリア 14 boarding area

**手荷物受取所 D Baggage Claim**

- 手荷物受取所 15 baggage claim (area)
- 回転式荷物受取台 16 baggage carousel
- 手荷物 17 baggage
- 荷物用カート 18 baggage cart/ luggage cart
- 荷物キャリア 19 luggage carrier
- ガーメントバッグ 20 garment bag
- 手荷物預り証 21 baggage claim check

**税関と入国審査 E Customs and Immigration**

- 税関 22 customs
- 税関職員 23 customs officer
- 税関申告書 24 customs declaration form
- 入国審査所 25 immigration
- 入国審査官 26 immigration officer
- パスポート 27 passport
- ビザ(査証) 28 visa

[2, 3, 5–9, 11, 13–16, 22, 23, 25, 26]
A. Excuse me. Where's the ________?*
B. Right over there.

* *With 22 and 25 use:* Excuse me. Where's ______?

[1, 4, 10, 12, 17–21, 24, 27, 28]
A. Oh, no! I think I've lost my ________!
B. I'll help you look for it.

Describe an airport you are familiar with. Tell about the check-in area, the security area, the gates, and the baggage claim area.

Have you ever gone through Customs and Immigration? Tell about your experience.

# 飛行機での移動

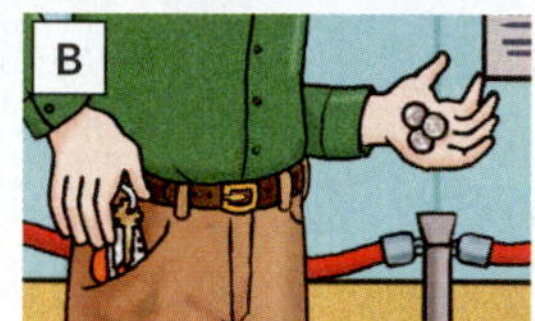

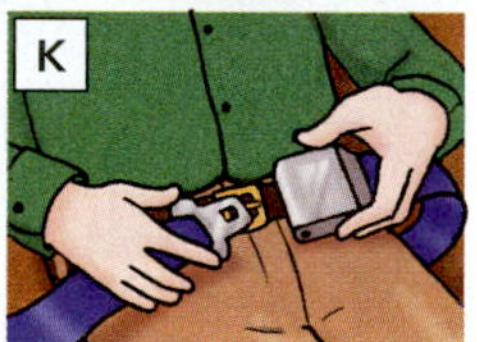

| | | |
|---|---|---|
| 操縦室 | 1 | cockpit |
| 機長 | 2 | pilot/captain |
| 副操縦士 | 3 | co-pilot |
| トイレ | 4 | lavatory/bathroom |
| 客室乗務員 | 5 | flight attendant |
| 荷物棚 | 6 | overhead compartment |
| 通路 | 7 | aisle |
| 窓側座席 | 8 | window seat |
| 中央座席 | 9 | middle seat |
| 通路側座席 | 10 | aisle seat |
| シートベルト着用ランプ | 11 | Fasten Seat Belt sign |
| 禁煙ランプ | 12 | No Smoking sign |
| 呼出ボタン | 13 | call button |
| 酸素マスク | 14 | oxygen mask |
| 非常口 | 15 | emergency exit |
| テーブル | 16 | tray (table) |
| 非常時手引き書 | 17 | emergency instruction card |
| エチケット袋 | 18 | air sickness bag |
| 救命胴衣 | 19 | life vest/life jacket |
| 滑走路 | 20 | runway |
| 空港ターミナル | 21 | terminal (building) |
| 管制塔 | 22 | control tower |
| 飛行機（ジェット機） | 23 | airplane/plane/jet |

| | | |
|---|---|---|
| 靴を脱ぐ | A | take off your shoes |
| ポケットのものを全部出す | B | empty your pockets |
| バッグをベルトコンベアに載せる | C | put your bag on the conveyor belt |
| コンピュータをトレイに入れる | D | put your computer in a tray |
| 金属探知機をくぐる | E | walk through the metal detector |
| 搭乗口でチェックインする | F | check in at the gate |
| 搭乗券を出す | G | get your boarding pass |
| 飛行機に乗る | H | board the plane |
| 機内持ち込み荷物をしまい込む | I | stow your carry-on bag |
| 座席を見つける | J | find your seat |
| シートベルトを締める | K | fasten your seat belt |

[1–23]
A. Where's the ______?
B. In/On/Next to/Behind/In front of/Above/Below the ______.

[A–K]
A. Please ______.
B. All right. Certainly.

Have you ever flown in an airplane? Tell about a flight you took.

Be an airport security officer! Give passengers instructions as they go through the security area. Now, be a flight attendant! Give passengers instructions before take-off.

# THE HOTEL

## ホテル

| | | | | | | | |
|---|---|---|---|---|---|---|---|
| ドアマン（玄関番） | **1** doorman | フロント係 | **9** desk clerk | エレベーター | **18** elevator |
| 係員による駐車サービス | **2** valet parking | 客 | **10** guest | 製氷機 | **19** ice machine |
| 駐車係員 | **3** parking attendant | 案内デスク | **11** concierge desk | 廊下 | **20** hall/hallway |
| ホテルのボーイ | **4** bellhop | 案内係 | **12** concierge | ルームキー | **21** room key |
| 荷物カート | **5** luggage cart | レストラン | **13** restaurant | 客室サービスカート | **22** housekeeping cart |
| ボーイ長 | **6** bell captain | 会議室 | **14** meeting room | 客室係 | **23** housekeeper |
| 玄関ホール／ロビー | **7** lobby | 売店 | **15** gift shop | 客室 | **24** guest room |
| フロント | **8** front desk | プール | **16** pool | ルームサービス | **25** room service |
| | | エクササイズルーム | **17** exercise room | | |

A. Where do you work?
B. I work at the *Grand* Hotel.
A. What do you do there?
B. I'm a/an ____[1, 3, 4, 6, 9, 12, 23]____.

A. Excuse me. Where's the ____[1–19, 22, 23]____?
B. Right over there.
A. Thanks.

Tell about a hotel you are familiar with. Describe the place and the people.

In your opinion, which hotel employee has the most interesting job? the most difficult job? Why?

# 趣味・クラフト・ゲーム

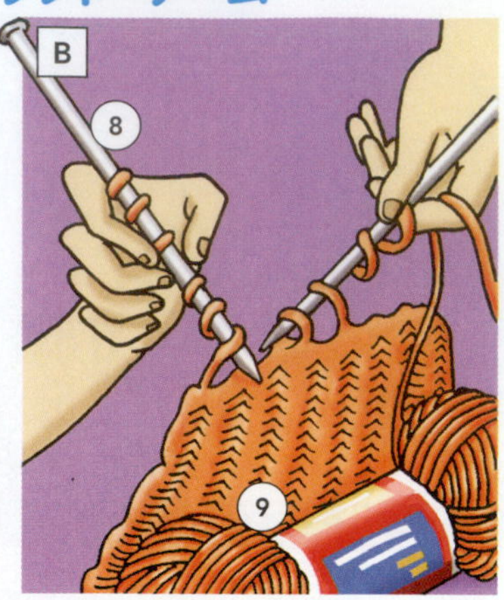

**縫う A sew**
ミシン 1 sewing machine
待ち針 2 pin
針さし 3 pin cushion
糸巻き 4 (spool of) thread
縫い針 5 (sewing) needle
指ぬき 6 thimble
安全ピン 7 safety pin

**編む B knit**
編み棒 8 knitting needle
編み糸 9 yarn

**かぎ針編みする C crochet**
かぎ針 10 crochet hook

**絵の具で描く D paint**
絵筆 11 paintbrush
イーゼル 12 easel
キャンバス 13 canvas
絵の具 14 paint
油絵の具 a oil paint
水彩絵の具 b watercolor

**鉛筆で描く E draw**
スケッチブック 15 sketch book
色鉛筆セット 16 (set of) colored pencils
図画用鉛筆 17 drawing pencil

**刺繍する F do embroidery**
刺繍 18 embroidery

**ニードルポイントをする G do needlepoint**
ニードルポイント 19 needlepoint
パターン 20 pattern

**木工する H do woodworking**
木工キット 21 woodworking kit

**折り紙をする I do origami**
折り紙 22 origami paper

**陶芸する J make pottery**
粘土 23 clay
ろくろ 24 potter's wheel

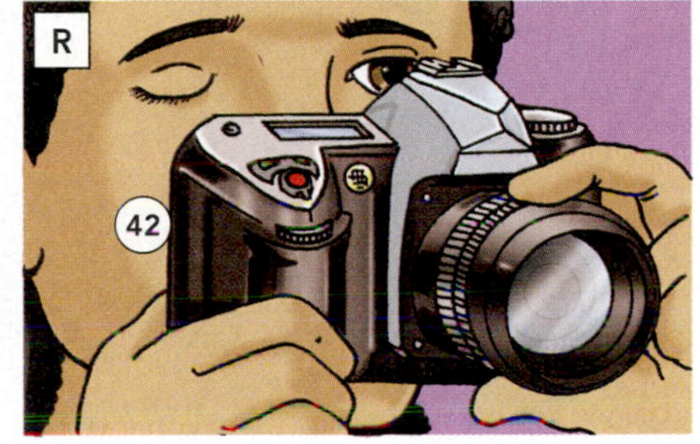

| | | |
|---|---|---|
| **切手収集をする** | **K** | **collect stamps** |
| 切手アルバム | **25** | stamp album |
| 虫めがね | **26** | magnifying glass |
| **コイン収集をする** | **L** | **collect coins** |
| コインカタログ | **27** | coin catalog |
| コインコレクション | **28** | coin collection |
| **プラモデルをする** | **M** | **build models** |
| プラモデル | **29** | model kit |
| 接着剤 | **30** | glue |
| アクリル絵の具 | **31** | acrylic paint |
| **バードウォッチングをする** | **N** | **go bird-watching** |
| 双眼鏡 | **32** | binoculars |
| フィールドガイド | **33** | field guide |
| **トランプをする** | **O** | **play cards** |
| トランプ(1組) | **34** | (deck of) cards |
| クラブ／クローバー | **a** | club |
| ダイヤ | **b** | diamond |
| ハート | **c** | heart |
| スペード | **d** | spade |
| **ボードゲームをする** | **P** | **play board games** |
| チェス | **35** | chess |
| チェッカー | **36** | checkers |
| バックギャモン | **37** | backgammon |
| モノポリー | **38** | Monopoly |
| さいころ | **a** | dice |
| スクラブル | **39** | Scrabble |
| **インターネットをする／ネットサーフィンする** | **Q** | **go online/ browse the Web/ "surf" the net** |
| ウェブブラウザ | **40** | web browser |
| ウェブアドレス／URL | **41** | web address/URL |
| **写真** | **R** | **photography** |
| カメラ | **42** | camera |
| **天文** | **S** | **astronomy** |
| 天体望遠鏡 | **43** | telescope |

A. What do you like to do in your free time?

B. {I like to ___[A–Q]___.
I enjoy ___[R, S]___.

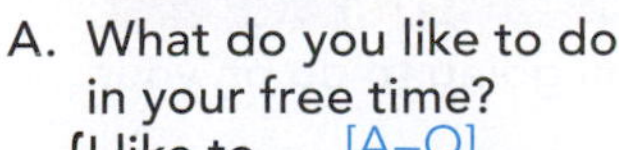

A. May I help you?

B. Yes, please. I'd like to buy (a/an) ___[1–34, 42, 43]___.

A. What do you want to do?

B. Let's play ___[35–39]___.

A. Good idea!

Do you like to do any of these activities in your free time? Which ones?

What games are popular in your country? Describe how to play one.

# 余暇での外出

| | | |
|---|---|---|
| 博物館 **1** museum | クラフトフェア **8** craft fair | 水族館 **14** aquarium |
| 美術館 **2** art gallery | ヤードセール **9** yard sale | 植物園 **15** botanical gardens |
| コンサート **3** concert | フリーマーケット **10** swap meet/ flea market | プラネタリウム **16** planetarium |
| 演劇 **4** play | 公園 **11** park | 動物園 **17** zoo |
| 遊園地 **5** amusement park | 浜辺 **12** beach | 映画 **18** movies |
| 史跡 **6** historic site | 山 **13** mountains | カーニバル **19** carnival |
| 国立公園 **7** national park | | フェア **20** fair |

A. What do you want to do today?

B. Let's go to { a/an __[1–9]__. / the __[10–20]__.

A. What did you do over the weekend?

B. I went to { a/an __[1–9]__. / the __[10–20]__.

A. What are you going to do on your day off?

B. I'm going to go to { a/an __[1–9]__. / the __[10–20]__.

What are some of your favorite places to go? Where are they? What do you do there?

# 公園・遊戯施設

| | | |
|---|---|---|
| サイクリングコース | 1 | bicycle path/ bike path/ bikeway |
| 池 | 2 | duck pond |
| ピクニック場 | 3 | picnic area |
| ごみ入れ | 4 | trash can |
| グリル | 5 | grill |
| ピクニック用テーブル | 6 | picnic table |
| 水飲み場 | 7 | water fountain |
| ジョギングコース | 8 | jogging path |
| ベンチ | 9 | bench |
| テニスコート | 10 | tennis court |
| 球場 | 11 | ballfield |
| 噴水 | 12 | fountain |
| 駐輪場 | 13 | bike rack |
| メリーゴーランド／回転木馬 | 14 | merry-go-round/ carousel |
| スケートボードランプ | 15 | skateboard ramp |
| 遊び場 | 16 | playground |
| クライミングウォール／人工壁 | 17 | climbing wall |
| ブランコ | 18 | swings |
| ジャングルジム | 19 | climber |
| すべり台 | 20 | slide |
| シーソー | 21 | seesaw |
| 砂場 | 22 | sandbox |
| 砂 | 23 | sand |

[1–22]
A. Excuse me. Does this park have (a) ________?
B. Yes. Right over there.

[17–23]
A. { Be careful on the ___[17–21]___!
Be careful in the ___[22, 23]___!
B. I will, Dad/Mom.

Describe a park and playground you are familiar with.

# 浜辺

| | | |
|---|---|---|
| 救助員 | 1 | lifeguard |
| 監視台 | 2 | lifeguard stand |
| 救命具 | 3 | life preserver |
| 売店 | 4 | snack bar/ refreshment stand |
| 物売り | 5 | vendor |
| 遊泳者 | 6 | swimmer |
| 波 | 7 | wave |
| サーファー | 8 | surfer |
| たこ | 9 | kite |
| ビーチチェア | 10 | beach chair |
| ビーチパラソル | 11 | beach umbrella |
| 砂の城 | 12 | sand castle |
| ブギボード | 13 | boogie board |
| 日光浴をしている人 | 14 | sunbather |
| サングラス | 15 | sunglasses |
| ビーチタオル | 16 | (beach) towel |
| ビーチボール | 17 | beach ball |
| サーフボード | 18 | surfboard |
| 貝殻 | 19 | seashell/shell |
| 岩場 | 20 | rock |
| アイスボックス | 21 | cooler |
| 日よけ帽子 | 22 | sun hat |
| サンスクリーン／日焼け止め／日焼けローション | 23 | sunscreen/ sunblock/ suntan lotion |
| レジャーシート | 24 | (beach) blanket |
| シャベル | 25 | shovel |
| バケツ | 26 | pail |

[1–26]
A. What a nice beach!
B. It is. Look at all the ______s!

[9–11, 13, 15–18, 21–26]
A. Are you ready for the beach?
B. Almost. I just have to get my ______.

Do you like to go to the beach? Describe your favorite beach. What do you take when you go there?

# 野外でのレクリエーション

**キャンプ A camping**
- テント 1 tent
- 寝袋 2 sleeping bag
- くい 3 tent stakes
- ランプ 4 lantern
- おの 5 hatchet
- キャンプストーブ 6 camping stove
- スイスアーミーナイフ 7 Swiss army knife
- 虫除け 8 insect repellent
- マッチ 9 matches

**ハイキング B hiking**
- リュックサック／バックパック 10 backpack
- 水筒 11 canteen
- コンパス／方位磁石 12 compass
- 地図 13 trail map
- GPS 14 GPS device
- 登山靴 15 hiking boots

**ロッククライミング／岩登り C rock climbing/ technical climbing**
- ハーネス 16 harness
- ロープ 17 rope

**マウンテンバイキング D mountain biking**
- マウンテンバイク 18 mountain bike
- 自転車用ヘルメット 19 (bike) helmet

**ピクニック E picnic**
- ピクニックシート 20 (picnic) blanket
- 魔法びん 21 thermos
- ピクニックバスケット 22 picnic basket

A. Let's go [A–E]* this weekend.
B. Good idea! We haven't gone [A–E]* in a long time.

**With E, say:* on a picnic.

A. Did you bring { the [1–9, 11–14, 16, 17, 20–22]? / your [10, 15, 18, 19]? }
B. Yes, I did.
A. Oh, good.

Have you ever gone camping, hiking, rock climbing, or mountain biking? Tell about it: What did you do? Where? What equipment did you use?

Do you like to go on picnics? Where? What picnic supplies and food do you take with you?

## スポーツ　個人競技・レクリエーション

**ジョギング　A　jogging**
ジョギングウェア　1　jogging suit
ジョギングシューズ　2　jogging shoes

**ランニング　B　running**
ランニングパンツ　3　running shorts
ランニングシューズ　4　running shoes

**ウォーキング　C　walking**
ウォーキングシューズ　5　walking shoes

**インラインスケート／ローラーブレード　D　inline skating/ rollerblading**
インラインスケート／ローラーブレード　6　inline skates/ rollerblades
ひざ当て　7　knee pads

**サイクリング　E　cycling/biking**
自転車　8　bicycle/bike
自転車用ヘルメット　9　(bicycle/bike) helmet

**スケートボード　F　skateboarding**
スケートボード　10　skateboard
ひじ当て　11　elbow pads

**ボウリング　G　bowling**
ボウリングボール　12　bowling ball
ボウリングシューズ　13　bowling shoes

**乗馬　H　horseback riding**
鞍／サドル　14　saddle
手綱　15　reins
あぶみ　16　stirrups

**テニス　I　tennis**
テニスラケット　17　tennis racket
テニスボール　18　tennis ball
テニス用ショートパンツ　19　tennis shorts

**バドミントン　J　badminton**
バドミントンラケット　20　badminton racket
バドミントンの羽　21　birdie/shuttlecock

**ラケットボール　K　racquetball**
保護ゴーグル　22　safety goggles
ラケットボール　23　racquetball
ラケット　24　racquet

**卓球　L　table tennis/ ping pong**
ラケット　25　paddle
卓球台　26　ping pong table
ネット　27　net
ピンポン球／ピンポン玉　28　ping pong ball

| | | |
|---|---|---|
| ゴルフ | **M** | **golf** |
| クラブ | **29** | golf clubs |
| ゴルフボール | **30** | golf ball |
| フリスビー | **N** | **Frisbee** |
| フリスビー | **31** | Frisbee/ flying disc |
| ビリヤード | **O** | **billiards/pool** |
| ビリヤード台 | **32** | pool table |
| キュー | **33** | pool stick |
| ビリヤードの球 | **34** | billiard balls |
| 武道 | **P** | **martial arts** |
| 黒帯 | **35** | black belt |
| 体操 | **Q** | **gymnastics** |
| 鞍馬（跳馬） | **36** | horse |
| 平行棒 | **37** | parallel bars |
| 床 | **38** | mat |
| 平均台 | **39** | balance beam |
| トランポリン | **40** | trampoline |
| ウェイトリフティング | **R** | **weightlifting** |
| バーベル | **41** | barbell |
| ウェイト（鉄アレー） | **42** | weights |
| アーチェリー | **S** | **archery** |
| 弓矢 | **43** | bow and arrow |
| 的 | **44** | target |
| ボクシング | **T** | **box** |
| ボクシンググローブ | **45** | boxing gloves |
| トランクス | **46** | (boxing) trunks |
| レスリング | **U** | **wrestle** |
| レスリングユニフォーム | **47** | wrestling uniform |
| マット | **48** | (wrestling) mat |
| トレーニング/フィットネス/エクササイズ | **V** | **work out/ exercise** |
| ランニングマシン | **49** | treadmill |
| ローイングマシン | **50** | rowing machine |
| エアロバイク | **51** | exercise bike |
| 多機能エクササイズマシーン | **52** | universal/ exercise equipment |

[A–V]
A. What do you like to do in your free time?
B. I like to go___[A–H]___.
I like to play ___[I–O]___.
I like to do ___[P–S]___.
I like to ___[T–V]___.

[1–52]
A. I really like this/these new ______.
B. It's/They're very nice.

Do you do any of these activities? Which ones? Which are popular in your country?

# スポーツ 団体競技

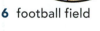

- 野球 **A baseball**
- 野球選手 1 baseball player
- 野球場 2 baseball field/ballfield
- ソフトボール **B softball**
- ソフトボール選手 3 softball player
- 球場 4 ballfield
- アメリカンフットボール **C football**
- アメリカンフットボール選手 5 football player
- アメリカンフットボール競技場 6 football field
- ラクロス **D lacrosse**
- ラクロス選手 7 lacrosse player
- ラクロス競技場 8 lacrosse field
- アイスホッケー **E (ice) hockey**
- アイスホッケー選手 9 hockey player
- アイスホッケーリンク 10 hockey rink
- バスケットボール **F basketball**
- バスケット選手 11 basketball player
- バスケットコート 12 basketball court
- バレーボール **G volleyball**
- バレー選手 13 volleyball player
- バレーコート 14 volleyball court
- サッカー **H soccer**
- サッカー選手 15 soccer player
- サッカー場 16 soccer field

[A–H]
A. Do you like to play **baseball**?
B. Yes. **Baseball** is one of my favorite sports.

A. ............ plays __[A–H]__ very well.
B. You're right. I think he's/she's one of the best ________s* on the team.

*Use 1, 3, 5, 7, 9, 11, 13, 15.

A. Now listen, team! I want all of you to go out on that ________† and play the best game of __[A–H]__ you've ever played!
B. All right, Coach!

† Use 2, 4, 6, 8, 10, 12, 14, 16.

Which sports in this lesson do you like to play? Which do you like to watch?

What are your favorite teams?

Name some famous players of these sports.

# 団体競技の用具

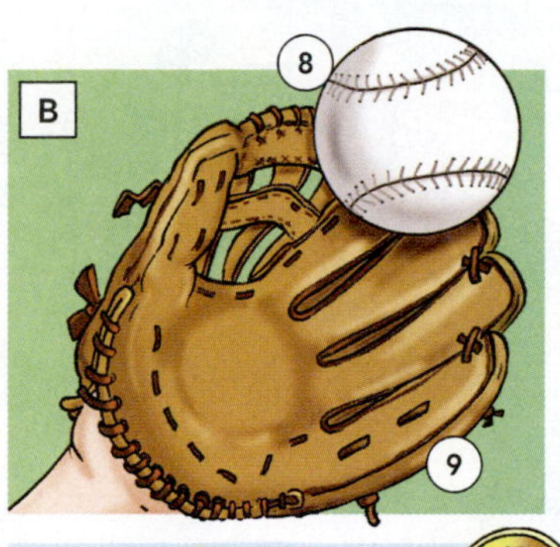

野球 **A baseball**
野球ボール **1** baseball
バット **2** bat
ヘルメット **3** batting helmet
野球ユニフォーム **4** (baseball) uniform
キャッチャーマスク **5** catcher's mask
グローブ **6** (baseball) glove
キャッチャーミット **7** catcher's mitt

ソフトボール **B softball**
ソフトボール **8** softball
ソフトボールグローブ **9** softball glove

アメリカンフットボール **C football**
フットボール **10** football
ヘルメット **11** football helmet
肩パッド **12** shoulder pads

ラクロス **D lacrosse**
ラクロスボール **13** lacrosse ball
ヘルメット **14** face guard
クロス **15** lacrosse stick

アイスホッケー **E (ice) hockey**
ホッケーパック **16** hockey puck
ホッケースティック **17** hockey stick
フェイスマスク **18** hockey mask
ホッケーグローブ **19** hockey glove
ホッケー用スケート靴 **20** hockey skates

バスケットボール **F basketball**
バスケットボール **21** basketball
バックボード **22** backboard
ゴール **23** basketball hoop

バレーボール **G volleyball**
バレーボール **24** volleyball
ネット **25** volleyball net

サッカー **H soccer**
サッカーボール **26** soccer ball
すね当て **27** shinguards

[1–27]
A. I can't find my **baseball**!
B. Look in the closet.*

*closet, basement, garage

[In a store]
A. Excuse me. I'm looking for (a) [1–27] .
B. All our [A–H] equipment is over there.
A. Thanks.

[At home]
A. I'm going to play [A–H] after school today.
B. Don't forget your [1–21, 24, 26, 27] !

Which sports in this lesson are popular in your country? Which sports do students play in high school?

# WINTER SPORTS AND RECREATION

## 冬のスポーツ・レクリエーション

**スキー** **A (downhill) skiing**
スキー板 **1** skis
スキー靴 **2** ski boots
ビンディング **3** bindings
ストック **4** (ski) poles

**クロスカントリースキー** **B cross-country skiing**
クロスカントリー用スキー板 **5** cross-country skis

**スケート** **C (ice) skating**
スケート靴 **6** (ice) skates
ブレード **7** blade
スケートガード **8** skate guard

**フィギュアスケート** **D figure skating**
フィギュア用スケート靴 **9** figure skates

**スノーボード** **E snowboarding**
スノーボード **10** snowboard

**そりすべり** **F sledding**
そり **11** sled
丸そり **12** sledding dish/saucer

**ボブスレー** **G bobsledding**
ボブスレー **13** bobsled

**スノーモービル** **H snowmobiling**
スノーモービル **14** snowmobile

[A–H]
A. What's your favorite winter sport?
B. **Skiing**.

[A–H]
[At work or at school on Friday]
A. What are you going to do this weekend?
B. I'm going to go ________.

[1–14]
[On the telephone]
A. Hello. *Sally's* Sporting Goods.
B. Hello. Do you sell ________(s)?
A. Yes, we do. / No, we don't.

Have you ever done any of these activities? Which ones?

Have you ever watched the Winter Olympics? Which event do you think is the most exciting? the most dangerous?

# 水上スポーツ・レクリエーション

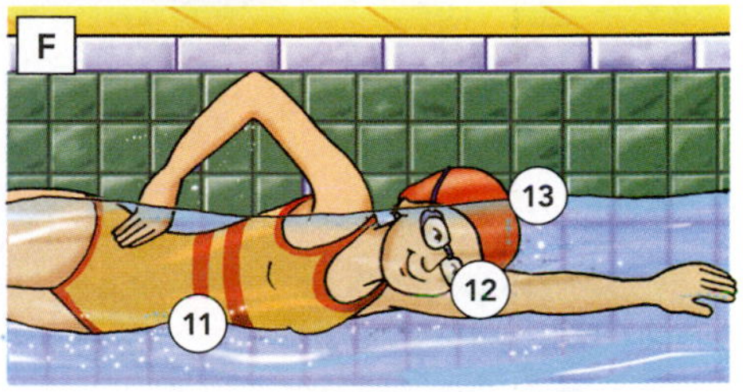

| | | |
|---|---|---|
| **ヨット** | **A** | **sailing** |
| ヨット | 1 | sailboat |
| 救命胴衣 | 2 | life jacket/life vest |
| **カヌー** | **B** | **canoeing** |
| カヌー | 3 | canoe |
| パドル | 4 | paddles |
| **ボート** | **C** | **rowing** |
| 手こぎボート | 5 | rowboat |
| オール | 6 | oars |
| **カヤック** | **D** | **kayaking** |
| カヤック | 7 | kayak |
| パドル | 8 | paddles |
| **ラフティング (川くだり)** | **E** | **(white-water) rafting** |
| ゴムボート(いかだ) | 9 | raft |
| 救命胴衣 | 10 | life jacket/ life vest |
| **水泳** | **F** | **swimming** |
| 水着 | 11 | swimsuit/ bathing suit |
| ゴーグル | 12 | goggles |
| 水泳帽 | 13 | bathing cap |
| **シュノーケリング** | **G** | **snorkeling** |
| 水中めがね | 14 | mask |
| シュノーケル | 15 | snorkel |
| フィン／足ひれ | 16 | fins |
| **スキューバダイビング** | **H** | **scuba diving** |
| ウエットスーツ | 17 | wet suit |
| 酸素ボンベ | 18 | (air) tank |
| 潜水マスク | 19 | (diving) mask |
| **サーフィン** | **I** | **surfing** |
| サーフボード | 20 | surfboard |
| **ウインドサーフィン** | **J** | **windsurfing** |
| セイルボード | 21 | sailboard |
| 帆 | 22 | sail |
| **水上スキー** | **K** | **waterskiing** |
| 水上スキー板 | 23 | water skis |
| 引き綱 | 24 | towrope |
| **釣り** | **L** | **fishing** |
| 釣り竿 | 25 | (fishing) rod/ pole |
| リール | 26 | reel |
| 釣り糸 | 27 | (fishing) line |
| 網 | 28 | (fishing) net |
| えさ | 29 | bait |

[A–L]
A. Would you like to go **sailing** tomorrow?
B. Sure. I'd love to.

A. Have you ever gone __[A–L]__?
B. Yes, I have./ No, I haven't.

A. Do you have everything you need to go __[A–L]__?
B. Yes. I have my __[1–29]__ (and my __[1–29]__).
A. Have a good time!

Which sports in this lesson have you tried? Which sports would you like to try?

Are any of these sports popular in your country? Which ones?

# SPORT AND EXERCISE ACTIONS

## スポーツや運動の動作

| | | |
|---|---|---|
| 打つ | 1 | hit |
| 投球する | 2 | pitch |
| 投げる | 3 | throw |
| つかむ／キャッチする | 4 | catch |
| パスする | 5 | pass |
| 蹴る | 6 | kick |
| サーブする | 7 | serve |
| バウンドする | 8 | bounce |
| ドリブルする | 9 | dribble |
| シュートする | 10 | shoot |
| 伸ばす | 11 | stretch |
| 曲げる | 12 | bend |
| 歩く | 13 | walk |
| 走る | 14 | run |
| 片足で跳ぶ | 15 | hop |
| スキップする | 16 | skip |
| ジャンプする（とび上がる） | 17 | jump |
| 腕を伸ばす | 18 | reach |
| 腕をふる | 19 | swing |
| もち上げる | 20 | lift |
| 泳ぐ | 21 | swim |
| 飛びこむ | 22 | dive |
| 射る | 23 | shoot |
| 腕立て伏せ | 24 | push-up |
| 上体起こし／腹筋運動 | 25 | sit-up |
| ひざの屈伸 | 26 | deep knee bend |
| ジャンピングジャック（準備体操の一種） | 27 | jumping jack |
| 宙返り／とんぼ返り | 28 | somersault |
| 側転 | 29 | cartwheel |
| 逆立ち | 30 | handstand |

[1–10]
A. ________ the ball!
B. Okay, Coach!

[11–23]
A. Now ________!
B. Like this?
A. Yes.

[24–30]
A. Okay, everybody. I want you to do twenty ________s!
B. Twenty ________s?!
A. That's right.

Do you exercise regularly?
Which exercises do you do?

Be an exercise instructor! Lead your friends in an exercise routine using the actions in this lesson.

# 娯楽

演劇 **A play**
劇場 1 theater
男優／俳優 2 actor
女優 3 actress

コンサート **B concert**
コンサートホール 4 concert hall
管弦楽団（オーケストラ） 5 orchestra
演奏者 6 musician
指揮者 7 conductor
バンド／楽隊 8 band

オペラ **C opera**
オペラ歌手 9 opera singer

バレエ **D ballet**
バレエダンサー 10 ballet dancer
バレリーナ 11 ballerina

ミュージッククラブ **E music club**
歌手 12 singer

映画 **F movies**
映画館 13 (movie) theater
スクリーン 14 (movie) screen
女優 15 actress
男優／俳優 16 actor

コメディクラブ **G comedy club**
コメディアン 17 comedian

[A–G]
A. What are you doing this evening?
B. I'm going to { a __[A, B, E, G]__. / the __[C, D, F]__.

[1–17]
A. What a magnificent _______!
B. I agree.

What kinds of entertainment in this lesson do you like?
What kinds of entertainment are popular in your country?

Who are some of your favorite actors? actresses? musicians? singers? comedians?

# 娯楽の種類

A

B

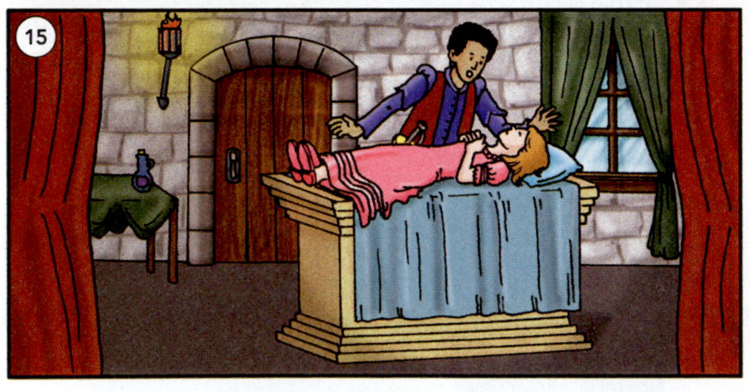

**音楽 A music**
クラシック 1 classical music
ポピュラー 2 popular music
カントリー 3 country music
ロック 4 rock music
フォーク 5 folk music
ラップ 6 rap music
ゴスペル 7 gospel music
ジャズ 8 jazz
ブルース 9 blues
ブルーグラス 10 bluegrass
ヒップポップ 11 hip hop
レゲエ 12 reggae

**演劇 B plays**
ドラマ 13 drama
喜劇 14 comedy
悲劇 15 tragedy
ミュージカルコメディ 16 musical (comedy)

映画 **C movies/films**

ドラマ **17** drama

喜劇 **18** comedy

西部劇 **19** western

ミステリー **20** mystery

ミュージカル **21** musical

アニメーション **22** cartoon

ドキュメンタリー **23** documentary

アクション映画／冒険映画 **24** action movie/ adventure movie

戦争映画 **25** war movie

ホラー映画 **26** horror movie

SF映画 **27** science fiction movie

外国映画 **28** foreign film

テレビ番組 **D TV programs**

ドラマ **29** drama

状況喜劇 **30** (situation) comedy/ sitcom

対談番組 **31** talk show

クイズ・ゲーム番組 **32** game show/ quiz show

リアリティ番組 **33** reality show

連続ドラマ **34** soap opera

アニメ番組 **35** cartoon

子供向番組 **36** children's program

ニュース番組 **37** news program

スポーツ番組 **38** sports program

自然番組 **39** nature program

ショッピング番組 **40** shopping program

A. What kind of __[A–D]__ do you like?

B. { I like __[1–12]__.
I like __[13–40]__s.

What's your favorite type of music?
Who is your favorite singer? musician? musical group?

What kind of movies do you like?
Who are your favorite movie stars?
What are the titles of your favorite movies?

What kind of TV programs do you like?
What are your favorite shows?

# 楽器

### 弦楽器 Strings

- バイオリン **1** violin
- ビオラ **2** viola
- チェロ **3** cello
- コントラバス **4** bass
- ギター **5** (acoustic) guitar
- エレキギター **6** electric guitar
- バンジョー **7** banjo
- ハープ **8** harp

### 木管楽器 Woodwinds

- ピッコロ **9** piccolo
- フルート **10** flute
- クラリネット **11** clarinet
- オーボエ **12** oboe
- リコーダー **13** recorder
- サキソホン **14** saxophone
- バスーン **15** bassoon

### 金管楽器 Brass

- トランペット **16** trumpet
- トロンボーン **17** trombone
- フレンチホルン **18** French horn
- チューバ **19** tuba

### 打楽器 Percussion

- ドラム **20** drums
- シンバル **a** cymbals
- タンバリン **21** tambourine
- 木琴 **22** xylophone

### 鍵盤楽器 Keyboard Instruments

- ピアノ **23** piano
- キーボード **24** electric keyboard
- オルガン **25** organ

### その他の楽器 Other Instruments

- アコーディオン **26** accordion
- ハーモニカ **27** harmonica

A. Do you play a musical instrument?
B. Yes. I play the **violin**.

A. You play the **trumpet** very well.
B. Thank you.

A. What's that noise?!
B. That's my son/daughter practicing the **drums**.

Do you play a musical instrument? Which one?

Which instruments are usually in an orchestra? a marching band? a rock group?

Name and describe typical musical instruments in your country.

# 農場・家畜

- 農家 **1** farmhouse
- 農夫 **2** farmer
- (野菜)畑 **3** (vegetable) garden
- かかし **4** scarecrow
- 干し草 **5** hay
- 作男 **6** hired hand
- 納屋 **7** barn
- 家畜小屋 **8** stable
- 馬 **9** horse
- 納屋の庭 **10** barnyard
- 七面鳥 **11** turkey
- ヤギ **12** goat
- 子羊 **13** lamb
- おんどり **14** rooster
- 豚飼育場 **15** pig pen
- 豚 **16** pig
- ニワトリ飼育場 **17** chicken coop
- ニワトリ **18** chicken
- ニワトリ小屋 **19** hen house
- メンドリ **20** hen
- 作物 **21** crop
- かんがい装置 **22** irrigation system
- トラクター **23** tractor
- 畑 **24** field
- 放牧場 **25** pasture
- 乳牛 **26** cow
- 羊 **27** sheep
- 果樹園 **28** orchard
- 果樹 **29** fruit tree
- 農場労働者 **30** farm worker
- アルファルファ **31** alfalfa
- トウモロコシ **32** corn
- 綿 **33** cotton
- 米 **34** rice
- 大豆 **35** soybeans
- 麦 **36** wheat

[1–30]
A. Where's the ______?
B. In/Next to the ______.

A. The [9, 11–14, 16, 18, 20, 26] s/ [27] are loose again!
B. Oh, no! Where are they?
A. They're in the [1, 3, 7, 8, 10, 15, 17, 19, 24, 25, 28].

[31–36]
A. Do you grow ______ on your farm?
B. No. We grow ______.

Tell about farms in your country. What crops and animals are common on these farms?

# ANIMALS AND PETS

## 動物・ペット

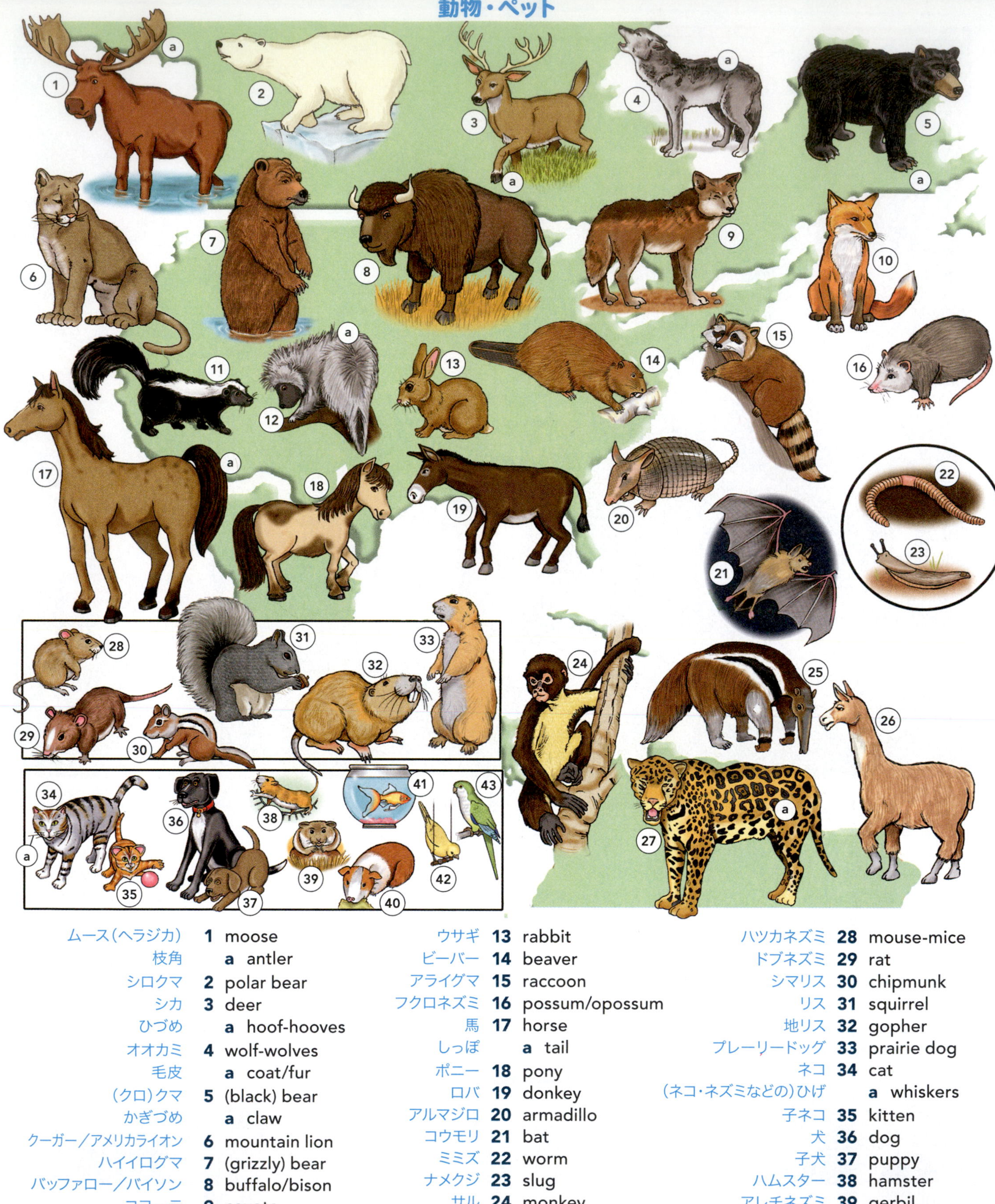

ムース（ヘラジカ） **1** moose
枝角 **a** antler
シロクマ **2** polar bear
シカ **3** deer
ひづめ **a** hoof-hooves
オオカミ **4** wolf-wolves
毛皮 **a** coat/fur
（クロ）クマ **5** (black) bear
かぎづめ **a** claw
クーガー／アメリカライオン **6** mountain lion
ハイイログマ **7** (grizzly) bear
バッファロー／バイソン **8** buffalo/bison
コヨーテ **9** coyote
キツネ **10** fox
スカンク **11** skunk
ヤマアラシ **12** porcupine
針／とげ **a** quill

ウサギ **13** rabbit
ビーバー **14** beaver
アライグマ **15** raccoon
フクロネズミ **16** possum/opossum
馬 **17** horse
しっぽ **a** tail
ポニー **18** pony
ロバ **19** donkey
アルマジロ **20** armadillo
コウモリ **21** bat
ミミズ **22** worm
ナメクジ **23** slug
サル **24** monkey
アリクイ **25** anteater
ラマ **26** llama
ジャガー **27** jaguar
はん点 **a** spots

ハツカネズミ **28** mouse-mice
ドブネズミ **29** rat
シマリス **30** chipmunk
リス **31** squirrel
地リス **32** gopher
プレーリードッグ **33** prairie dog
ネコ **34** cat
（ネコ・ネズミなどの）ひげ **a** whiskers
子ネコ **35** kitten
犬 **36** dog
子犬 **37** puppy
ハムスター **38** hamster
アレチネズミ **39** gerbil
テンジクネズミ／モルモット **40** guinea pig
金魚 **41** goldfish
カナリア **42** canary
インコ **43** parakeet

レイヨウ **44** antelope
ヒヒ **45** baboon
サイ **46** rhinoceros
角 **a** horn
パンダ **47** panda
オランウータン **48** orangutan
ヒョウ **49** panther
テナガザル **50** gibbon

トラ **51** tiger
足 **a** paw
ラクダ **52** camel
こぶ **a** hump
ゾウ **53** elephant
きば **a** tusk
(ゾウの)鼻 **b** trunk
ハイエナ **54** hyena

ライオン **55** lion
たてがみ **a** mane
キリン **56** giraffe
シマウマ **57** zebra
しま **a** stripes
チンパンジー **58** chimpanzee
カバ **59** hippopotamus
ヒョウ **60** leopard

ゴリラ **61** gorilla
カンガルー **62** kangaroo
袋 **a** pouch
コアラ **63** koala (bear)
カモノハシ **64** platypus

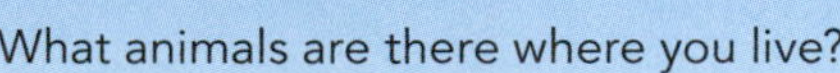

[1–33, 44–64]
A. Look at that ________!
B. Wow! That's the biggest ________ I've ever seen!

[34–43]
A. Do you have a pet?
B. Yes. I have a ________.
A. What's your ________'s name?
B. ................

What animals are there where you live?

Is there a zoo near where you live? What animals does it have?

What are some common pets in your country?

If you could be an animal, which animal would you like to be? Why?

Does your culture have any popular folk tales or children's stories about animals? Tell a story you know.

# BIRDS AND INSECTS

## 鳥類・昆虫類

### 鳥類 Birds

- コマドリ **1** robin
  - 巣 **a** nest
  - 卵 **b** egg
- アオカケス **2** blue jay
  - 翼 **a** wing
  - 尾 **b** tail
  - 羽 **c** feather
- コウカンチョウ／ベニスズメ **3** cardinal
- カラス **4** crow
- カモメ **5** seagull
- キツツキ **6** woodpecker
  - くちばし **a** beak
- ハト **7** pigeon
- フクロウ **8** owl
- タカ **9** hawk
- ワシ **10** eagle
  - かぎつめ **a** claw
- ハクチョウ **11** swan
- ハチドリ **12** hummingbird
- カモ／アヒル **13** duck
  - くちばし **a** bill
- スズメ **14** sparrow
- ガチョウ **15** goose-geese
- ペンギン **16** penguin
- フラミンゴ **17** flamingo
- ツル **18** crane
- コウノトリ **19** stork
- ペリカン **20** pelican
- クジャク **21** peacock
- オウム（インコを含む） **22** parrot
- ダチョウ **23** ostrich

### 昆虫 Insects

- ハエ **24** fly
- テントウムシ **25** ladybug
- ホタル **26** firefly/lightning bug
- ガ **27** moth
- イモムシ／毛虫 **28** caterpillar
  - まゆ **a** cocoon
- チョウ **29** butterfly
- ダニ **30** tick
- カ **31** mosquito
- トンボ **32** dragonfly
- クモ **33** spider
  - クモの巣 **a** web
- カマキリ **34** praying mantis
- スズメバチ **35** wasp
- ハチ **36** bee
  - ハチの巣 **a** beehive
- バッタ **37** grasshopper
- カブトムシ **38** beetle
- サソリ **39** scorpion
- ムカデ **40** centipede
- コオロギ **41** cricket

[1–41]

A. Is that a/an _______?

B. No. I think it's a/an _______.

[24–41]

A. Hold still! There's a _______ on your shirt!

B. Oh! Can you get it off me?

A. There! It's gone!

What birds and insects are there where you live?

Does your culture have any popular folk tales or children's stories about birds or insects? Tell a story you know.

# 魚類・海洋動物・爬虫類

## 魚類 Fish

| | | |
|---|---|---|
| マス | 1 | trout |
| 背びれ | a | fin |
| えら | b | gill |
| うろこ | c | scales |
| カレイ | 2 | flounder |
| マグロ | 3 | tuna |
| メカジキ | 4 | swordfish |
| スズキ | 5 | bass |
| サメ | 6 | shark |
| ウナギ | 7 | eel |
| タラ | 8 | cod |
| エイ／アカエイ | 9 | ray/stingray |
| タツノオトシゴ | 10 | sea horse |

## 海洋動物 Sea Animals

| | | |
|---|---|---|
| クジラ | 11 | whale |
| イルカ | 12 | dolphin |
| イルカ／ネズミイルカ | 13 | porpoise |
| クラゲ | 14 | jellyfish |
| タコ | 15 | octopus |
| 触腕 | a | tentacle |
| アザラシ | 16 | seal |
| アシカ／トド | 17 | sea lion |
| ラッコ | 18 | otter |
| セイウチ | 19 | walrus |
| きば | a | tusk |
| カニ | 20 | crab |
| イカ | 21 | squid |
| カタツムリ | 22 | snail |
| ヒトデ | 23 | starfish |
| ウニ | 24 | sea urchin |
| イソギンチャク | 25 | sea anemone |

## 両生類・爬虫類 Amphibians and Reptiles

| | | |
|---|---|---|
| 陸ガメ | 26 | tortoise |
| こうら | a | shell |
| 海ガメ | 27 | turtle |
| ワニ(アリゲーター) | 28 | alligator |
| ワニ(クロコダイル) | 29 | crocodile |
| トカゲ | 30 | lizard |
| イグアナ | 31 | iguana |
| カエル | 32 | frog |
| イモリ | 33 | newt |
| サンショウウオ | 34 | salamander |
| ガマガエル／ヒキガエル | 35 | toad |
| ヘビ | 36 | snake |
| ガラガラヘビ | 37 | rattlesnake |
| ボア | 38 | boa constrictor |
| コブラ | 39 | cobra |

[1–39]
A. Is that a/an ________?
B. No. I think it's a/an ________.

[26–39]
A. Are there any ________s around here?
B. No. But there are lots of ________!

What fish, sea animals, and reptiles can be found in your country? Which ones are endangered and need to be protected? Why?

In your opinion, which ones are the most interesting? the most beautiful? the most dangerous?

## 樹木・草木・花

木 **1** tree
葉 **2** leaf-leaves
小枝 **3** twig
枝 **4** branch
大枝 **5** limb
幹 **6** trunk
樹皮 **7** bark
根 **8** root
針状葉 **9** needle

松かさ **10** pine cone
ハナミズキ **11** dogwood
ヒイラギ **12** holly
モクレン **13** magnolia
ニレ **14** elm
サクラ **15** cherry
ヤシ **16** palm
カバ **17** birch
カエデ **18** maple

ナラ・カシ類 **19** oak
マツ **20** pine
アカスギ **21** redwood
ヤナギ **22** (weeping) willow
低木／低木のしげみ **23** bush
ヒイラギ **24** holly
ベリー類 **25** berries

低木 **26** shrub
シダ **27** fern
植物 **28** plant
サボテン **29** cactus-cacti
つる植物 **30** vine
ツタウルシ **31** poison ivy
ウルシ **32** poison sumac
ポイズンオーク／ウルシ **33** poison oak

花 **34** flower
花びら **35** petal
茎 **36** stem
つぼみ **37** bud
とげ **38** thorn
球根 **39** bulb
キク **40** chrysanthemum
ラッパスイセン **41** daffodil
ヒナギク **42** daisy

マリーゴールド **43** marigold
カーネーション **44** carnation
クチナシ **45** gardenia
ユリ **46** lily
アヤメ **47** iris
パンジー **48** pansy
ペチュニア **49** petunia
ラン **50** orchid
バラ **51** rose

ヒマワリ **52** sunflower
クロッカス **53** crocus
チューリップ **54** tulip
ゼラニウム **55** geranium
スミレ **56** violet
ポインセチア **57** poinsettia
ジャスミン **58** jasmine
ハイビスカス **59** hibiscus

[11–22]
A. What kind of tree is that?
B. I think it's a/an ________ tree.

[31–33]
A. Watch out for the ________ over there!
B. Oh. Thanks for the warning.

[40–57]
A. Look at all the ________s!*
B. They're beautiful!

**With 58 and 59, use:* Look at all the ___!

Describe your favorite tree and your favorite flower.

What kinds of trees and flowers grow where you live?

In your country, what flowers do you see at weddings? at funerals? during holidays? in hospital rooms? Tell which flowers people use for different occasions.

# ENERGY, CONSERVATION, AND THE ENVIRONMENT

## エネルギー・資源節約・環境

### エネルギー源 Sources of Energy

| | | |
|---|---|---|
| 石油 | **1** | oil/petroleum |
| (天然)ガス | **2** | (natural) gas |
| 石炭 | **3** | coal |
| 核エネルギー／原子力 | **4** | nuclear energy |
| 太陽エネルギー | **5** | solar energy |
| 水力発電 | **6** | hydroelectric power |
| 風力 | **7** | wind |
| 地熱エネルギー | **8** | geothermal energy |

### 資源節約 Conservation

| | | |
|---|---|---|
| リサイクルする | **9** | recycle |
| エネルギーを節約する | **10** | save energy/ conserve energy |
| 水を節約する | **11** | save water/ conserve water |
| カープール(相乗り通勤)する | **12** | carpool |

### 環境問題 Environmental Problems

| | | |
|---|---|---|
| 大気汚染 | **13** | air pollution |
| 水質汚濁 | **14** | water pollution |
| 有毒廃棄物 | **15** | hazardous waste/ toxic waste |
| 酸性雨 | **16** | acid rain |
| 放射線 | **17** | radiation |
| 地球温暖化 | **18** | global warming |

[1–8]

A. In my opinion, ______ will be our best source of energy in the future.
B. I disagree. I think our best source of energy will be ______.

[9–12]

A. Do you ______?
B. Yes. I'm very concerned about the environment.

[13–18]

A. Do you worry about the environment?
B. Yes. I'm very concerned about ______.

What kind of energy do you use to heat your home? to cook? In your opinion, which will be the best source of energy in the future?

Do you practice conservation? What do you do to help the environment?

In your opinion, what is the most serious environmental problem in the world today? Why?

# 自然災害

| | | |
|---|---|---|
| 地震 | **1** | earthquake |
| ハリケーン | **2** | hurricane |
| 台風 | **3** | typhoon |
| 暴風雪 | **4** | blizzard |
| 竜巻 | **5** | tornado |
| 洪水 | **6** | flood |
| 津波 | **7** | tsunami |
| 干ばつ | **8** | drought |
| 森林火災 | **9** | forest fire |
| 野火 | **10** | wildfire |
| 山崩れ／地すべり | **11** | landslide |
| 泥滑動 | **12** | mudslide |
| 雪崩 | **13** | avalanche |
| 火山噴火 | **14** | volcanic eruption |

A. Did you hear about the ______ in ......(country)......?
B. Yes, I did. I saw it on the news.

Have you or someone you know ever experienced a natural disaster? Tell about it.

Which natural disasters sometimes happen where you live? How do people prepare for them?

# 旅行

## 旅行の種類 Types of Travel

出張 **1** business trip
家族旅行 **2** family trip
クルーズ **3** cruise
ガイド付きツアー **4** (guided) tour
バスツアー **5** bus tour
電車の旅 **6** train trip
船の旅 **7** boat trip
スキー旅行 **8** ski trip
研修旅行 **9** study tour
エコツアー **10** eco-tour
サファリ **11** safari
遠征／探検 **12** expedition

## 旅行を予約する Booking a Trip

旅行会社 **13** travel agency
ツアー会社 **14** tour company
オンライン **15** online
電話で **16** over the phone

[1–12]
A. Are you planning to travel soon?
B. Yes. I'm going on a ______ to (country).
A. A ______ to (country)? That's wonderful!

[13–16]
A. How did you make the arrangements for your trip?
B. I booked it { through a [13, 14]. / [15, 16]. }

Tell about a trip you took: Where did you travel? What kind of trip was it? How did you book the trip?

# 目的地にて

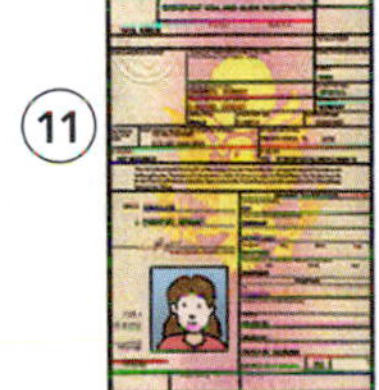

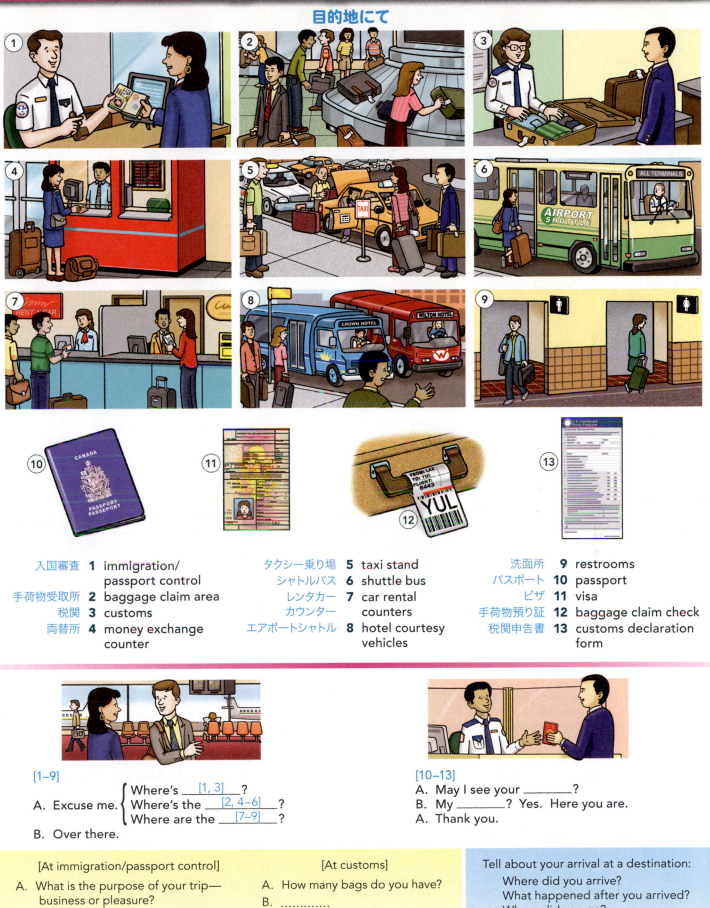

入国審査 **1** immigration/ passport control
手荷物受取所 **2** baggage claim area
税関 **3** customs
両替所 **4** money exchange counter
タクシー乗り場 **5** taxi stand
シャトルバス **6** shuttle bus
レンタカー カウンター **7** car rental counters
エアポートシャトル **8** hotel courtesy vehicles
洗面所 **9** restrooms
パスポート **10** passport
ビザ **11** visa
手荷物預り証 **12** baggage claim check
税関申告書 **13** customs declaration form

[1–9]

A. Excuse me. Where's ___[1, 3]___?
Where's the ___[2, 4–6]___?
Where are the ___[7–9]___?
B. Over there.

[10–13]

A. May I see your _______?
B. My _______? Yes. Here you are.
A. Thank you.

[At immigration/passport control]

A. What is the purpose of your trip—business or pleasure?
B. ............
A. How long do you plan to stay?
B. ............

[At customs]

A. How many bags do you have?
B. ............
A. Can you open them, please? I need to inspect them.
B. Certainly.

Tell about your arrival at a destination:
Where did you arrive?
What happened after you arrived?
Where did you go?
What did you do?

# HOTEL COMMUNICATION

## ホテルでの会話

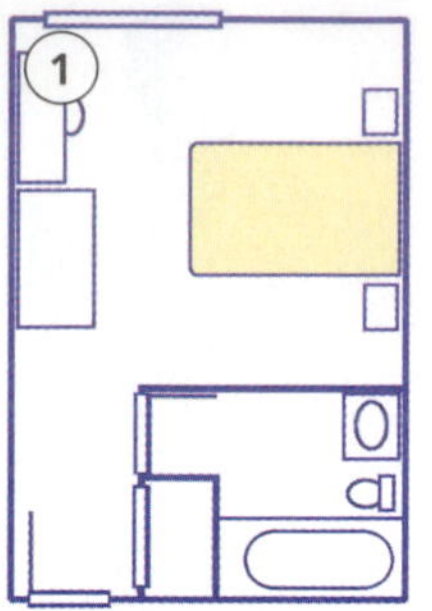

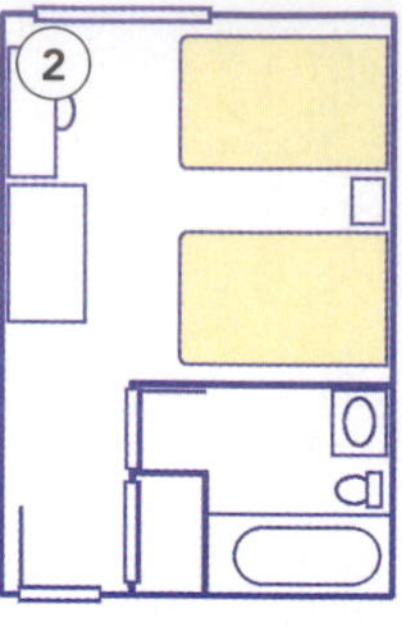

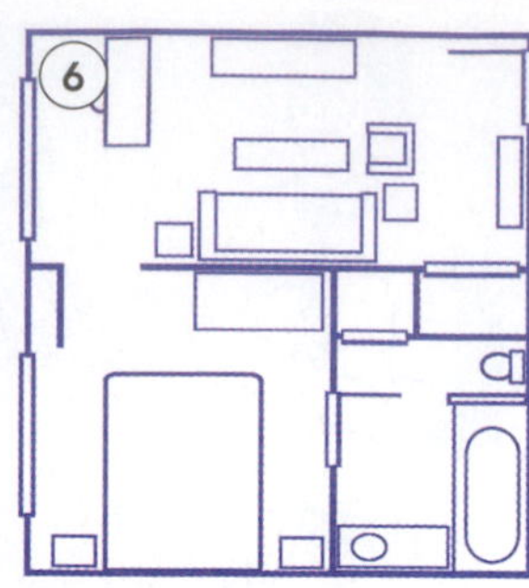

| | | |
|---|---|---|
| シングル | 1 | single room |
| ダブル | 2 | room with double beds |
| 禁煙室 | 3 | non-smoking room |
| バリアフリールーム | 4 | handicapped-accessible room |
| 景色のよい部屋 | 5 | room with a view |
| スイート | 6 | suite |
| ルームサービス係 | 7 | Room Service |
| 客室係 | 8 | Housekeeping |
| メンテナンス係 | 9 | Maintenance |
| フロント | 10 | Front Desk |
| 案内係 | 11 | Concierge |
| ベルデスク | 12 | Bell Desk |
| ディナーを注文したいのです。 | a | I'd like to order dinner. |
| タオルをください。 | b | We need some towels. |
| 部屋の洗面台が壊れています。 | c | The sink in our room is broken. |
| 朝7時にモーニングコールをお願いします。 | d | I'd like a wake-up call at 7 a.m., please. |
| ショーのチケットが買いたいのです。 | e | I'd like to get tickets for a show. |
| チェックアウトします。バッグを運んでもらえますか。 | f | I'm checking out. Can you please send someone to get my bags? |

[1-6]
A. I'd like a ______, please.
B. Let me see if that's available.
A. Thank you.

A. [7–12].
B. [a–f].
A. Certainly.

Tell about a hotel you stayed in: What type of room did you have? What hotel services did you use?

# 旅先での活動

観光する **1** go sightseeing
歩いて観光する **2** take a walking tour
バスツアーに参加する **3** take a bus tour
両替する **4** exchange money
おみやげを買う **5** buy souvenirs
絵はがきを送る **6** mail some postcards

レストランの予約をする **7** make a restaurant reservation
車を借りる **8** rent a car
ショー／コンサートのチケットを買う **9** get tickets for a *show/concert*
名所旧跡を訪れる **10** visit an historic site
買い物に行く **11** go shopping

公園に行く **12** go to a park
博物館に行く **13** go to a museum
フィットネスクラブに行く **14** go to a health club/fitness club
インターネットカフェに行く **15** go to an Internet cafe
クラブに行く **16** go to a club

A. May I help you?
B. Yes, please. I'd like to ________.

A. What did you do today?
B. We ________ed.

Tell about a tourist experience you had: Where did you go? What did you do there?

# 旅先での会話

## Tourist Requests 旅先でよく使われる表現

## Asking Permission 許可を得る

## Talking with Local People 地元の人と会話する

| | | |
|---|---|---|
| 両替する | 1 | exchange money |
| トラベラーズチェックを現金化する | 2 | cash a traveler's check |
| これを買う | 3 | buy this |
| チケットを2枚買う | 4 | buy two tickets |
| 私の国へこれを送る | 5 | mail this to my country |
| ここで写真を撮る | 6 | take photographs here |
| ここで食べる | 7 | eat here |
| 入る | 8 | go in |
| ここで携帯電話を使う | 9 | use a cell phone here |
| クレジットカードで払う | 10 | pay with a credit card |
| 私は ～ から来ました。 | 11 | I'm from (country). |
| 私はここに5日間います。 | 12 | I'm here for five days. |
| 私は ～ と ～ を見ました。 | 13 | I've seen ............ and ............. |
| 私はあなたの町がとても好きです。ここはとても ～ です。 | 14 | I like your city very much. It's very ............. |

[1–5]
A. May I help you?
B. Yes, please. I'd like to ________.

[6–10]
A. Can I ________?
B. { Yes, you can. / No, you can't.

[11–14]
A. ___[a–d]___?
B. ___[11–14]___.

## Emergency Expressions 非常時の表現

## Useful Expressions 役に立つ表現

| | | |
|---|---|---|
| 助けて! | **15** | Help! |
| 警察を呼んで! | **16** | Police! |
| じゃましないで! / あっちへ行って! | **17** | Please don't bother me! / Please go away! / Get away from me! |
| 火事だ! | **18** | Fire! |
| 注意して! | **19** | Look out! |
| 動くな! / 止まれ! / 動かないで! | **20** | Freeze! / Stop! / Don't move! |
| (〜語)を話せますか。 | **21** | Do you speak ......(language)......? |
| それを書いてください。 | **22** | Please write that down for me. |
| あれを英語でなんと言いますか。 | **23** | What do you call that in English? |
| もう一度言ってください。 | **24** | Please repeat that. |
| もう少しゆっくり言ってください。 | **25** | Please speak slowly. |
| すみません。今なんと言ったのですか。 | **26** | I'm sorry. What did you say? |

Be a tourist! Practice conversations with other students. Use all the expressions on pages 164 and 165.

世界

ARCTIC OCEAN
Baffin Bay
GREENLAND
ICELAND
Hudson Bay
Bering Sea
CANADA
ALEUTIAN ISLANDS
NORTH AMERICA
UNITED STATES OF AMERICA
AZORES (Portugal)
ATLANTIC OCEAN
BERMUDA
MOROCCO
CANARY ISLANDS (Spain)
WESTERN SAHARA
HAWAIIAN ISLANDS (US)
MEXICO
Gulf of Mexico
THE BAHAMAS
CUBA
DOMINICAN REPUBLIC
JAMAICA
PUERTO RICO
BELIZE
HAITI
HONDURAS
GUATEMALA
NICARAGUA
EL SALVADOR
COSTA RICA
PANAMA
MAURITANIA
SENEGAL
CAPE VERDE
GAMBIA
GUINEA-BISSAU
GUINEA
SIERRA LEONE
LIBERIA
GHANA
EQUATORIAL GUINEA
PACIFIC OCEAN
LINE ISLANDS
PHOENIX ISLANDS
KIRIBATI
AMERICAN SAMOA
Equator
GALÁPAGOS ISLANDS
ECUADOR
VENEZUELA
GUYANA
SURINAME
FRENCH GUIANA
COLOMBIA
SOUTH AMERICA
PERU
BRAZIL
MARQUESAS ISLANDS
COOK ISLANDS
WESTERN SAMOA
TONGA
TAHITI
FRENCH POLYNESIA
SOCIETY ISLANDS
AUSTRAL ISLANDS
BOLIVIA
PARAGUAY
CHILE
ARGENTINA
URUGUAY
FALKLAND/MALVINAS ISLANDS
N
W
E
S

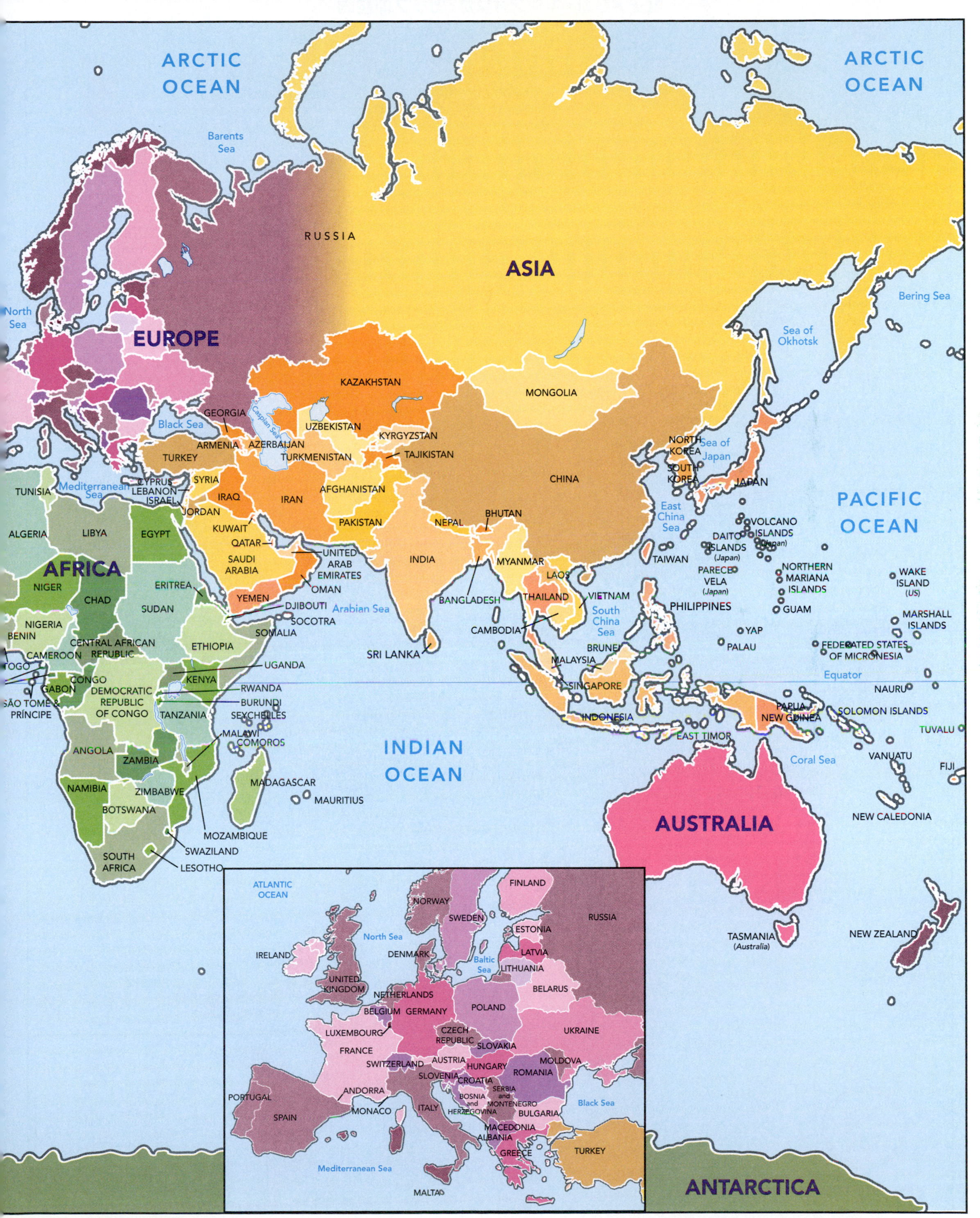

ARCTIC OCEAN
ARCTIC OCEAN
Barents Sea
RUSSIA
ASIA
EUROPE
AFRICA
AUSTRALIA
ANTARCTICA
PACIFIC OCEAN
INDIAN OCEAN
North Sea
Bering Sea
Sea of Okhotsk
KAZAKHSTAN
MONGOLIA
GEORGIA
Caspian Sea
Black Sea
UZBEKISTAN
KYRGYZSTAN
ARMENIA
AZERBAIJAN
TAJIKISTAN
TURKEY
TURKMENISTAN
NORTH KOREA
Sea of Japan
SOUTH KOREA
JAPAN
CHINA
TUNISIA
Mediterranean Sea
CYPRUS
LEBANON
ISRAEL
SYRIA
IRAQ
IRAN
AFGHANISTAN
JORDAN
East China Sea
ALGERIA
LIBYA
EGYPT
KUWAIT
PAKISTAN
NEPAL
BHUTAN
QATAR
VOLCANO ISLANDS (Japan)
DAITO ISLANDS (Japan)
UNITED ARAB EMIRATES
SAUDI ARABIA
INDIA
MYANMAR
TAIWAN
PARECE VELA (Japan)
NORTHERN MARIANA ISLANDS
WAKE ISLAND (US)
NIGER
ERITREA
OMAN
LAOS
CHAD
SUDAN
YEMEN
DJIBOUTI
Arabian Sea
BANGLADESH
THAILAND
VIETNAM
PHILIPPINES
GUAM
NIGERIA
SOCOTRA
South China Sea
MARSHALL ISLANDS
BENIN
CENTRAL AFRICAN REPUBLIC
SOMALIA
CAMBODIA
YAP
TOGO
CAMEROON
ETHIOPIA
BRUNEI
PALAU
FEDERATED STATES OF MICRONESIA
SRI LANKA
MALAYSIA
UGANDA
CONGO
KENYA
Equator
GABON
DEMOCRATIC REPUBLIC OF CONGO
RWANDA
SINGAPORE
NAURU
SÃO TOMÉ & PRÍNCIPE
BURUNDI
PAPUA NEW GUINEA
TANZANIA
SEYCHELLES
INDONESIA
SOLOMON ISLANDS
MALAWI
TUVALU
COMOROS
EAST TIMOR
ANGOLA
ZAMBIA
Coral Sea
VANUATU
FIJI
MADAGASCAR
NAMIBIA
ZIMBABWE
MAURITIUS
BOTSWANA
NEW CALEDONIA
MOZAMBIQUE
SOUTH AFRICA
SWAZILAND
LESOTHO
ATLANTIC OCEAN
FINLAND
NORWAY
SWEDEN
RUSSIA
ESTONIA
North Sea
LATVIA
IRELAND
DENMARK
Baltic Sea
LITHUANIA
UNITED KINGDOM
BELARUS
NETHERLANDS
POLAND
BELGIUM
GERMANY
LUXEMBOURG
CZECH REPUBLIC
UKRAINE
SLOVAKIA
FRANCE
AUSTRIA
MOLDOVA
SWITZERLAND
HUNGARY
ROMANIA
SLOVENIA
CROATIA
ANDORRA
SERBIA and MONTENEGRO
PORTUGAL
BOSNIA and HERZEGOVINA
Black Sea
SPAIN
MONACO
ITALY
BULGARIA
MACEDONIA
ALBANIA
GREECE
TURKEY
Mediterranean Sea
MALTA
TASMANIA (Australia)
NEW ZEALAND

北アメリカ・中央アメリカ・カリブ海諸国

南アメリカ

Caribbean Sea
Barranquilla
Cartagena
Maracaibo
Valencia
Barquisimeto
Caracas
VENEZUELA
Georgetown
Paramaribo
Cayenne
GUYANA
SURINAME
FRENCH GUIANA
ATLANTIC OCEAN
Medellín
Bogotá
Cali
COLOMBIA
Equator
Quito
ECUADOR
Gulf of Guayaquil
Guayaquil
Belém
Manaus
Fortaleza
Teresina
Recife
PERU
BRAZIL
Lima
Salvador
Brasília
La Paz
Goiânia
BOLIVIA
Sucre
Belo Horizonte
Rio de Janeiro
Campinas
São Paulo
CHILE
PARAGUAY
Asuncion
Curitiba
PACIFIC OCEAN
ARGENTINA
Pôrto Alegre
Córdoba
Rosario
Santiago
URUGUAY
Buenos Aires
Montevideo
Gulf of San Matías
ATLANTIC OCEAN
Gulf of San Jorge
N
W
E
S
FALKLAND ISLANDS
Port Stanley
Strait of Magellan
SOUTH GEORGIA ISLAND
0
500 Miles
0
500 KM

ヨーロッパ

Denmark Strait
Reykjavik
ICELAND
Norwegian Sea
White Sea
SWEDEN
FINLAND
NORWAY
Helsinki
RUSSIA
Oslo
Tallinn
Stockholm
Baltic Sea
ESTONIA
North Sea
Moscow
Riga
LATVIA
LITHUANIA
Copenhagen
DENMARK
Dublin
Vilnius
Minsk
IRELAND
UNITED KINGDOM
BELARUS
NETHERLANDS
Amsterdam
Berlin
The Hague
London
Warsaw
POLAND
ATLANTIC OCEAN
Brussels
GERMANY
Kiev
English Channel
BELGIUM
LUXEMBOURG
Prague
UKRAINE
Luxembourg
Paris
CZECH REPUBLIC
SLOVAKIA
MOLDOVA
LIECHTENSTEIN
Vienna
Bratislava
Sea of Azov
Chisinau
Bay of Biscay
Bern
AUSTRIA
Budapest
FRANCE
SWITZERLAND
HUNGARY
SLOVENIA
ROMANIA
Ljubljana
Zagreb
CROATIA
Belgrade
Bucharest
Black Sea
MONACO
SAN MARINO
Adriatic Sea
BOSNIA and HERZEGOVINA
Sarajevo
SERBIA and MONTENEGRO
SPAIN
ANDORRA
BULGARIA
ITALY
Sofia
PORTUGAL
CORSICA (France)
Madrid
Skopje
Rome
MACEDONIA
Lisbon
Tirana
Ankara
ALBANIA
SARDINIA (Italy)
BALEARIC ISLANDS (Spain)
Tyrrhenian Sea
Aegean Sea
TURKEY
GREECE
Mediterranean Sea
Strait of Gibraltar
Ionian Sea
Athens
GIBRALTAR
SICILY (Italy)
Nicosia
Valletta
CYPRUS
MALTA
CRETE (Greece)
Mediterranean Sea
N
W
E
S
0
500 Miles
0
500KM

アフリカ・中東

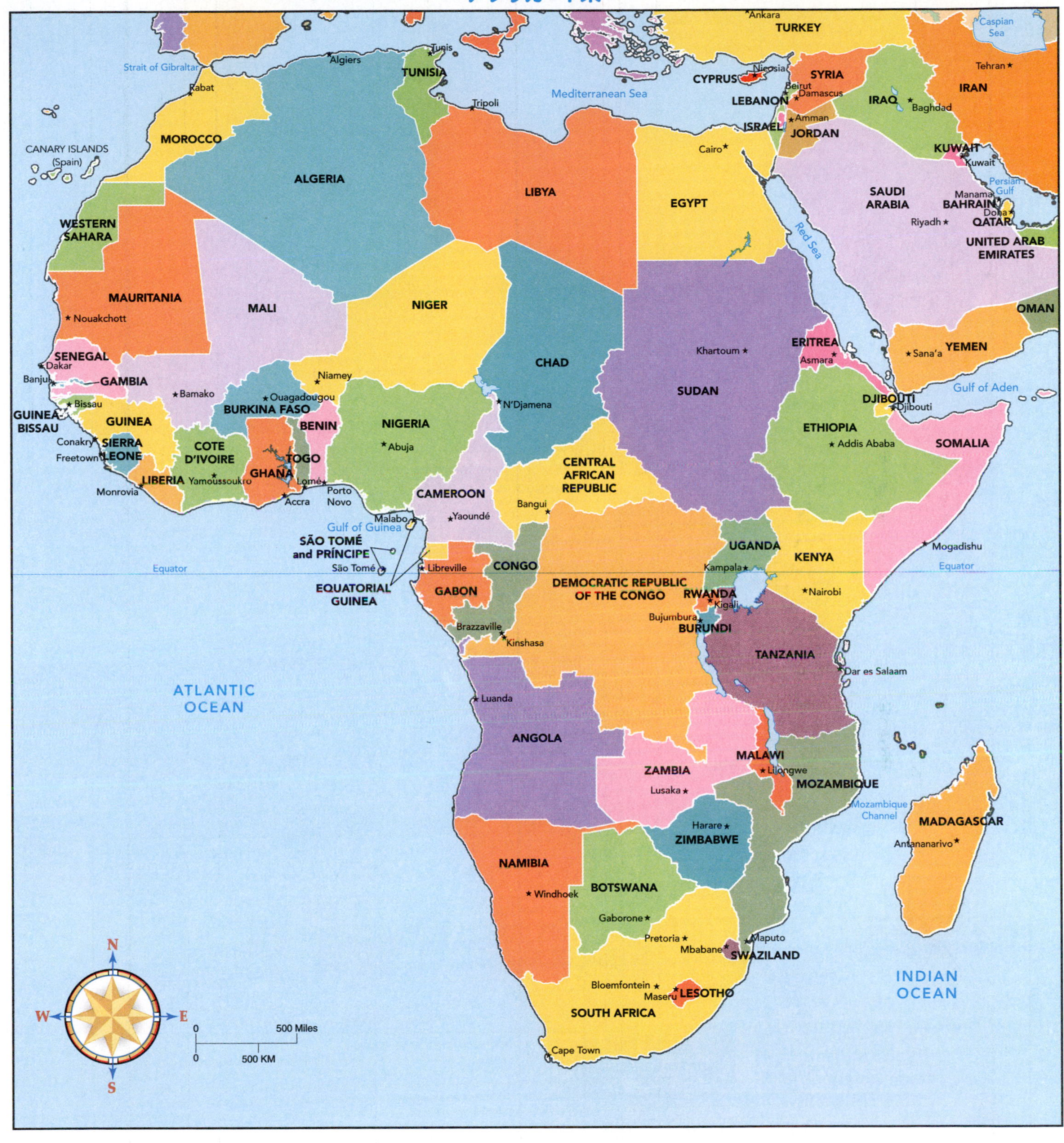
Ankara
TURKEY
Caspian Sea
Tehran
IRAN
Strait of Gibraltar
Algiers
Tunis
TUNISIA
CYPRUS
Nicosia
SYRIA
Rabat
Mediterranean Sea
Beirut
Damascus
Tripoli
LEBANON
IRAQ
Baghdad
ISRAEL
Amman
JORDAN
MOROCCO
CANARY ISLANDS (Spain)
Cairo
KUWAIT
Kuwait
ALGERIA
LIBYA
EGYPT
SAUDI ARABIA
Persian Gulf
Manama
BAHRAIN
Doha
QATAR
Riyadh
WESTERN SAHARA
Red Sea
UNITED ARAB EMIRATES
MAURITANIA
Nouakchott
MALI
NIGER
OMAN
ERITREA
Asmara
Khartoum
YEMEN
Sana'a
SENEGAL
Dakar
CHAD
Banjul
GAMBIA
Niamey
SUDAN
Gulf of Aden
Bamako
Ouagadougou
DJIBOUTI
Djibouti
GUINEA-BISSAU
Bissau
BURKINA FASO
N'Djamena
GUINEA
BENIN
NIGERIA
ETHIOPIA
Addis Ababa
SOMALIA
Conakry
SIERRA LEONE
COTE D'IVOIRE
Abuja
Freetown
TOGO
CENTRAL AFRICAN REPUBLIC
GHANA
LIBERIA
Yamoussoukro
Lomé
Monrovia
Porto Novo
CAMEROON
Accra
Bangui
Malabo
Yaoundé
Gulf of Guinea
SÃO TOMÉ and PRÍNCIPE
UGANDA
Mogadishu
KENYA
São Tomé
Libreville
CONGO
Kampala
Equator
EQUATORIAL GUINEA
GABON
DEMOCRATIC REPUBLIC OF THE CONGO
RWANDA
Kigali
Nairobi
Bujumbura
BURUNDI
Brazzaville
Kinshasa
TANZANIA
Dar es Salaam
ATLANTIC OCEAN
Luanda
ANGOLA
MALAWI
Lilongwe
ZAMBIA
Lusaka
MOZAMBIQUE
Mozambique Channel
Harare
ZIMBABWE
MADAGASCAR
Antananarivo
NAMIBIA
Windhoek
BOTSWANA
Gaborone
Pretoria
Maputo
Mbabane
SWAZILAND
INDIAN OCEAN
Bloemfontein
Maseru
LESOTHO
SOUTH AFRICA
Cape Town
N
S
E
W
0
500 Miles
500 KM

# アジア・オーストラリア

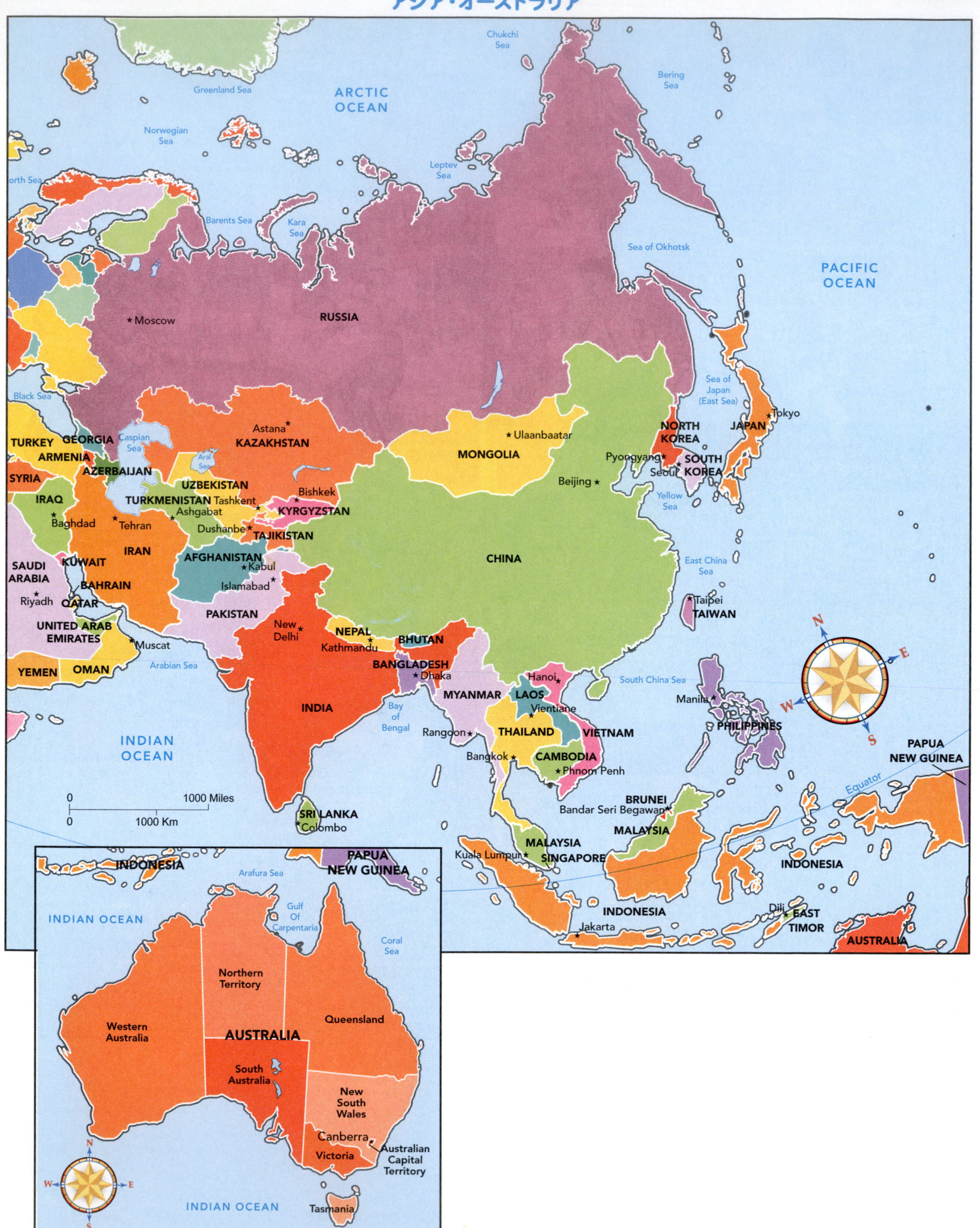

Chukchi Sea
Bering Sea
Greenland Sea
ARCTIC OCEAN
Norwegian Sea
Laptev Sea
North Sea
Barents Sea
Kara Sea
Sea of Okhotsk
PACIFIC OCEAN
Moscow
RUSSIA
Sea of Japan (East Sea)
Black Sea
Tokyo
JAPAN
NORTH KOREA
Astana
KAZAKHSTAN
Ulaanbaatar
MONGOLIA
TURKEY
GEORGIA
Caspian Sea
ARMENIA
Aral Sea
Pyongyang
SOUTH KOREA
Seoul
AZERBAIJAN
SYRIA
UZBEKISTAN
Beijing
Bishkek
IRAQ
TURKMENISTAN
Tashkent
Yellow Sea
Ashgabat
KYRGYZSTAN
Baghdad
Tehran
Dushanbe
TAJIKISTAN
IRAN
AFGHANISTAN
CHINA
East China Sea
SAUDI ARABIA
KUWAIT
Kabul
BAHRAIN
Islamabad
Riyadh
QATAR
Taipei
TAIWAN
PAKISTAN
UNITED ARAB EMIRATES
New Delhi
NEPAL
BHUTAN
Muscat
Kathmandu
Arabian Sea
BANGLADESH
YEMEN
OMAN
Dhaka
Hanoi
South China Sea
MYANMAR
LAOS
Manila
INDIA
Bay of Bengal
Vientiane
Rangoon
THAILAND
VIETNAM
PHILIPPINES
INDIAN OCEAN
Bangkok
CAMBODIA
PAPUA NEW GUINEA
Phnom Penh
Equator
0 1000 Miles
0 1000 Km
BRUNEI
Bandar Seri Begawan
SRI LANKA
Colombo
MALAYSIA
MALAYSIA
Kuala Lumpur
SINGAPORE
INDONESIA
INDONESIA
PAPUA NEW GUINEA
Arafura Sea
INDONESIA
Dili
EAST TIMOR
Jakarta
AUSTRALIA
INDIAN OCEAN
Gulf Of Carpentaria
Coral Sea
Northern Territory
Western Australia
Queensland
AUSTRALIA
South Australia
New South Wales
Canberra
Australian Capital Territory
Victoria
INDIAN OCEAN
Tasmania
N
E
S
W

世界の国々・国籍・言語

       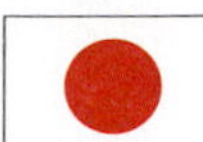 

| Country | Nationality | Language |
|---|---|---|
| Afghanistan | Afghan | Afghan |
| Argentina | Argentine | Spanish |
| Australia | Australian | English |
| Bolivia | Bolivian | Spanish |
| Brazil | Brazilian | Portuguese |
| Bulgaria | Bulgarian | Bulgarian |
| Cambodia | Cambodian | Cambodian |
| Canada | Canadian | English/French |
| Chile | Chilean | Spanish |
| China | Chinese | Chinese |
| Colombia | Colombian | Spanish |
| Costa Rica | Costa Rican | Spanish |
| Cuba | Cuban | Spanish |
| (The) Czech Republic | Czech | Czech |
| Denmark | Danish | Danish |
| (The) Dominican Republic | Dominican | Spanish |
| Ecuador | Ecuadorian | Spanish |
| Egypt | Egyptian | Arabic |
| El Salvador | Salvadorean | Spanish |
| England | English | English |
| Estonia | Estonian | Estonian |
| Ethiopia | Ethiopian | Amharic |
| Finland | Finnish | Finnish |
| France | French | French |
| Germany | German | German |
| Greece | Greek | Greek |
| Guatemala | Guatemalan | Spanish |
| Haiti | Haitian | Haitian Kreyol |
| Honduras | Honduran | Spanish |
| Hungary | Hungarian | Hungarian |
| India | Indian | Hindi |
| Indonesia | Indonesian | Indonesian |
| Israel | Israeli | Hebrew |

| Country | Nationality | Language |
|---|---|---|
| Italy | Italian | Italian |
| Japan | Japanese | Japanese |
| Jordan | Jordanian | Arabic |
| Korea | Korean | Korean |
| Laos | Laotian | Laotian |
| Latvia | Latvian | Latvian |
| Lebanon | Lebanese | Arabic |
| Lithuania | Lithuanian | Lithuanian |
| Malaysia | Malaysian | Malay |
| Mexico | Mexican | Spanish |
| New Zealand | New Zealander | English |
| Nicaragua | Nicaraguan | Spanish |
| Norway | Norwegian | Norwegian |
| Pakistan | Pakistani | Urdu |
| Panama | Panamanian | Spanish |
| Peru | Peruvian | Spanish |
| (The) Philippines | Filipino | Tagalog |
| Poland | Polish | Polish |
| Portugal | Portuguese | Portuguese |
| Puerto Rico | Puerto Rican | Spanish |
| Romania | Romanian | Romanian |
| Russia | Russian | Russian |
| Saudi Arabia | Saudi | Arabic |
| Slovakia | Slovak | Slovak |
| Spain | Spanish | Spanish |
| Sweden | Swedish | Swedish |
| Switzerland | Swiss | German/French/Italian |
| Taiwan | Taiwanese | Chinese |
| Thailand | Thai | Thai |
| Turkey | Turkish | Turkish |
| Ukraine | Ukrainian | Ukrainian |
| (The) United States | American | English |
| Venezuela | Venezuelan | Spanish |
| Vietnam | Vietnamese | Vietnamese |

A. Where are you from?
B. I'm from **Mexico**.

A. What's your nationality?
B. I'm **Mexican**.

A. What language do you speak?
B. I speak **Spanish**.

Tell about yourself: Where are you from? What's your nationality? What languages do you speak?

Now interview and tell about a friend.

# 動詞リスト

## 規則動詞

規則動詞は以下の4通りに語形変化して過去形、過去分詞形を作ります。

### 1 動詞の語尾に **ed** をつける。例：

act → acte**d**

act
add
answer
appear
ask
assist
attack
attend
bank
board
boil
box
brainstorm
broil
brush
burn
burp
carpool
cash
check
clean
clear
collect
comb
construct
cook
correct
cough
cover
crash
cross (out)
deliver
deposit
design
discuss
dress
drill
dust
edit
end
enter
establish
explain
faint
fasten
fix
floss
fold
follow
form
grill
guard
hand (in)
help
insert
invent
iron
kick
land
leak
learn
lengthen
lift
listen
load
look
lower
mark
match
mix
mow
obey
open
paint
park
pass
peel
plant
play
polish
pour
print
reach
record
register
relax
repair
repeat
request
respond
rest
return
roast
rock
saute
scratch
seat
select
shorten
sign
simmer
sort
spell
sprain
steam
stow
stretch
surf
swallow
talk
turn
twist
unload
vacuum
vomit
walk
wash
watch
wax
weed
whiten
work

### 2 動詞の語尾に **d** をつける。例：

assemble → assemble**d**

assemble
bake
balance
barbecue
bathe
bounce
browse
bruise
bubble
change
circle
close
combine
declare
describe
dislocate
dive
dribble
enforce
erase
examine
exchange
exercise
experience
file
gargle
grate
hire
manage
measure
microwave
move
nurse
operate
organize
overdose
practice
prepare
produce
pronounce
prune
raise
rake
recite
recycle
remove
revise
rinse
save
scrape
serve
share
shave
slice
sneeze
state
style
supervise
translate
type
underline
unscramble
use
vote
wheeze

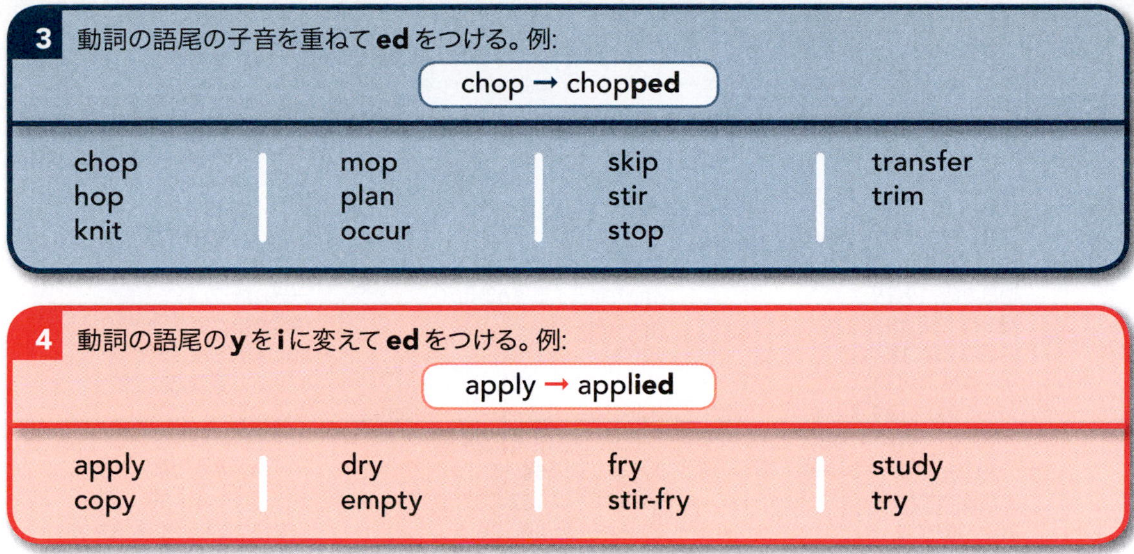

**3** 動詞の語尾の子音を重ねて **ed** をつける。例:

chop → chop**ped**

| | | | |
|---|---|---|---|
| chop | mop | skip | transfer |
| hop | plan | stir | trim |
| knit | occur | stop | |

**4** 動詞の語尾の **y** を **i** に変えて **ed** をつける。例:

apply → appl**ied**

| | | | |
|---|---|---|---|
| apply | dry | fry | study |
| copy | empty | stir-fry | try |

**不規則動詞**

以下の動詞は不規則に変化して過去形、過去分詞形を作ります。

| | | | | | |
|---|---|---|---|---|---|
| be | was/were | been | know | knew | known |
| beat | beat | beaten | leave | left | left |
| become | became | become | let | let | let |
| bend | bent | bent | make | made | made |
| begin | began | begun | meet | met | met |
| bleed | bled | bled | pay | paid | paid |
| break | broke | broken | put | put | put |
| bring | brought | brought | read | read | read |
| build | built | built | rewrite | rewrote | rewritten |
| buy | bought | bought | run | ran | run |
| catch | caught | caught | ring | rang | rung |
| choose | chose | chosen | say | said | said |
| come | came | come | see | saw | seen |
| cut | cut | cut | sell | sold | sold |
| do | did | done | set | set | set |
| draw | drew | drawn | shoot | shot | shot |
| drink | drank | drunk | sing | sang | sung |
| drive | drove | driven | sit | sat | sat |
| eat | ate | eaten | sleep | slept | slept |
| fall | fell | fallen | speak | spoke | spoken |
| feed | fed | fed | stand | stood | stood |
| fly | flew | flown | sweep | swept | swept |
| get | got | gotten | swim | swam | swum |
| give | gave | given | swing | swung | swung |
| go | went | gone | take | took | taken |
| grow | grew | grown | teach | taught | taught |
| hang | hung | hung | throw | threw | thrown |
| have | had | had | understand | understood | understood |
| hit | hit | hit | withdraw | withdrew | withdrawn |
| hold | held | held | write | wrote | written |
| hurt | hurt | hurt | | | |

# 日本語索引

太字の数字は各語句の掲載ページを示し、右側の細字の数字はそのページ上のイラスト番号および語句リスト番号を示しています。例えば、"アイロン台 73-17" は、「アイロン台」という単語が73ページの項目17に掲載されていることを意味します。

## さ



## し

**ひ**



**ふ**

## へ



## ほ

## 英語索引

太字の数字は各語句の掲載ページを示し、右側の細字の数字はそのページ上のイラスト番号および語句リスト番号を示しています。例えば、"address **1**-5" は、addressという単語が１ページの項目5に掲載されていることを意味します。

**Expressions**

数・曜日・月

## Cardinal Numbers

| | |
|---|---|
| 1 | one |
| 2 | two |
| 3 | three |
| 4 | four |
| 5 | five |
| 6 | six |
| 7 | seven |
| 8 | eight |
| 9 | nine |
| 10 | ten |
| 11 | eleven |
| 12 | twelve |
| 13 | thirteen |
| 14 | fourteen |
| 15 | fifteen |
| 16 | sixteen |
| 17 | seventeen |
| 18 | eighteen |
| 19 | nineteen |
| 20 | twenty |
| 21 | twenty-one |
| 22 | twenty-two |
| 30 | thirty |
| 40 | forty |
| 50 | fifty |
| 60 | sixty |
| 70 | seventy |
| 80 | eighty |
| 90 | ninety |
| 100 | one hundred |
| 101 | one hundred (and) one |
| 102 | one hundred (and) two |
| 1,000 | one thousand |
| 10,000 | ten thousand |
| 100,000 | one hundred thousand |
| 1,000,000 | one million |
| 1,000,000,000 | one billion |

## Ordinal Numbers

| | |
|---|---|
| 1st | first |
| 2nd | second |
| 3rd | third |
| 4th | fourth |
| 5th | fifth |
| 6th | sixth |
| 7th | seventh |
| 8th | eighth |
| 9th | ninth |
| 10th | tenth |
| 11th | eleventh |
| 12th | twelfth |
| 13th | thirteenth |
| 14th | fourteenth |
| 15th | fifteenth |
| 16th | sixteenth |
| 17th | seventeenth |
| 18th | eighteenth |
| 19th | nineteenth |
| 20th | twentieth |
| 21st | twenty-first |
| 22nd | twenty-second |
| 30th | thirtieth |
| 40th | fortieth |
| 50th | fiftieth |
| 60th | sixtieth |
| 70th | seventieth |
| 80th | eightieth |
| 90th | ninetieth |
| 100th | one hundredth |
| 101st | one hundred (and) first |
| 102nd | one hundred (and) second |
| 1,000th | one thousandth |
| 10,000th | ten thousandth |
| 100,000th | one hundred thousandth |
| 1,000,000th | one millionth |
| 1,000,000,000th | one billionth |

## Days of the Week

Sunday
Monday
Tuesday
Wednesday
Thursday
Friday
Saturday

## Months of the Year

| | |
|---|---|
| January | July |
| February | August |
| March | September |
| April | October |
| May | November |
| June | December |

## 項目別索引